Hutchinson's
Tree Book

A reference guide to
Popular Landscape Trees

Bob H. Head

Hutchinson Publishing Corporation
Taylors, South Carolina
2006

First Edition 2006

Published by:
Hutchinson Publishing Corporation
102 East Lee Road
Taylors, South Carolina 29687
www.plantlocator.com

Library of Congress Cataloging-in-Publication Date
Head, Bob H., 2006
Hutchinson's Tree Book / Head, Bob H.
Library of Congress 2006927551
ISBN 0-9773952-0-0

Front and back cover design: Leigh Judy, Stuart Littleton and Brad Shipman
Front cover photos: (top left) - Moon's Tree Farm
(top center) - Horticultural Portraits
(top right) - Bold Spring Nursery
(bottom left) - Images by BA
(bottom center) - Ray Bracken Nursery
(bottom right) - Southeastern Growers
Back cover photo: Bill Hutchinson
Inside front and back cover photo: Bill Hutchinson
Typesetting, page layout, production: Holley Stokely and April Hutchinson

Printed in the United States of America

Dedication

This book is dedicated to my father and mother, Charlie and Rita Hutchinson. Thank you both so much for all you have taught me throughout the years and for always being there. My father Charlie passed away Feb. 6, 1995 at the age of 75, but the lessons he taught us all will live on forever. His incredible work ethic began as a young boy during the Depression and continued throughout his life, including a four year term in World War II as a Marine in the Pacific. Both of you taught us all that dedication and perseverance are an absolute necessity in life. Thank you both so much for everything. I would also like to include my beautiful daughter, Tyler, Charlie and Rita's granddaughter. Charlie would be proud of the beautiful young lady you have become, just as we all are.

Bill Hutchinson

Publisher's Acknowledgments

Numerous people have helped make this book a reality. We have seen a need for this type of book in both the horticulture industry and for the typical home gardener for many years. All of us here at Hutchinson Publishing Corporation, along with Bob and Lisa Head (Head Ornamentals, Inc.), would like to thank all of our friends and colleagues for all of their help, enthusiasm, and dedication to bringing this project together. Our sincerest appreciation goes out to the entire staff at Hutchinson Publishing Corporation for their relentless determination in making this book one of the most valuable and functional guides for ornamental trees ever published. Leigh Judy was the captain of the Project Team at Hutchinson Publishing and truly made it happen in an organized and timely manner. Holley Stokely, Nancy Drummond, and April Hutchinson were instrumental in all page layouts, and the overall flow and functionality of the text, photos, indices, etc. Holley has been a great addition to the team, having a degree from Clemson University in Landscape Architecture and several years experience working with a design-build firm and commercial tree grower. We would also like to thank Jeremy Willis and Rob Wentzky for all of their help in choosing varieties and photos for the book. Their knowledge of the demand and availability of trees throughout the industry, has been an invaluable resource in determining the trees featured in this book. Thanks also to Jennifer Orr, Tyler Mills, Stuart Littleton, Nikki Betrock, Marta Hutchinson, Denis Bedu, and Brad Shipman for all of their help compiling data and photos for this project. Lisa Head was a tremendous help regarding plant patents and her extensive knowledge of all aspects of the horticultural industry. Our sincerest gratitude to B.A. Waddell (Images by BA) and Heather Leyer (Horticultural Portraits) for their contribution of many beautiful color photographs in several of the page layouts.

In addition, we would like to thank Irv and Bette Betrock (Betrock Information Systems, Inc., Publisher's of the PlantFinder® and PlantFinder West® magazines, Betrock's Guide to Florida Landscape Plants, Betrock's Guide to Landscape Palms, Betrock's Florida Plant Guide, and Betrock's Cold Hardy Palms) for all of their help and guidance over the last two decades. Their knowledge of the horticultural publishing arena and their market knowledge, has made it truly phenomenal to be associated with them.

Author's Dedication

I write this book for my wife Lisa, and sons, Tyler and Brantley and for my parents, Roberta and Harold Head.

I gratefully dedicate this book to the Green Industry.

Bob H. Head

Author's Acknowledgments

There are many people who have contributed their time and energy to make this book possible. First, I have to thank my wife, Lisa, for her knowledge and hard work over the many long hours. I'd like to also thank my son, Tyler, for his help in editing all of the first revisions. Thanks also, to my other son, Brantley, for his patience in my absence during all of the research and writing.

Special thanks to Holley Stokely for her hours spent organizing and reading my notes and then preparing the first drafts. We couldn't have accomplished it without her. Thanks to Jennifer Orr and Nancy Drummond for their hours of invaluable research. Leigh Judy has been phenomenal in his efforts to pull it all together and help us meet the deadline. Rob Wentzky and Jeremy Willis kept us on track with their perceptive editing of the final revisions. April Hutchinson inspired us with her creative design of the beautiful book cover and all of the page layouts. Lastly, thanks to Bill Hutchinson for his insight in seeing the need for this type of book in our industry and his confidence in me to write it. The encouragement of the Hutchinson staff has been wonderful for both Lisa and me during this entire project.

Bob H. Head

Table of Contents

Preface

Trees have always been the focal point of any quality landscape. Having personally been part of the horticultural industry for over twenty-five years, all of us here at Hutchinson Publishing Corporation wanted to provide our valued customers with a very concise compilation of the most popular and new varieties of trees in the horticultural industry. There have been hundreds of books published on trees over the last several years, but we've decided to publish a book that would be a truly functional guide to landscape trees that will serve as an excellent source of color pictures and concise cultural information for each of the trees. The trees represented in this book are utilized by landscape professionals as well as your average home gardener. We have chosen trees that are typically available from both wholesale and retail nurseries and we have also included a special index in the book to give our readers a general availability of the trees featured in the book. This important section will help any landscape designer determine how readily available a tree is, prior to specifying it on a new project. Each tree featured here has a very simple, easy-to-read format of technical information, that allows the reader to quickly determine the varieties that they are looking for in their landscape. Several hundred color photographs have been utilized here to help our readers determine the visual characteristics of each tree. Most of the trees featured in the book have close-up photos to help with identification, full color shots of the individual trees, and seasonal pictures. In addition, many are pictured in a landscape.

The author, Bob Head, is currently president of Head-Lee Nursery, supplying a wide variety of woody ornamentals to both the wholesale and retail nursery trade for over thirty years. Bob, along with his wife Lisa and brother Bill, also own and operate Head Ornamentals, Inc., a company established to introduce new plant cultivars into the industry. Bob has a very broad background in the horticultural industry, beginning with fourteen years experience as an Ornamental Horticulture Specialist for Clemson University. He has been involved with the horticultural industry as a landscaper and as one of the premier propagators and nurserymen in the industry. His vast knowledge of all aspects of the horticulture industry from design to growing and installation, have made us proud to be associated with him in producing this book. We, at Hutchinson Publishing Corporation, would like to thank Bob and Lisa Head, along with Jennifer Orr and Tyler Mills, for all of their hard work and dedication to this project. We believe that this tree guide will make a valuable addition to the bookshelves of landscape professionals and enthusiasts throughout the Southeast, Southwest, Mid-Atlantic, and Northeast regions.

Bill Hutchinson, President
Hutchinson Publishing Corp.

About the Author

Bob Head is a second-generation nurseryman. He earned his B.S. degree in Ornamental Horticulture from Clemson University, and he worked fourteen years as an Area Ornamental Horticultural Specialist for Clemson University Cooperative Extension Service. While with the Extension Service, he consulted over a seven county area with commercial growers in the wholesale and retail green industry trade and commercial fruit and vegetable producers.

Bob is President of Head-Lee Nursery, Inc. in Seneca, South Carolina, a thirty year old family owned retail-wholesale nursery specializing in a wide variety of plants and hard goods for retail and landscape professionals. The wholesale division focuses on supplying difficult to propagate plants such as *Magnolias* and conifers. They also propagate many varieties of maples and other woody shrubs. In 1997, he received the South Carolina Nursery Professional of the Year Award for his outstanding work and contributions to the nursery industry.

An extensive collection of plants evaluated over a thirty year period yielded many exceptional plant cultivars. In 1999 he, along with his wife Lisa and brother Bill, formed Head Ornamentals, Inc. Through their website at www.gardendebut.com and their trademark, Garden Debut®, they have introduced several plant cultivars that include *Magnolia grandiflora* Teddy Bear®, *Acer rubrum* Summer Red®, *Wisteria frutescens* 'Amethyst Falls' and *Loropetalum chinense* Snow Muffin®, among others.

Bob is a member of the International Plant Propagator's Society and serves on the South Carolina Nursery and Landscape Association's Board of Directors. He continues to teach and lecture at the International Plant Propagators Conference, Southern Plant Conference and the Cullowhee Native Plant Conference, as well as State Master Gardener Conferences and local meetings.

Introduction

Attractive landscaping is appealing to everyone. The beauty of Spring blooms gives way to the lustrous greens of Summer days only to be eclipsed by the majestic colors of Fall. Winter finds us with a seemingly barren landscape until you look further and see the artistry in the bark and detail of the branch structure of any tree. Granted, some are more attractive than others, and what one person may find appealing may not be of any interest to the next. The trained horticulturist, landscape contractor, designer or landscape architect is familiar with the traits and characteristics of individual trees, but may not have access to a single source of pictures of the many tree varieties available and suitable to a particular landscape for their clients. Untrained homeowners know what they like when they see it but might not be able to identify a particular tree when searching for the perfect addition to their yard without some assistance. This book is designed to provide color photos and concise information that describe many trees commonly used in the Eastern United States.

How to Use This Book

This book is divided into four sections. Section I contains plant description pages which provide a detailed description and full color pictures of each showcased tree. Section II is a selection of various landscape information that reference topics such as market availability, a tree planting guide, rootball sizes and weight, and a USDA Hardiness Zone Map. This section provides useful resource guides commonly used by individuals that work with or within the horticulture industry. Section III consists of several appendices that lists trees by various categories such as flowering season, salt tolerance and other additional categories. These appendices are useful to designers, landscape architects and landscape contractors when specifying materials or substitutions in sites with limiting or specific factors. Section IV contains the glossary and index, photo acknowledgments and bibliography.

Section I is the most comprehensive section, as it consists of detailed descriptions of each tree. Each page has been set up in a consistent format with the plant names listed at the top. Each tree is listed first by its botanical name, which is made up of a three part name consisting of the genus, species and cultivar (variety). Below the botanical name is the common name used within the horticulture industry. The plant patent or trademark is noted for each plant requiring that information. Each of the tree pages include several color pictures ranging from full shots to close-up images of the foliage, flowers, fruit or bark. Following is a brief explanation of the data categories used in this book. Please check the glossary in the back of the book for further information about any topic.

USDA Hardiness Zones: The region a plant commonly grows best based on a region's climate, average temperatures and common weather extremes. The USDA has divided the United States into these different zones, that are commonly used in the horticulture industry (see page 185 for the USDA Hardiness Zone Map).

Native Habitat: The origin or geographical location from which a tree has originated or is naturally found.

Plant Type: A general description of the plant including whether it is deciduous or evergreen, leaf type, size and other notable characteristics.

Mature Size: The average height and width that the tree will reach under normal growing conditions in 25-40 years.

Form/Shape: The typical growth habit of the plant (ie. upright, full to ground) and the general appearance of the plant (ie. oval, rounded, denseness, vase shaped).

Bark: The color, characteristics, and interesting traits of the bark and stems for each tree. Information can be helpful when identifying a deciduous tree during Winter months when leaves are absent.

Flower: Description of the flower including the color, size, shape, bloom season and additional notable information.

Fruit: Description of the fruit including type, size, color, season and additional notable information.

Foliage: Description of the leaf arrangement, shape, form, color, Fall color (if applicable) and additional notable information.

Growth Rate: The typical rate of growth that a particular tree undergoes in a year under normal conditions.

> *Slow*: typically six inches or less in a year
>
> *Moderate*: typically six inches to three feet in a year
>
> *Fast*: typically three feet or more in a year

Drought Tolerance: The ability of an established plant, either transplanted or growing in a site for three or more years, to withstand periods of no rainfall or supplemental irrigation and thrive.

> *Low*: tree will not survive unless irrigated regularly
>
> *Moderate*: tree will survive with some irrigation
>
> *High*: tree can survive in dry conditions without irrigation

Salt Tolerance: The extent to which a tree can survive in conditions where salt is present in the air and/or soil.

> *Low*: tree is highly intolerant of excess salt on the leaves or in the soil
>
> *Moderate*: tree can tolerate minimal amounts of salt on the leaves or in the soil
>
> *High*: tree will tolerate above average levels of salt on the leaves or in the soil; ideal for coastal sites or where salt is used for de-icing of walks or roadways

Soil Requirements: Soil characteristics required by a tree to achieve optimal growth. Trees can survive in different types of soil, but certain combinations of soil type and moisture are better than others.

Light Requirements: The relative amount of sunlight required for a tree to grow.

> *Full sun*: the tree requires a minimum of six hours of direct sun per day; some trees may require more than six hours for optimum foliage color and best flowering
>
> *Part shade*: tree should receive direct sunlight for approximately four to six hours or filtered shade throughout the day
>
> *Light shade*: trees should be planted in an area that receives indirect sunlight, filtered sun, or three to four hours of direct sunlight
>
> *Shade*: tree should have protection from direct sun, but may tolerate filtered sunlight or a couple hours of direct sunlight

Pest Problems: Insects that may infest or attack the tree.

Disease Problems: Common diseases that may affect the health of the tree.

Environmental Factors: A list of common factors that the tree may cause or encounter in the landscape.

Pruning: Recommendations for pruning and plant maintenance that are commonly practiced.

Uses: List of common or recommended landscape uses for the tree in the landscape.

Urban Uses: Recommendations for uses in urban environments including attributes and common problems found to occur from harsh city conditions.

Substitutions: Trees that are of similar size, shape and growing characteristics and would be suitable in place of the tree listed.

Comments: Additional notes and personal experiences from the author about the tree.

Other Cultivars: List of additional cultivars of the same species of the showcased tree.

Deciduous Trees

Acer buergerianum
Trident Maple
USDA Hardiness Zones: 5-9

DESCRIPTION

NATIVE HABITAT: Korea and Eastern China
PLANT TYPE: Deciduous, broadleaf, medium size tree
MATURE SIZE: 20-35' tall by 20-35' wide
FORM/SHAPE: Oval, rounded outline
BARK: Smooth; grayish tan when young; gray when mature
FLOWER: Greenish yellow; blooms in Spring
FRUIT: Green, winged samara; ripens to reddish brown in Fall
FOLIAGE: Opposite, simple; new growth emerges bronze; becomes dark green in Summer; turns yellow, orange, and red in Fall

LANDSCAPE CHARACTERISTICS

GROWTH RATE: Moderate   **DROUGHT TOLERANCE:** High   **SALT TOLERANCE:** Low
SOIL REQUIREMENTS: Well-drained, moist, fertile, humus rich, slightly acidic soil
LIGHT REQUIREMENTS: Full sun to part shade
PEST PROBLEMS: Thrips, caterpillars, Mapleworm, bagworm, gall making insects, leaf miner, Maple petiole borer, mites, sawfly, ambrosia beetles, twig pruner, flatheaded Apple tree borer, aphids, mealybugs, scales, sapsucker birds and black vine beetle
DISEASE PROBLEMS: Anthracnose, canker rot, dieback, leaf blight, *Nectria*, nematodes, *Phomopsis*, powdery mildew, *Verticillium* wilt, tar spot and wetwood
ENVIRONMENTAL FACTORS: Girdling roots from limited soil growing area; lack of root pruning results in circling roots in container grown plant; Winter or Summer sunscald to the bark; ice and snowstorm damage
PRUNING: Prune to develop crown and strong limb angles; remove crossing limbs and low hanging limbs to allow pedestrian or vehicular circulation

ADDITIONAL NOTES

USES: Patio, lawn or street tree, container plantings
URBAN USES: Good for streets, medians and planter boxes
SUBSTITUTIONS: *Lagerstroemia* cultivars, *Malus* cultivars, *Pyrus* cultivars, *Styrax japonica* cultivars
COMMENTS: Trident Maple is a very adaptable tree for small spaces.
OTHER CULTIVARS: 'ABTIR' PP 9576 Streetwise® - dark green foliage; strong, upright, oval crown form

Acer buergerianum 'ABMTF' PP 16,629
Aeryn® Trident Maple
USDA Hardiness Zones: 5-9

DESCRIPTION

NATIVE HABITAT: Korea and Eastern China
PLANT TYPE: Deciduous, broadleaf, medium size tree
MATURE SIZE: 20-35' tall by 20-35' wide
FORM/SHAPE: Broad, pyramidal when young; oval, rounded outline when mature
BARK: Smooth; grayish tan when young; somewhat gray when mature
FLOWER: Yellow-green; small; inconspicuous
FRUIT: Green, winged samara about 1" long by 1/4" wide; changes to brown when mature
FOLIAGE: Opposite, simple; medium-sized, five-lobed; glossy, dark green leaves turn a consistent yellowish orange in Fall

LANDSCAPE CHARACTERISTICS

GROWTH RATE: Moderate   **DROUGHT TOLERANCE:** Moderate to High   **SALT TOLERANCE:** Low
SOIL REQUIREMENTS: Adaptable to sandy, loam or clay soil; adaptable to many pH and fertility levels; best growth in well-drained, moist, fertile, humus rich, slightly acidic soil
LIGHT REQUIREMENTS: Full sun to part shade
PEST PROBLEMS: Thrips, caterpillars, Mapleworm, bagworm, gall making insects, leaf miner, Maple petiole borer, mites, sawfly, ambrosia beetles, twig pruner, flatheaded Apple tree borer, aphids, mealybugs, scales, sapsucker birds and black vine beetle
DISEASE PROBLEMS: Anthracnose, canker rot, dieback, leaf blight, *Nectria*, nematodes, *Phomopsis*, powdery mildew, *Verticillium* wilt, tar spot and wetwood
ENVIRONMENTAL FACTORS: Girdling roots from limited soil growing area; lack of root pruning results in circling roots in container grown plant; Winter or Summer sunscald to the bark; ice and snowstorm damage
PRUNING: Prune to develop crown and strong limb angles; remove crossing limbs and low hanging limbs to allow pedestrian or vehicular circulation

ADDITIONAL NOTES

USES: Small specimen or shade tree, parking lot buffer, group planting with other trees, planter boxes and street tree for difficult sites and space limitations
URBAN USES: Very adaptable to urban growing sites; moderately tolerant of air pollutants, compacted soil and moderately dry planting sites
SUBSTITUTIONS: *Acer palmatum* cultivars, *Lagerstroemia* cultivars, *Pyrus* cultivars, *Prunus* cultivars, *Chionanthus retusus, Ulmus* cultivars
COMMENTS: Aeryn® is a very uniform, fast growing Trident Maple with an upright, broad crown. This plant has glossy, dark green foliage and uniform, yellowish orange Fall foliage with strong limb angles and excellent drought tolerance.
OTHER CULTIVARS: 'ABTIR' PP 9576 Streetwise® - dark green foliage; strong, upright, oval crown form

Acer palmatum
Japanese Maple
USDA Hardiness Zones: 5-8

DESCRIPTION

NATIVE HABITAT: Japan, Korea and Central China
PLANT TYPE: Deciduous, broadleaf, small tree
MATURE SIZE: 15-25' tall by 10-25' wide
FORM/SHAPE: Spreading branches; low, rounded with layered look; sometimes multi-stemmed
BARK: Smooth; light gray
FLOWER: Red; blooms in Spring
FRUIT: Greenish yellow, winged samara forms in Spring; persistent throughout Summer into Fall; matures to grayish brown
FOLIAGE: Opposite, simple; palmate; new leaves emerge green and turn yellow, bronze to red-purple in Fall

LANDSCAPE CHARACTERISTICS

GROWTH RATE: Moderate   **DROUGHT TOLERANCE:** Moderate once established   **SALT TOLERANCE:** Low
SOIL REQUIREMENTS: Well-drained, moist, fertile, humus rich, slightly acidic soil
LIGHT REQUIREMENTS: Part shade to light shade
PEST PROBLEMS: Thrips, caterpillars, Mapleworm, bagworm, gall making insects, leaf miner, Maple petiole borer, mites, sawfly, ambrosia beetles, twig pruner, flatheaded Apple tree borer, aphids, mealybugs, scales, sapsucker birds and black vine beetle
DISEASE PROBLEMS: Anthracnose, canker rot, dieback, leaf blight, *Nectria*, nematodes, *Phomopsis*, powdery mildew, *Verticillium* wilt, tar spot and wetwood
ENVIRONMENTAL FACTORS: Girdling roots from limited soil growing area; lack of root pruning results in circling roots in container grown plant; Winter or Summer sunscald to the bark; ice and snowstorm damage
PRUNING: Prune to develop crown and strong limb angles; remove crossing limbs and low hanging limbs to allow pedestrian or vehicular circulation

ADDITIONAL NOTES

USES: Small specimen or shade tree, parking lot buffer, group planting with other trees, planter boxes and street tree for difficult sites and space limitations
URBAN USES: Very adaptable to urban growing sites; moderately tolerant of air pollutants, compacted soil and moderately dry planting sites
SUBSTITUTIONS: *Lagerstroemia* cultivars, *Malus* cultivars, *Pyrus* cultivars, *Prunus* cultivars, *Styrax* cultivars
COMMENTS: Japanese Maple is an excellent small tree useful in landscape settings where proper soil and light conditions are present.
OTHER CULTIVARS: Many cultivars as well as seedlings of the species are available with varying plant forms

Acer palmatum 'Bloodgood'
Bloodgood Japanese Maple
USDA Hardiness Zones: 5b-8

DESCRIPTION

NATIVE HABITAT: Japan, Korea and Central China
PLANT TYPE: Deciduous, broadleaf, small tree
MATURE SIZE: 15-20' tall by 12-20' wide
FORM/SHAPE: Globose, spreading
BARK: Greenish red when young; light gray when mature
FLOWER: Red; blooms in Spring
FRUIT: Burgundy, winged samara forms in Spring; persistent throughout Summer into Fall; matures to grayish brown
FOLIAGE: Opposite, simple, palmate; purple-red; greenish red leaves in hot Summer conditions with red Fall color

LANDSCAPE CHARACTERISTICS

GROWTH RATE: Moderate   **DROUGHT TOLERANCE:** Moderate once established   **SALT TOLERANCE:** Low
SOIL REQUIREMENTS: Well-drained, moist, fertile, humus rich, slightly acidic soil
LIGHT REQUIREMENTS: Part sun to light shade
PEST PROBLEMS: Thrips, caterpillars, Mapleworm, bagworm, gall making insects, leaf miner, Maple petiole borer, mites, sawfly, ambrosia beetles, twig pruner, flatheaded Apple tree borer, aphids, mealybugs, scales, sapsucker birds and black vine beetle
DISEASE PROBLEMS: Anthracnose, canker rot, dieback, leaf blight, *Nectria*, nematodes, *Phomopsis*, powdery mildew, *Verticillium* wilt, tar spot and wetwood
ENVIRONMENTAL FACTORS: Girdling roots from limited soil growing area; lack of root pruning results in circling roots in container grown plant; Winter or Summer sunscald to the bark; ice and snowstorm damage
PRUNING: Prune to develop crown and strong limb angles; remove crossing limbs and low hanging limbs to allow pedestrian or vehicular circulation

ADDITIONAL NOTES

USES: Patio tree, containers, specimen, multi-trunk form, bonsai and accent tree with other landscape plants
URBAN USES: Moderate tolerance to urban environments; needs a shaded site and moist, well-drained soil for best survival
SUBSTITUTIONS: *Lagerstroemia* cultivars, *Malus* cultivars, *Pyrus* cultivars, *Prunus* cultivars, *Styrax japonica* cultivars
COMMENTS: Bloodgood Japanese Maple is the most well-known of the *atropurpureum* type of Japanese Maples. Bright light brings out the best leaf color, but too much direct sunlight during Summer damages and discolors the foliage.
OTHER CULTIVARS: 'Burgundy Lace' - burgundy-red leaves with sharply serrated lobes

Acer palmatum 'Sango kaku'
Coral Bark Japanese Maple
USDA Hardiness Zones: 5-9

DESCRIPTION

NATIVE HABITAT: Japan, Korea and Central China
PLANT TYPE: Deciduous, broadleaf, small tree
MATURE SIZE: 18-20' tall by 10-15' wide
FORM/SHAPE: Upright, compact, densely-branched crown
BARK: Smooth; orange-green in Summer; darkens to bright, coral-red in Winter
FLOWER: Yellowish green; small; inconspicuous; blooms in Spring
FRUIT: Greenish yellow, winged samara forms in Spring; persistent throughout Summer and into Fall; matures to grayish brown
FOLIAGE: Opposite, simple, palmate; mature leaves medium green with variable Fall color that ranges from yellow to orange depending on the region

LANDSCAPE CHARACTERISTICS

GROWTH RATE: Moderate   **DROUGHT TOLERANCE:** Low   **SALT TOLERANCE:** Low
SOIL REQUIREMENTS: Well-drained, moist, fertile, humus rich, slightly acidic soil
LIGHT REQUIREMENTS: Part sun to light shade
PEST PROBLEMS: Thrips, caterpillars, Mapleworm, bagworm, gall making insects, leaf miner, Maple petiole borer, mites, sawfly, ambrosia beetles, twig pruner, flatheaded Apple tree borer, aphids, mealybugs, scales, sapsucker birds and black vine beetle
DISEASE PROBLEMS: Anthracnose, canker rot, dieback, leaf blight, *Nectria*, nematodes, *Phomopsis*, powdery mildew, *Verticillium* wilt, tar spot and wetwood
ENVIRONMENTAL FACTORS: Girdling roots from limited soil growing area; lack of root pruning results in circling roots in container grown plant; Winter or Summer sunscald to the bark; ice and snowstorm damage
PRUNING: Prune to develop crown and strong limb angles; remove crossing limbs and low hanging limbs to allow pedestrian or vehicular circulation

ADDITIONAL NOTES

USES: Patio tree, containers, specimen, multi-trunk form, bonsai and accent tree with other landscape plants
URBAN USES: Moderate tolerance to urban environments; needs a shaded site and moist, well-drained soil for best survival
SUBSTITUTIONS: *Lagerstroemia* cultivars, *Prunus* cultivars, *Malus* cultivars, *Cornus* cultivars, *Cercis* cultivars
COMMENTS: The group, *Acer palmatum,* is the most planted small tree group in urban environments. 'Sango kaku' has shown good adaptability to Southern soils and climates throughout its range in USDA Hardiness Zones 5-9. It does not tolerate tight, compacted, wet soil or the air pollution of some urban areas.
OTHER CULTIVARS: 'Beni-Kawa' - burgundy-coral bark, green leaves; 'Sunrise' - yellow-coral bark, green leaves

Acer palmatum dissectum 'Seiryu'
Seiryu Japanese Maple
USDA Hardiness Zones: 6-8

DESCRIPTION

NATIVE HABITAT: Japan, Korea and Central China
PLANT TYPE: Deciduous, broadleaf, small tree
MATURE SIZE: 15-18' tall by 10-15' wide
FORM/SHAPE: Upright, compact when young; becomes broad, oval when mature
BARK: Young bark is smooth, dark green and matures to tannish gray with shallow fissures and ridges
FLOWER: Yellowish green; small; inconspicuous; appears in Spring
FRUIT: Greenish yellow, winged samara forms in Spring; persistent throughout Summer into Fall; matures to grayish brown
FOLIAGE: Opposite, simple, palmate, finely dissected; medium bright green leaves turn yellowish green to yellow, orange and red in Fall; changes color very late in Fall and may be damaged by frost

LANDSCAPE CHARACTERISTICS

GROWTH RATE: Slow to Moderate   **DROUGHT TOLERANCE:** Moderate once established   **SALT TOLERANCE:** Low
SOIL REQUIREMENTS: Well-drained, moist, fertile, humus rich, slightly acidic soil
LIGHT REQUIREMENTS: Part sun to light shade
PEST PROBLEMS: Thrips, caterpillars, Mapleworm, bagworm, gall making insects, leaf miner, Maple petiole borer, mites, sawfly, ambrosia beetles, twig pruner, flatheaded Apple tree borer, aphids, mealybugs, scales, sapsucker birds and black vine beetle
DISEASE PROBLEMS: Anthracnose, canker rot, dieback, leaf blight, *Nectria*, nematodes, *Phomopsis*, powdery mildew, *Verticillium* wilt, tar spot and wetwood
ENVIRONMENTAL FACTORS: Girdling roots from limited soil growing area; lack of root pruning results in circling roots in container grown plant; Winter or Summer sunscald to the bark; ice and snowstorm damage
PRUNING: Prune to develop crown and strong limb angles; remove crossing limbs and low hanging limbs to allow pedestrian or vehicular circulation

ADDITIONAL NOTES

USES: Patio tree, containers, specimen, multi-trunk form, bonsai and accent tree with other landscape plants
URBAN USES: Moderate tolerance to urban environments; needs a shaded site and moist, well-drained soil for best survival
SUBSTITUTIONS: *Lagerstroemia* cultivars, *Loropetalum* cultivars, *Malus* cultivars, *Prunus* cultivars, *Styrax japonica* cultivars
COMMENTS: Seiryu Japanese Maple is one of the few *Acer palmatum dissectum* cultivars with upright limb habit. This plant forms an accent tree to lightly shade other plants or flowers growing underneath it in the landscape.
OTHER CULTIVARS: 'Red Dragon' PVR - deep purple-red foliage, weeping, mounding form; 'Lionheart' - purplish red foliage turning bronze; upright trunk growth with horizontal branches and drooping limb tips

Acer platanoides 'Crimson King'
Crimson King Norway Maple
USDA Hardiness Zones: 3-7

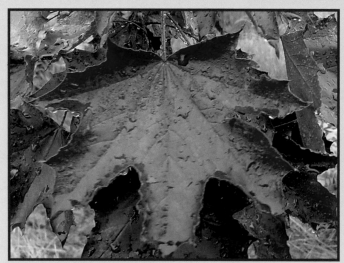

DESCRIPTION

NATIVE HABITAT: Northern Europe
PLANT TYPE: Deciduous, broadleaf, medium to large tree
MATURE SIZE: 15-25' tall by 10-20' wide (USDA Hardiness Zones 6-7); 50-60' tall by 20-30' wide (USDA Hardiness Zones 5 and colder)
FORM/SHAPE: Upright, oval to dome
BARK: Smooth, young bark; blackish purple turns pale and gray; matures to grayish brown with fissures and ridges
FLOWER: Reddish yellow to burgundy-yellow; blooms in Spring
FRUIT: Burgundy, winged samara; rarely produced
FOLIAGE: Opposite, simple, broad, five-lobed, coarsely toothed; leaves emerge in Spring and remain a dark black purple color throughout the growing season; Fall color is rusty, maroon or purple

LANDSCAPE CHARACTERISTICS

GROWTH RATE: Slow to Moderate   **DROUGHT TOLERANCE:** Moderate   **SALT TOLERANCE:** Moderate to High
SOIL REQUIREMENTS: Very adaptable to many soil types, pH and moisture levels; best growth in well-drained, moist, fertile, humus rich soil
LIGHT REQUIREMENTS: Full sun to part shade; best foliage color in full sun; in USDA Hardiness Zone 7, Summer heat may scorch the leaves and reduce the foliage color and quality
PEST PROBLEMS: Thrips, caterpillars, Mapleworm, bagworm, gall making insects, leaf miner, Maple petiole borer, mites, sawfly, ambrosia beetles, twig pruner, flatheaded Apple tree borer, aphids, mealybugs, scales, sapsucker birds and black vine beetle
DISEASE PROBLEMS: Anthracnose, canker rot, dieback, leaf blight, *Nectria*, nematodes, *Phomopsis*, powdery mildew, *Verticillium* wilt, tar spot and wetwood
ENVIRONMENTAL FACTORS: Girdling roots from limited soil growing area; lack of root pruning results in circling roots in container grown plant; Winter or Summer sunscald to the bark; ice and snowstorm damage; very prone to summer leaf scorch and winter bark splitting in USDA Hardiness Zone 7; better plant growth and quality in colder climate
PRUNING: Prune to develop crown and strong limb angles; remove crossing limbs and low hanging limbs to allow pedestrian or vehicular circulation

ADDITIONAL NOTES

USES: Large accent tree, specimen and lawn shade tree in Northern USDA Hardiness Zones
URBAN USES: Tolerant of cold temperature, air pollutants and poor soil conditions
SUBSTITUTIONS: Red leaf *Acer palmatum* cultivars, burgundy leaf *Loropetalum*, *Malus* cultivars, *Prunus* cultivars, *Cercis canadensis* 'Forest Pansy'
COMMENTS: 'Crimson King' has very dramatic foliage color but limited excessive use. Does not grow well in zones warmer than USDA Hardiness Zone 7, but some attractive specimens may be found in USDA Hardiness Zone 7 where cooler micro-climates prevail.
OTHER CULTIVARS: 'Faassen's Black' - dark purple foliage; similar form to 'Crimson King'; 'Crimson Sentry' dark red-purple foliage, smaller than species; more compact plant form; 25-30' tall by 10-15' wide

Acer rubrum
Red Maple
USDA Hardiness Zones: 4-9

DESCRIPTION

NATIVE HABITAT: Eastern United States
PLANT TYPE: Deciduous, broadleaf, large tree
MATURE SIZE: 40-60' tall by 25-35' wide
FORM/SHAPE: Pyramidal, elliptical when young; oval, rounded when mature
BARK: Smooth; grayish tan; develops shallow fissures, ridges and plates when mature
FLOWER: Bronze-red; blooms in Spring
FRUIT: Brownish green winged samara; color varies on each tree
FOLIAGE: Opposite, simple, three to five-lobed; new growth emerges somewhat red and turns medium green in Summer; Fall leaves are brilliant red, orange, purple and yellow to yellowish green; color varies on each tree

LANDSCAPE CHARACTERISTICS

GROWTH RATE: Moderate to Fast   **DROUGHT TOLERANCE:** Moderate once established   **SALT TOLERANCE:** Low
SOIL REQUIREMENTS: Well-drained, moist, fertile, humus rich, slightly acidic soil; tolerates wet sites
LIGHT REQUIREMENTS: Sun to part shade
PEST PROBLEMS: Thrips, caterpillars, Mapleworm, bagworm, gall making insects, leaf miner, Maple petiole borer, mites, sawfly, ambrosia beetles, twig pruner, flatheaded Apple tree borer, aphids, mealybugs, scales, sapsucker birds and black vine beetle
DISEASE PROBLEMS: Anthracnose, canker rot, dieback, leaf blight, *Nectria*, nematodes, *Phomopsis*, powdery mildew, *Verticillium* wilt, tar spot and wetwood
ENVIRONMENTAL FACTORS: Girdling roots from limited soil growing area; lack of root pruning results in circling roots in container grown plant; Winter or Summer sunscald to the bark; ice and snowstorm damage
PRUNING: Prune to develop crown and strong limb angles; remove crossing limbs and low hanging limbs to allow pedestrian or vehicular circulation

ADDITIONAL NOTES

USES: Large specimen or shade tree in group plantings
URBAN USES: Good for streets and medians but does not tolerate heavy air pollution
SUBSTITUTIONS: *Lagerstroemia* cultivars, *Pyrus* cultivars, *Nyssa* species, small *Quercus* species
COMMENTS: Red Maple is one of the most commonly used landscape trees for its shade in Summer and brilliant colors in Fall.
OTHER CULTIVARS: Autumn Flame® - early Fall color, smaller leaves; Autumn Blaze® - resembles Silver Maple, upright growth, crimson Fall color, fast growing; October Glory® - oval crown, colors later than other Maples with brilliant orange-red-purple color; Red Sunset® - orange-red Fall color, colors before October Glory®; 'HOSR' Summer Red® - new growth emerges burgundy-red through Summer, Fall color is yellow, orange and purple; heat tolerant

Acer rubrum
Autumn Flame® Red Maple
USDA Hardiness Zones: 3b-8

DESCRIPTION

NATIVE HABITAT: Eastern United States; cultivar of nursery origin
PLANT TYPE: Deciduous, broadleaf, large tree
MATURE SIZE: 35-40' tall by 35-40' wide
FORM/SHAPE: Broad dome to round, dense crown
BARK: Smooth; grayish tan and develops shallow fissures, ridges and plates when mature
FLOWER: Yellowish green; small; inconspicuous; blooms in Spring
FRUIT: Green, winged samara
FOLIAGE: Opposite, simple, medium-sized, five-lobed; glossy, dark green leaves in Summer turn yellowish orange to red in acidic soil in Fall

LANDSCAPE CHARACTERISTICS

GROWTH RATE: Moderate to Fast   **DROUGHT TOLERANCE:** Moderate once established   **SALT TOLERANCE:** Low
SOIL REQUIREMENTS: Well-drained, moist, fertile, humus rich, slightly acidic soil; tolerates wet sites
LIGHT REQUIREMENTS: Full sun to part shade; best growth and color in full sun
PEST PROBLEMS: Thrips, caterpillars, Mapleworm, bagworm, gall making insects, leaf miner, Maple petiole borer, mites, sawfly, ambrosia beetles, twig pruner, flatheaded Apple tree borer, aphids, mealybugs, scales, sapsucker birds and black vine beetle
DISEASE PROBLEMS: Anthracnose, canker rot, dieback, leaf blight, *Nectria*, nematodes, *Phomopsis*, powdery mildew, *Verticillium* wilt, tar spot and wetwood
ENVIRONMENTAL FACTORS: Girdling roots from limited soil growing area; lack of root pruning results in circling roots in container grown plant; Winter or Summer sunscald to the bark; ice and snowstorm damage
PRUNING: Prune to develop crown and strong limb angles; remove crossing limbs and low hanging limbs to allow pedestrian or vehicular circulation

ADDITIONAL NOTES

USES: Large shade tree, street tree, specimen tree, group plantings, buffer and naturalizing
URBAN USES: Very adaptable to urban growing sites; moderately tolerant of air pollutants, compacted soil and moderately dry planting sites
SUBSTITUTIONS: Other *Acer rubrum* cultivars, small *Quercus* species, *Lagerstroemia* cultivars
COMMENTS: Autumn Flame® is dense, compact and very cold hardy with an earlier Fall color than other cultivars. Autumn Flame® has good tolerance to potato leafhopper injury and heat.
OTHER CULTIVARS: 'Brandywine' - moderately upright, oval form, orange to red to purplish red Fall foliage, good tolerance to heat and leafhopper damage, U.S. National Arboretum introduction

Acer rubrum
October Glory® Red Maple
USDA Hardiness Zones: 5-8

DESCRIPTION

NATIVE HABITAT: Eastern United States; cultivar of nursery origin
PLANT TYPE: Deciduous, broadleaf, large tree
MATURE SIZE: 40-50' high by 25-35' wide
FORM/SHAPE: Oval, rounded, generally smooth outline
BARK: Smooth; grayish tan and develops shallow fissures, ridges and plates when mature
FLOWER: Red; showy before leaves emerge; blooms in Spring
FRUIT: Somewhat red, winged samara
FOLIAGE: Opposite, simple, medium-sized, five-lobed; green to dark green leaves in Summer turn orange, red or purple in Fall

LANDSCAPE CHARACTERISTICS

GROWTH RATE: Moderate   **DROUGHT TOLERANCE:** Moderate once established   **SALT TOLERANCE:** Low
SOIL REQUIREMENTS: Well-drained, moist, fertile, humus rich, slightly acidic soil; tolerates wet sites
LIGHT REQUIREMENTS: Full sun to part shade; best growth and color in full sun
PEST PROBLEMS: Thrips, caterpillars, Mapleworm, bagworm, gall making insects, leaf miner, Maple petiole borer, mites, sawfly, ambrosia beetles, twig pruner, flatheaded Apple tree borer, aphids, mealybugs, scales, sapsucker birds and black vine beetle
DISEASE PROBLEMS: Anthracnose, canker rot, dieback, leaf blight, *Nectria*, nematodes, *Phomopsis*, powdery mildew, *Verticillium* wilt, tar spot and wetwood
ENVIRONMENTAL FACTORS: Girdling roots from limited soil growing area; lack of root pruning results in circling roots in container grown plant; Winter or Summer sunscald to the bark; ice and snowstorm damage
PRUNING: Prune to develop crown and strong limb angles; remove crossing limbs and low hanging limbs to allow pedestrian or vehicular circulation

ADDITIONAL NOTES

USES: Large shade tree, street tree, specimen tree, group plantings, buffer and naturalizing
URBAN USES: Very adaptable to urban growing sites; moderately tolerant of air pollutants, compacted soil and moderately dry planting sites
SUBSTITUTIONS: Other *Acer rubrum* cultivars, *Lagerstroemia* cultivars, *Nyssa* species, small *Quercus* species, *Pyrus* and *Prunus* cultivars
COMMENTS: October Glory® is the most widely planted and grown *Acer rubrum* cultivar with consistent plant growth, form and Fall coloration over USDA Hardiness Zones 5-8.
OTHER CULTIVARS: 'Sun Valley' - early, orange-red Fall color; broad, uniform, oval crown, tolerant of leafhopper damage; 'HOSR' Summer Red® - heat tolerant to USDA Hardiness Zone 9, uniform, well-branched, dense, round, oval crown; Fall color is yellow, orange and purple

Acer rubrum 'Brandywine'
Brandywine Red Maple
USDA Hardiness Zones: 4-8

DESCRIPTION

NATIVE HABITAT: Eastern United States; cultivar of nursery origin
PLANT TYPE: Deciduous, broadleaf, large tree
MATURE SIZE: 30-40' tall by 20-25' wide
FORM/SHAPE: Moderately upright, oval
BARK: Smooth; grayish tan and develops shallow fissures, ridges and plates when mature
FLOWER: Yellowish green; small; inconspicuous; blooms in Spring
FRUIT: Green, winged samara; turns reddish green to reddish brown
FOLIAGE: Opposite, simple, medium-sized, five-lobed, heavily textured; glossy, dark green leaves turn orange to red to purple-red in Fall

LANDSCAPE CHARACTERISTICS

GROWTH RATE: Moderate to Fast   **DROUGHT TOLERANCE:** Moderate once established   **SALT TOLERANCE:** Low
SOIL REQUIREMENTS: Well-drained, moist, fertile, humus rich, slightly acidic soil; tolerates wet sites
LIGHT REQUIREMENTS: Full sun to part shade
PEST PROBLEMS: Thrips, caterpillars, Mapleworm, bagworm, gall making insects, leaf miner, Maple petiole borer, mites, sawfly, ambrosia beetles, twig pruner, flatheaded Apple tree borer, aphids, mealybugs, scales, sapsucker birds and black vine beetle
DISEASE PROBLEMS: Anthracnose, canker rot, dieback, leaf blight, *Nectria*, nematodes, *Phomopsis*, powdery mildew, *Verticillium* wilt, tar spot and wetwood
ENVIRONMENTAL FACTORS: Girdling roots from limited soil growing area; lack of root pruning results in circling roots in container grown plant; Winter or Summer sunscald to the bark; ice and snowstorm damage
PRUNING: Prune to develop crown and strong limb angles; remove crossing limbs and low hanging limbs to allow pedestrian or vehicular circulation

ADDITIONAL NOTES

USES: Large shade tree, street tree, specimen tree, group plantings, buffer and naturalizing
URBAN USES: Very adaptable to urban growing sites; moderately tolerant of air pollutants, compacted soil and moderately dry planting sites
SUBSTITUTIONS: Other *Acer rubrum* cultivars, small *Quercus* species, *Lagerstroemia* cultivars
COMMENTS: 'Brandywine' is a U.S. National Arboretum cultivar resulting from a cross between October Glory® and Autumn Flame®. It is compact, more heat and leafhopper tolerant and has a better Fall color in Southern hardiness regions.
OTHER CULTIVARS: 'Sun Valley' - early, orange-red Fall color; broad, uniform, oval crown, tolerant of leafhopper damage; 'HOSR' Summer Red® - heat tolerant to USDA Hardiness Zone 9, uniform, well-branched, dense, round, oval crown; Fall color is yellow, orange and purple

Acer rubrum 'Franksred'
Red Sunset® Red Maple
USDA Hardiness Zones: 4-7

DESCRIPTION

NATIVE HABITAT: Eastern United States; cultivar of nursery origin
PLANT TYPE: Deciduous, broadleaf, large tree
MATURE SIZE: 40-45' tall by 30-35' wide
FORM/SHAPE: Upright, oval
BARK: Smooth; grayish tan and develops shallow fissures, ridges and plates when mature
FLOWER: Greenish yellow; inconspicuous; blooms in Spring
FRUIT: Fruitless; male flowering cultivar
FOLIAGE: Opposite, simple, large, five-lobed, leathery; glossy, dark green leaves turn orange-red to dark red in Fall

LANDSCAPE CHARACTERISTICS

GROWTH RATE: Moderate to Fast   **DROUGHT TOLERANCE:** Moderate once established   **SALT TOLERANCE:** Low
SOIL REQUIREMENTS: Well-drained, moist, fertile, humus rich, slightly acidic soil; tolerates wet sites
LIGHT REQUIREMENTS: Full sun to part shade
PEST PROBLEMS: Thrips, caterpillars, Mapleworm, bagworm, gall making insects, leaf miner, Maple petiole borer, mites, sawfly, ambrosia beetles, twig pruner, flatheaded Apple tree borer, aphids, mealybugs, scales, sapsucker birds and black vine beetle
DISEASE PROBLEMS: Anthracnose, canker rot, dieback, leaf blight, *Nectria*, nematodes, *Phomopsis*, powdery mildew, *Verticillium* wilt, tar spot and wetwood
ENVIRONMENTAL FACTORS: Girdling roots from limited soil growing area; lack of root pruning results in circling roots in container grown plant; Winter or Summer sunscald to the bark; ice and snowstorm damage
PRUNING: Prune to develop crown and strong limb angles; remove crossing limbs and low hanging limbs to allow pedestrian or vehicular circulation

ADDITIONAL NOTES

USES: Large shade tree, street tree, specimen tree, group plantings, buffer and naturalizing
URBAN USES: Very adaptable to urban growing sites; moderately tolerant of air pollutants, compacted soil and moderately dry planting sites
SUBSTITUTIONS: Other *Acer rubrum* cultivars, small *Quercus* species, *Lagerstroemia* cultivars
COMMENTS: Red Sunset® shows its best qualities of vigorous growth, strong, well-balanced branching habit and brilliant Fall color in USDA Hardiness Zone 7a and colder. Potato leafhopper is a serious plant pest that must be controlled on young trees.
OTHER CULTIVARS: 'Brandywine' - moderately upright, oval form, orange to red to purplish red Fall foliage, good tolerance to heat and leafhopper damage, U.S. National Arboretum introduction; 'HOSR' Summer Red® heat tolerant to USDA Hardiness Zone 9, uniform, well-branched, dense, round, oval, crown; Fall color is yellow, orange and purple

Acer rubrum 'HOSR'
Summer Red® Red Maple
USDA Hardiness Zones: 5-9

DESCRIPTION

NATIVE HABITAT: Eastern United States; nursery selection by Head Ornamentals, Inc.
PLANT TYPE: Deciduous, broadleaf, large tree
MATURE SIZE: 35-40' tall by 20-25' wide
FORM/SHAPE: Upright, oval, rounded
BARK: Smooth; burgundy when young and matures to brownish gray; develops shallow fissures, ridges and plates when mature
FLOWER: Dark burgundy-red; blooms in late Winter
FRUIT: Purplish red, winged samara
FOLIAGE: Opposite, simple, medium-sized, three to five-lobed; very distinctive leaf color; new growth is burgundy-red; mature leaves are glossy, dark, purplish green with a silvery white leaf back; yellow, orange and purple Fall color

LANDSCAPE CHARACTERISTICS

GROWTH RATE: Moderate to Fast   **DROUGHT TOLERANCE:** Moderate   **SALT TOLERANCE:** Low
SOIL REQUIREMENTS: Well-drained, moist, fertile, humus rich soil; tolerates wet sites
LIGHT REQUIREMENTS: Full sun to part shade; best growth and color in full sun
PEST PROBLEMS: Thrips, caterpillars, Mapleworm, bagworm, gall making insects, leaf miner, Maple petiole borer, mites, sawfly, ambrosia beetles, twig pruner, flatheaded Apple tree borer, aphids, mealybugs, scales, sapsucker birds and black vine beetle
DISEASE PROBLEMS: Anthracnose, canker rot, dieback, leaf blight, *Nectria*, nematodes, *Phomopsis*, powdery mildew, *Verticillium* wilt, tar spot and wetwood
ENVIRONMENTAL FACTORS: Girdling roots from limited soil growing area; lack of root pruning results in circling roots in container grown plant; Winter or Summer sunscald to the bark; ice and snowstorm damage
PRUNING: Prune to develop crown and strong limb angles; remove crossing limbs and low hanging limbs to allow pedestrian or vehicular circulation

ADDITIONAL NOTES

USES: Large tree, accent foliage, street tree, specimen, lawn tree, group plantings, buffer and naturalizing
URBAN USES: Very adaptable to urban growing sites; moderately tolerant of air pollutants, compacted soil and moderately dry planting sites; good in areas where other *Acer rubrum* cultivars do not receive enough Winter cold, chilling hours for proper growth
SUBSTITUTIONS: Other *Acer rubrum* cultivars, small *Quercus* species, *Lagerstroemia* cultivars, *Ginkgo* cultivars
COMMENTS: Summer Red® is adaptable to the deep South. It's not affected by low chilling hours from mild Winters. Fall leaf color on older foliage is yellow with younger foliage orange to purple.
OTHER CULTIVARS: October Glory® - purplish red Fall color, compact plant form; Burgundy Bell® - reddish green new growth

Acer saccharum
Sugar Maple or Northern Sugar Maple
USDA Hardiness Zones: 3-8

DESCRIPTION

NATIVE HABITAT: Eastern North America and Southern Canada
PLANT TYPE: Deciduous, broadleaf, large tree
MATURE SIZE: 40-60' tall by 20-40' wide
FORM/SHAPE: Oval, rounded, upright
BARK: Smooth; tannish gray; matures to blackish gray and develops deep fissures and ridges
FLOWER: Light green; inconspicuous; produced in short, round umbels; blooms in Spring
FRUIT: Light yellowish green, winged samara; turns brown in Fall
FOLIAGE: Opposite, simple, three to five-lobed; medium dark green leaves turn bright yellow, orange and red in Fall

LANDSCAPE CHARACTERISTICS

GROWTH RATE: Slow to Moderate   **DROUGHT TOLERANCE:** Moderate once established   **SALT TOLERANCE:** Low
SOIL REQUIREMENTS: Adaptable to sandy, loam or clay soil; adaptable to many pH and fertility levels; best growth in well-drained, moist, fertile, humus rich, slightly acidic soil; not tolerant of compacted or wet soil sites
LIGHT REQUIREMENTS: Full sun to part shade; best growth and color in full sun
PEST PROBLEMS: Thrips, caterpillars, Mapleworm, bagworm, gall making insects, leaf miner, Maple petiole borer, mites, sawfly, ambrosia beetles, twig pruner, flatheaded Apple tree borer, aphids, mealybugs, scales, sapsucker birds and black vine beetle
DISEASE PROBLEMS: Anthracnose, canker rot, dieback, leaf blight, *Nectria*, nematodes, *Phomopsis*, powdery mildew, *Verticillium* wilt, tar spot and wetwood
ENVIRONMENTAL FACTORS: Girdling roots from limited soil growing area; lack of root pruning results in circling roots in container grown plant; Winter or Summer sunscald to the bark; ice and snowstorm damage; not tolerant of water-logged, compacted soils; may be slow growing and poorly formed in USDA Hardiness Zones warmer than 7a
PRUNING: Prune to develop crown and strong limb angles; remove crossing limbs and low hanging limbs to allow pedestrian or vehicular circulation

ADDITIONAL NOTES

USES: Large shade and lawn tree, commercial and urban plantings
URBAN USES: Golf courses, lawns, parks, streets and medians
SUBSTITUTIONS: *Acer rubrum* and cultivars, *Acer barbatum*, *Pyrus* cultivars, *Lagerstroemia* cultivars, *Quercus* species
COMMENTS: Sugar Maples grow best in colder regions. Some cultivars are more tolerant of Southeastern conditions.
OTHER CULTIVARS: Green Mountain® - dark green leaves, orange-scarlet Fall color; 'Legacy' - good resistance to leaf tatter, yellowish orange Fall color, drought tolerant; 'Commemoration' - fast growing, dense canopy, orange to orange-red Fall color, colors early; Steeple® - narrow, oval, heat and drought tolerant, yellowish orange Fall color

Acer saccharum
Green Mountain® Sugar Maple
USDA Hardiness Zones: 3-8

DESCRIPTION

NATIVE HABITAT: Eastern North America and Southern Canada; cultivar of nursery origin
PLANT TYPE: Deciduous, broadleaf, large tree
MATURE SIZE: 45' tall by 35' wide
FORM/SHAPE: Broad, oval to rounded
BARK: Smooth; tannish gray; matures to blackish gray and develops deep fissures and ridges
FLOWER: Light green; inconspicuous; produced in short, round umbels; blooms in Spring
FRUIT: Light yellowish green, winged samara; turns brown in Fall
FOLIAGE: Opposite, simple, three to five-lobed, broad and heavily textured, leaves typically shaped like species; in acidic soils, dark green leaves turn reddish orange in Fall

LANDSCAPE CHARACTERISTICS

GROWTH RATE: Moderate   **DROUGHT TOLERANCE:** Moderate   **SALT TOLERANCE:** Low
SOIL REQUIREMENTS: Adaptable to sandy, loam or clay soil; adaptable to many pH and fertility levels; best growth in well-drained, moist, fertile, humus rich, slightly acidic soil; not tolerant of compacted or wet soil sites
LIGHT REQUIREMENTS: Full sun to part shade; best growth and color in full sun
PEST PROBLEMS: Thrips, caterpillars, Mapleworm, bagworm, gall making insects, leaf miner, Maple petiole borer, mites, sawfly, ambrosia beetles, twig pruner, flatheaded Apple tree borer, aphids, mealybugs, scales, sapsucker birds and black vine beetle
DISEASE PROBLEMS: Anthracnose, canker rot, dieback, leaf blight, *Nectria*, nematodes, *Phomopsis*, powdery mildew, *Verticillium* wilt, tar spot and wetwood
ENVIRONMENTAL FACTORS: Girdling roots from limited soil growing area; lack of root pruning results in circling roots in container grown plant; Winter or Summer sunscald to the bark; ice and snowstorm damage; not tolerant of water-logged, compacted soil; may be slow growing and poorly formed in Zones warmer than USDA Hardiness Zone 7a
PRUNING: Prune to develop crown and strong limb angles; remove crossing limbs and low hanging limbs to allow pedestrian or vehicular circulation

ADDITIONAL NOTES

USES: Large shade tree, lawn tree, park tree and golf courses; needs large space for crown to spread and roots to develop
URBAN USES: Moderately tolerant of air pollutants; not tolerant of water-logged soil or excessively dry soil; best growth and stress tolerance in colder climates
SUBSTITUTIONS: *Acer rubrum* and cultivars, *Quercus* species and cultivars
COMMENTS: Green Mountain® is very cold hardy and does not perform well in zones warmer than USDA Hardiness Zone 7a. The best plant form, dark green foliage, Fall foliage color and consistent plant quality are in USDA Hardiness Zones 6 and colder.
OTHER CULTIVARS: 'Bonfire' - fast plant growth, broad, oval form, Fall foliage orange to red, adaptable to a wide range of conditions; 'Commemoration' - fast growing, broad, oval to rounded, dark green leaves turn orange to orange-red in Fall

Acer saccharum 'Astis'
Steeple® Sugar Maple
USDA Hardiness Zones: 4-8

DESCRIPTION

NATIVE HABITAT: Eastern North America and Southern Canada; southern selected cultivar
PLANT TYPE: Deciduous, broadleaf, large tree
MATURE SIZE: 45' tall by 20-25' wide
FORM/SHAPE: Narrow, symmetrical, oval crown
BARK: Smooth; tannish gray; matures to blackish gray and develops deep fissures and ridges
FLOWER: Greenish yellow; inconspicuous; produced in short, round umbels; blooms in Spring
FRUIT: Yellowish green samara with slightly divergent wings; turns brown in Fall
FOLIAGE: Opposite, simple, three to five-lobed; dark green leaves turn yellow-orange in Fall

LANDSCAPE CHARACTERISTICS

GROWTH RATE: Slow to Moderate   **DROUGHT TOLERANCE:** Moderate to High   **SALT TOLERANCE:** Low
SOIL REQUIREMENTS: Adaptable to sandy, loam or clay soil; adaptable to many pH and fertility levels; best growth in well-drained, moist, fertile, humus rich, slightly acidic soil; not tolerant of compacted or wet soil sites
LIGHT REQUIREMENTS: Full sun to part shade; best growth and color in full sun
PEST PROBLEMS: Thrips, caterpillars, Mapleworm, bagworm, gall making insects, leaf miner, Maple petiole borer, mites, sawfly, ambrosia beetles, twig pruner, flatheaded Apple tree borer, aphids, mealybugs, scales, sapsucker birds and black vine beetle
DISEASE PROBLEMS: Anthracnose, canker rot, dieback, leaf blight, *Nectria*, nematodes, *Phomopsis*, powdery mildew, *Verticillium* wilt, tar spot and wetwood
ENVIRONMENTAL FACTORS: Girdling roots from limited soil growing area; lack of root pruning results in circling roots in container grown plant; Winter or Summer sunscald to the bark; ice and snowstorm damage; Sugar Maples do not typically perform well in tight, compacted soil
PRUNING: Prune to develop crown and strong limb angles; remove crossing limbs and low hanging limbs to allow pedestrian or vehicular circulation

ADDITIONAL NOTES

USES: Large shade tree, lawn tree, park tree and golf courses; needs large space for crown to spread and roots to develop
URBAN USES: Moderately tolerant of air pollutants; not tolerant of water-logged soil or excessively dry soil; best growth and stress tolerance in colder climates; narrow, oval, compact, upright growth habit for street trees and other restricted above ground spaces
SUBSTITUTIONS: *Acer rubrum* 'Brandywine', *Zelkova serrata* 'Musashino', *Lagerstroemia* cultivars, Rotundiloba Sweetgum, Slender Silouette Sweetgum, *Carpinus betulus* 'Fastigiata', Gold Falls® *Zelkova*
COMMENTS: Steeple® Sugar Maple has shown good heat tolerance for the South. Selected by Dr. Michael Dirr for its excellent narrow, oval crown form and heat tolerant foliage.
OTHER CULTIVARS: 'Barrett Cole' PP 10,590 Apollo™ - dwarf, densely-branched, very narrow, columnar form, foliage dark green and heat tolerant, Fall foliage yellow-orange-red, 25' tall; 'Endowment' - large, broad, columnar form, 50' tall by 20' wide, dark green foliage, turns bright gold in Fall

Acer saccharum 'Legacy'
Legacy Sugar Maple
USDA Hardiness Zones: 5-9

DESCRIPTION

NATIVE HABITAT: Eastern North America and Southern Canada; cultivar of nursery origin
PLANT TYPE: Deciduous, broadleaf, large tree
MATURE SIZE: 40-60' tall by 20-40' wide
FORM/SHAPE: Dense, oval
BARK: Smooth; tannish gray; matures to blackish gray and develops deep fissures and ridges
FLOWER: Yellow-green; inconspicuous; produced in short round umbels; blooms in Spring
FRUIT: Green samara; turns light brown in Fall
FOLIAGE: Opposite, simple, three to five-lobed; dark green leaves turn yellow, orange and red in Fall

LANDSCAPE CHARACTERISTICS

GROWTH RATE: Moderate to Fast   **DROUGHT TOLERANCE:** Moderate   **SALT TOLERANCE:** Low
SOIL REQUIREMENTS: Adaptable to sandy, loam or clay soil; adaptable to many pH and fertility levels; best growth in well-drained, moist, fertile, humus rich, slightly acidic soil; not tolerant of compacted or wet soil sites
LIGHT REQUIREMENTS: Full sun to part shade; best growth and color in full sun
PEST PROBLEMS: Thrips, caterpillars, Mapleworm, bagworm, gall making insects, leaf miner, Maple petiole borer, mites, sawfly, ambrosia beetles, twig pruner, flatheaded Apple tree borer, aphids, mealybugs, scales, sapsucker birds and black vine beetle
DISEASE PROBLEMS: Anthracnose, canker rot, dieback, leaf blight, *Nectria*, nematodes, *Phomopsis*, powdery mildew, *Verticillium* wilt, tar spot and wetwood
ENVIRONMENTAL FACTORS: Girdling roots from limited soil growing area; lack of root pruning results in circling roots in container grown plant; Winter or Summer sunscald to the bark; ice and snowstorm damage; not tolerant of water-logged, compacted soil; may be slow growing and poorly formed in USDA Hardiness Zones warmer than 7a
PRUNING: Prune to develop crown and strong limb angles; remove crossing limbs and low hanging limbs to allow pedestrian or vehicular circulation

ADDITIONAL NOTES

USES: Large shade tree, lawn tree, park tree and golf courses; needs large space for crown to spread and roots to develop
URBAN USES: Moderately tolerant of air pollutants; not tolerant of water-logged soil or excessively dry soil; best growth and stress tolerance in colder climates
SUBSTITUTIONS: *Acer barbatum, Acer leucoderme, Acer nigrum, Acer rubrum* cultivars, *Quercus* species
COMMENTS: 'Legacy' exhibits dead, brown leaf retention after Fall coloration is gone, but the tree is clean of old leaves by late Winter.
OTHER CULTIVARS: 'Bonfire' - fast growth, broad, oval form, Fall foliage orange to red, adaptable to a wide range of conditions; 'Commemoration' - fast growing, broad, oval to rounded, dark green leaves turn orange to orange-red in Fall

Acer x freemanii 'Jeffers Red'
Autumn Blaze® Maple
USDA Hardiness Zones: 3-8

DESCRIPTION

NATIVE HABITAT: Hybrid of nursery origin
PLANT TYPE: Deciduous, broadleaf, large tree
MATURE SIZE: 50' tall by 40' wide
FORM/SHAPE: Oval, upright
BARK: Smooth; silvery gray
FLOWER: Red; inconspicuous; blooms in Spring
FRUIT: Green, winged samara, if produced; turns to brown in Fall
FOLIAGE: Opposite, simple; medium green leaves turn red, orange or reddish orange in Fall

LANDSCAPE CHARACTERISTICS

GROWTH RATE: Fast   **DROUGHT TOLERANCE:** Moderate   **SALT TOLERANCE:** Low
SOIL REQUIREMENTS: Well-drained, moist, fertile, humus rich, slightly acidic soil
LIGHT REQUIREMENTS: Full sun
PEST PROBLEMS: Thrips, caterpillars, Mapleworm, bagworm, gall making insects, leaf miner, Maple petiole borer, mites, sawfly, ambrosia beetles, twig pruner, flatheaded Apple tree borer, aphids, mealybugs, scales, sapsucker birds and black vine beetle
DISEASE PROBLEMS: Anthracnose, canker rot, dieback, leaf blight, *Nectria*, nematodes, *Phomopsis*, powdery mildew, *Verticillium* wilt, tar spot and wetwood
ENVIRONMENTAL FACTORS: Very fast growth can lead to limb damage from ice; aggressive root system; girdling roots from limited soil growing area
PRUNING: Prune to develop crown and strong limb angles; remove crossing limbs and low hanging limbs to allow pedestrian or vehicular circulation

ADDITIONAL NOTES

USES: Parking lot buffers, Fall color accent, large shade tree, streets and parks
URBAN USES: Good for streets and medians
SUBSTITUTIONS: *Acer rubrum* and cultivars, *Acer saccharum*, *Lagerstroemia* cultivars, *Quercus* species, *Nyssa* species
COMMENTS: Autumn Blaze®is a cross between a Red Maple and a Silver Maple, with better branching habit than Silver Maple. This tree has good Fall color and an aggressive root system with fast growth. Autumn Blaze® has the best traits of both species.
OTHER CULTIVARS: 'Marmo' - upright, oval shape, orange to orange-red Fall color; USDA Hardiness Zone 3; 'DTR102' PP 7655 Autumn Fantasy® - broad, oval shape, bright red Fall color, USDA Hardiness Zone 4

Aesculus x carnea 'Fort McNair'
Fort McNair Red Horse Chestnut
USDA Hardiness Zones: 5-7

DESCRIPTION

NATIVE HABITAT: Hybrid of garden origin
PLANT TYPE: Deciduous, broadleaf, medium size flowering tree
MATURE SIZE: 30-40' tall by 25-30' wide
FORM/SHAPE: Pyramidal when young; round and dense when mature
BARK: Smooth, thick; light brown or tan
FLOWER: Bright coral-pink; blooms in Spring; very showy
FRUIT: Brown nut; attracts wildlife; poisonous to humans; messy
FOLIAGE: Opposite, palmately compound; green leaves turn yellow in Fall; some leaves drop early in Fall before changing color

LANDSCAPE CHARACTERISTICS

GROWTH RATE: Slow   **DROUGHT TOLERANCE:** Moderate   **SALT TOLERANCE:** Moderate
SOIL REQUIREMENTS: Well-drained, moist, fertile, humus rich, sandy, clay or loam soil
LIGHT REQUIREMENTS: Full sun; afternoon shade can benefit the plant
PEST PROBLEMS: Bagworm, mites, lacebug, scales, oyster scale
DISEASE PROBLEMS: *Ganoderma*, *Hypoxylon*, *Verticillium* wilt, *Nectria*, anthracnose, *Phomopsis*, bleeding canker and root rot
ENVIRONMENTAL FACTORS: Trunk bark tends to crack in full sun
PRUNING: Do not over prune; keep limbs low to ground so shade protects trunk bark from hot sun exposure

ADDITIONAL NOTES

USES: Specimen tree, shade tree, screen, medians and parking lots
URBAN USES: Can be used in urban areas, but leaf and flower litter can be messy
SUBSTITUTIONS: *Aesculus pavia* or hybrid cultivars, *Cornus* cultivars, *Malus* cultivars, *Prunus* cultivars, *Styrax japonica* cultivars
COMMENTS: Leaf and flower litter can become very messy. Use away from pedestrian and traffic areas where plant litter will not be a problem.
OTHER CULTIVARS: 'Briotti' - symmetrical tree with bright red flowers

Amelanchier x grandiflora 'Autumn Brilliance'
Autumn Brilliance® Serviceberry
USDA Hardiness Zones: 4-7b

DESCRIPTION

NATIVE HABITAT: Hybrid between *A. arborea* and *A. laevis*
PLANT TYPE: Deciduous, broadleaf, multi-trunk, small flowering tree
MATURE SIZE: 15-20' tall by 15-20' wide
FORM/SHAPE: Upright, symmetrical canopy; moderately spreading and heavily branched
BARK: Smooth; thin chalk-gray
FLOWER: Pink in bud fading to white; held in larger clusters than other Serviceberry; blooms early to late Spring; attracts insects
FRUIT: Round, less than 1/2", fleshy and red; edible; attracts birds and animals; not messy
FOLIAGE: Alternate, simple, elliptical, oblong; young leaves purplish and pubescent; medium green mature leaves finely textured and serrated; leaves turn bright red to yellow-orange in Fall

LANDSCAPE CHARACTERISTICS

GROWTH RATE: Slow   **DROUGHT TOLERANCE:** Moderate   **SALT TOLERANCE:** Moderate
SOIL REQUIREMENTS: Well-drained, moist, fertile, humus rich, slightly acidic soil; adaptable to a wide range of soils including clay, loam and sandy; benefits from well-limed soil
LIGHT REQUIREMENTS: Full sun to light shade; best growth and development in full sun; prefers shade in warmer regions
PEST PROBLEMS: Skeletonizing insects, leaf miner, cambium miners, Pear sawfly larvae, borers, spider mites, aphids, scales, wooly Elm aphid, flatheaded Apple tree borer and wooly Alder aphid
DISEASE PROBLEMS: Black mildew, leaf blight, fireblight, powdery mildew, fruit rot, Cedar rust, *Nectria, Taphrina* and *Verticillium* wilt
ENVIRONMENTAL FACTORS: Not tolerant of extremely wet or dry planting sites; drought stress and water-logged soil may result in pest and disease damage; sensitive to air pollution
PRUNING: Can be pruned to a single trunk, but needs little pruning to develop a strong tree with minimal limb breakage

ADDITIONAL NOTES

USES: Excellent landscape tree with four season interest, buffer strips, parking lots, medians, patio specimen tree, residential street tree and naturalizing
URBAN USES: Drought and poor water drainage may result in pest and disease problems
SUBSTITUTIONS: *Chionanthus retusus* and *virginicus*, *Loropetalum chinense* and *rubrum* 'Zhuzhou Fuchsia', *Malus* cultivars, *Prunus* cultivars, *Lagerstroemia* cultivars, *Ilex* cultivars
COMMENTS: Autumn Brilliance® has strong branching, reliable Spring blooms and bright Fall color. Also known as Apple Serviceberry, it is more resistant to leaf spot than the species. The plant has spectacular large white flowers, but bark is easily damaged.
OTHER CULTIVARS: 'Cole's Select' - similar size and shape, smaller foliage, orange-red Fall color, thick glossy foliage in mid-Summer; 'Robin Hill' - upright tree form, sensitive to drought, pink buds open white; 'Rubescens' - similar to 'Robin Hill', flower buds rose-red, opening soft pink

Betula nigra
River Birch

USDA Hardiness Zones: 6-9

DESCRIPTION

NATIVE HABITAT: Eastern and Central United States through the South and into Eastern Texas

PLANT TYPE: Deciduous, broadleaf, large tree

MATURE SIZE: 30-60' tall by 20-50' wide

FORM/SHAPE: Upright, open oval, can be multi or single-stemmed

BARK: Smooth; greenish brown when young; mature bark exfoliates in large, papery sheets with a gray-brown to chalky tan to beige-white color

FLOWER: Catkins, 2-4" long; blooms in Spring

FRUIT: Nutlet produced in Spring

FOLIAGE: Alternate, simple; medium to dark green, serrated leaves turn shades of yellow in Fall

LANDSCAPE CHARACTERISTICS

GROWTH RATE: Moderate to Fast   **DROUGHT TOLERANCE:** Low   **SALT TOLERANCE:** Low

SOIL REQUIREMENTS: Well-drained, moist, fertile, humus rich soil; very tolerant of moist sites

LIGHT REQUIREMENTS: Full sun to part shade

PEST PROBLEMS: Sawfly, mites, bronze Birch borer, Poplar and Willow borer, skeletonizer, Elm leaf beetle, Japanese beetle, thrips, caterpillars, leaf miner, leafroller, Dogwood borer, Birch lacebug, aphids, leaf gall aphid, leafhopper, scales and treehopper

DISEASE PROBLEMS: Anthracnose, *Armillaria* root rot, canker, butt rot, dieback, *Discula, Hypoxylon*, leaf blotch, *Nectria,* powdery mildew and *Taphrina* leaf blister

ENVIRONMENTAL FACTORS: Nickel element deficiency causes mouse ear and stem dwarfness; drought stress causes some early leaf drop

PRUNING: Do not prune or trim late Winter through Spring when sap is flowing; prune to maintain central leaders; remove low hanging limbs

ADDITIONAL NOTES

USES: Specimen tree, buffer areas, lawns, parks, as a Winter accent with bark interest and reclamation plantings

URBAN USES: Good in urban areas as a street tree or in medians

SUBSTITUTIONS: *Taxodium* species and cultivars or *Nyssa* species

COMMENTS: A native tree adaptable to wet soil sites. Drought stress causes leaf drop. This is not a good tree for pedestrian areas due to constant leaf and twig drop. The exfoliating bark provides great Winter interest.

OTHER CULTIVARS: Dura-Heat® - smaller, dense branching with less leaf drop; Heritage® - large Northern selection; 'Little King' - dwarf selection for small areas; 'Summer Cascade' PP 15,105 - small, weeping selection that has to be staked to obtain height and form, needs part shade

Betula nigra 'BNMTF'
Dura-Heat® River Birch
USDA Hardiness Zones: 4-9

DESCRIPTION

NATIVE HABITAT: Eastern and Central United States through the South and into Eastern Texas; cultivar of nursery origin
PLANT TYPE: Deciduous, broadleaf, large tree
MATURE SIZE: 40-50' tall by 25-35' wide
FORM/SHAPE: Upright, open oval, can be multi or single-stemmed
BARK: Smooth; greenish brown when young; mature bark exfoliates in large, papery sheets with a gray-brown to chalky tan to beige color
FLOWER: Catkins, 2-4" long; blooms in Spring
FRUIT: Nutlet produced in Spring
FOLIAGE: Alternate, simple; medium to dark green, serrated leaves turn shades of yellow in Fall

LANDSCAPE CHARACTERISTICS

GROWTH RATE: Moderate to Fast   **DROUGHT TOLERANCE:** Low   **SALT TOLERANCE:** Low
SOIL REQUIREMENTS: Well-drained, moist, fertile, humus rich soil; very tolerant of moist sites
LIGHT REQUIREMENTS: Full sun to part shade
PEST PROBLEMS: Sawfly, mites, bronze Birch borer, Poplar and Willow borer, skeletonizer, Elm leaf beetle, Japanese beetle, thrips, caterpillars, leaf miner, leafroller, Dogwood borer, Birch lacebug, aphids, leaf gall aphid, leafhopper, scale and treehopper
DISEASE PROBLEMS: Anthracnose, *Armillaria* root rot, canker, butt rot, dieback, *Discula, Hypoxylon*, leaf blotch, *Nectria,* powdery mildew and *Taphrina* leaf blister
ENVIRONMENTAL FACTORS: Nickel element deficiency causes mouse ear and stem dwarfness; drought stress causes some early leaf drop
PRUNING: Do not prune or trim late Winter through Spring when sap is flowing; prune to maintain central leaders; remove low hanging limbs

ADDITIONAL NOTES

USES: Specimen tree, buffer areas, lawns, parks, as a Winter accent with bark interest and reclamation plantings
URBAN USES: Good in urban areas as a street tree or in medians
SUBSTITUTIONS: *Taxodium* species and cultivars or *Nyssa* species
COMMENTS: Dura Heat® River Birch has chalky tan to beige colored inner bark that is exposed as older bark exfoliates. Dura Heat® has a smaller leaf than that typical of the species. The tree has a dense and compact limb structure. The thick, durable leaves of Dura Heat® are less prone to drop during Summer drought stress than the species and other River Birch cultivars.
OTHER CULTIVARS: Heritage® - large Northern selection; 'Little King' - dwarf selection for small areas; 'Summer Cascade' PP 15,105 - small, weeping selection that has to be staked to obtain height and form, needs part shade

Betula nigra 'Cully'
Heritage® River Birch
USDA Hardiness Zones: 4-9

DESCRIPTION

NATIVE HABITAT: Eastern and Central United States through the South and into Eastern Texas; Northern selection
PLANT TYPE: Deciduous, broadleaf, large tree
MATURE SIZE: 50-60' tall by 30-40' wide
FORM/SHAPE: Upright, open oval, can be multi or single-stemmed
BARK: Smooth; greenish brown when young; mature bark exfoliates in large, papery sheets with a chalky tan to beige-white color
FLOWER: Catkins, 2-4" long; blooms in Spring
FRUIT: Nutlet produced in Spring
FOLIAGE: Alternate, simple; medium to dark green, serrated leaves turn shades of yellow in Fall

LANDSCAPE CHARACTERISTICS

GROWTH RATE: Moderate to Fast   **DROUGHT TOLERANCE:** Low   **SALT TOLERANCE:** Low
SOIL REQUIREMENTS: Well-drained, moist, fertile, humus rich soil; very tolerant of moist sites
LIGHT REQUIREMENTS: Full sun to part shade
PEST PROBLEMS: Sawfly, mites, bronze Birch borer, Poplar and Willow borer, skeletonizer, Elm leaf beetle, Japanese beetle, thrips, caterpillars, leaf miner, leafroller, Dogwood borer, Birch lacebug, aphids, leaf gall aphid, leafhopper, scale and treehopper
DISEASE PROBLEMS: Anthracnose, *Armillaria* root rot, canker, butt rot, dieback, *Discula, Hypoxylon*, leaf blotch, *Nectria,* powdery mildew and *Taphrina* leaf blister
ENVIRONMENTAL FACTORS: Nickel element deficiency causes mouse ear and stem dwarfness; drought stress causes some early leaf drop
PRUNING: Do not prune or trim late Winter or Spring when sap is flowing; prune to maintain central leaders; remove low hanging limbs

ADDITIONAL NOTES

USES: Specimen tree, buffer areas, lawns, parks, as a Winter accent with bark interest and reclamation plantings
URBAN USES: Good in urban areas as a street tree or in medians
SUBSTITUTIONS: *Taxodium* species and cultivars or *Nyssa* species
COMMENTS: Heritage® River Birch has the whitest exfoliating bark on mature trees or any River Birch cultivar. Heritage® is a vigorous grower, and develops into a very large growing tree. The tree tends to shed leaves during Summer drought stress. Heritage® is a Northern selection.
OTHER CULTIVARS: Dura-Heat® - smaller, dense branching with less leaf drop; 'Little King' - dwarf selection for small areas; 'Summer Cascade' PP 15,105 - small, weeping selection that has to be staked to obtain height and form, needs part shade

Carpinus betulus 'Fastigiata'
Pyramidal European Hornbeam
USDA Hardiness Zones: 5-8

DESCRIPTION

NATIVE HABITAT: Asia Minor to Europe (British Isles)
PLANT TYPE: Deciduous, broadleaf, large tree
MATURE SIZE: 30-40' tall by 15-20' wide
FORM/SHAPE: Upright, columnar tree; becomes oval as tree ages
BARK: Smooth; gray; develops fluted ridges and muscular features
FLOWER: White; inconspicuous; blooms in Spring
FRUIT: Small brown nutlet forms in clusters at the base of the bracts; inconspicuous
FOLIAGE: Alternate, simple, serrate; medium green leaves turn yellow in Fall

LANDSCAPE CHARACTERISTICS

GROWTH RATE: Moderate   **DROUGHT TOLERANCE:** Low to Moderate   **SALT TOLERANCE:** Low
SOIL REQUIREMENTS: Well-drained, moist, fertile, humus rich soil
LIGHT REQUIREMENTS: Part shade to full sun
PEST PROBLEMS: Ambrosia beetles, Japanese beetle, and lacebug
DISEASE PROBLEMS: Trunk cankers, leaf spot, and anthracnose
ENVIRONMENTAL FACTORS: Bark is thin and easily damaged; needs moist soil; dry soil and compaction may cause dieback
PRUNING: Prune to remove low limbs, improve shape and allow for vehicular and pedestrian circulation

ADDITIONAL NOTES

USES: Specimen, shade tree, screening in narrow or tight spaces
URBAN USES: Good for urban areas, especially as a street or median tree
SUBSTITUTIONS: Columnar shaped *Lagerstroemia* cultivars, *Zelkova*, *Prunus*, *Pyrus*, *Malus* cultivars
COMMENTS: Pyramidal European Hornbeam is a very desirable small tree for use where space is limited.
OTHER CULTIVARS: 'Frans Fontaine' - maintains columnar growth as tree ages

Carpinus caroliniana
American Hornbeam or Blue Beech
USDA Hardiness Zones: 3-9

DESCRIPTION

NATIVE HABITAT: Minnesota, Eastern United States to East Texas

PLANT TYPE: Deciduous, broadleaf, small tree

MATURE SIZE: 20-30' tall by 20-30' wide

FORM/SHAPE: Broad, oval crown; some columnar varieties available; seedling tree will vary in shape

BARK: Smooth; gray; develops fluted ridges and muscular features

FLOWER: Orange to yellow; inconspicuous; blooms in Spring

FRUIT: Oval; small, brown nutlet; inconspicuous; attracts wildlife

FOLIAGE: Alternate, simple, serrate; green leaves turn orange, red or yellow in Fall; leaves persist on tree in Winter

LANDSCAPE CHARACTERISTICS

GROWTH RATE: Slow to Moderate   **DROUGHT TOLERANCE:** Low to Moderate   **SALT TOLERANCE:** Low

SOIL REQUIREMENTS: Well-drained, moist, fertile, humus rich soil

LIGHT REQUIREMENTS: Part shade to full sun

PEST PROBLEMS: Ambrosia beetles, Japanese beetle and lacebug

DISEASE PROBLEMS: Trunk cankers, leaf spot and anthracnose

ENVIRONMENTAL FACTORS: Bark is thin and easily damaged; needs moist soil; dry soil and compaction may cause dieback

PRUNING: Prune to remove low limbs, improve shape and allow for vehicular and pedestrian circulation

ADDITIONAL NOTES

USES: Specimen, hedge, street tree or in smaller spaces

URBAN USES: Good for urban areas, especially as a street or median tree

SUBSTITUTIONS: *Lagerstroemia* cultivars, *Acer palmatum* cultivars, *Amelanchier* cultivars, *Betula nigra* 'Little King'

COMMENTS: *Carpinus caroliniana* is a very attractive, small native tree with variable form, size and Fall foliage color. It has nice, showy stem interest.

OTHER CULTIVARS: Palisade® - columnar form

Cercis canadensis
Eastern Redbud Tree
USDA Hardiness Zones: 4-9

DESCRIPTION

NATIVE HABITAT: Throughout Eastern United States, from the Northeast to Florida, along the Gulf Coast to Texas and into Northern Mexico

PLANT TYPE: Deciduous, broadleaf, small Spring flowering tree

MATURE SIZE: 20-30' tall by 15-25' wide

FORM/SHAPE: Irregular, upright, rounded, vase-shaped

BARK: Smooth; thin, brownish gray to black bark; matures to black with rough, checkered ridges and plates

FLOWER: Lavender-purple or pink, sometimes white; blooms in early Spring before leaves emerge; attracts insects

FRUIT: Green; changes to brownish black; 1-3" flat bean-like pod; persistent

FOLIAGE: Alternate, simple, entire, broad-ovate to heart-shaped; medium to dark green leaves in Summer turn yellow in Fall

LANDSCAPE CHARACTERISTICS

GROWTH RATE: Moderate to Fast   **DROUGHT TOLERANCE:** High   **SALT TOLERANCE:** Low

SOIL REQUIREMENTS: Well-drained, moist, fertile, humus rich, well-limed, sandy, clay or loam soil; not tolerant of water-logged soil, short duration flooding or compacted soil

LIGHT REQUIREMENTS: Part shade to full sun; flowers best in full sun

PEST PROBLEMS: Texas leafcutter ants, mites, redheaded Ash borer, treehopper, caterpillars, scales, ambrosia beetles, black twig borer, whitefly, mealybugs, Oleander scale, white Peach scale and Oak weevil

DISEASE PROBLEMS: Anthracnose, downy mildew, *Nectria*, root rot, canker, leaf spot, *Verticillium* wilt and wetwood; virus-like disorders cause decline of Redbuds; *Xylaria polymorpha* root rot can occur in urban areas

ENVIRONMENTAL FACTORS: Not tolerant of wet or flooded soil conditions; injured by ozone, sulfur dioxide and fluoride

PRUNING: Prune for stronger structure; to remove low hanging limbs, to reduce the spread, to thin out over crowded and shaded inner limbs

ADDITIONAL NOTES

USES: Specimen tree, containers, flowering, native tree, naturalizing and group plantings

URBAN USES: Injured by urban air pollution

SUBSTITUTIONS: *Cornus* species and cultivars, *Lagerstroemia* cultivars, *Malus* cultivars, *Prunus* cultivars, *Styrax japonica* and cultivars

COMMENTS: Eastern Redbud Tree is a small flowering tree that easily adapts to many regions and soil types. Many cultivars are grown providing a variety of sizes, forms, foliage and flower color.

OTHER CULTIVARS: 'Appalachian Red' - bright, rose-pink flower color; 'Covey' - weeping form; 'Forest Pansy' - purple to bronze-green foliage; *var. texensis* 'Oklahoma' - deep purple flower color, dark, shiny green foliage; *var. texensis* 'Traveller' PP 8640 - weeping, mounding plant form with shiny, dark green foliage

Cercis canadensis 'Covey'
Lavender Twist Weeping Redbud Tree
USDA Hardiness Zones: 5-8

DESCRIPTION

NATIVE HABITAT: Cultivar of garden origin
PLANT TYPE: Deciduous, broadleaf, weeping, small Spring flowering tree
MATURE SIZE: 5' tall by 5-10' wide; height depends on staking or plant manipulation
FORM/SHAPE: Weeping; branches arch to create an umbrella-shaped crown
BARK: Smooth; black to brownish black
FLOWER: Reddish purple bud; opens to rosy pink-purple; fascicled blooms; blooms from March to April before leaves emerge; attracts insects
FRUIT: Green; changes to brownish black; 1-3" flat bean-like pod; persistent
FOLIAGE: Alternate, simple, entire, broad-ovate to heart-shaped; medium to dark green leaves in Summer turn yellow in Fall

LANDSCAPE CHARACTERISTICS

GROWTH RATE: Moderate   **DROUGHT TOLERANCE:** Moderate once established   **SALT TOLERANCE:** Low
SOIL REQUIREMENTS: Well-drained, moist, fertile, humus rich, well-limed, sandy, clay or loam soil; not tolerant of water-logged soil, short duration flooding or compacted soil
LIGHT REQUIREMENTS: Sun to light shade; light shade will reduce sunburn damage to top surface of limbs that have direct exposure to sunlight
PEST PROBLEMS: Texas leafcutter ants, mites, redheaded Ash borer, treehopper, caterpillars, scales, ambrosia beetles, black twig borer, whitefly, mealybugs, Oleander scale, white Peach scale and Oak weevil
DISEASE PROBLEMS: Anthracnose, downy mildew, *Nectria*, root rot, canker, leaf spot, *Verticillium* wilt and wetwood; virus-like disorders cause decline of Redbuds; *Xylaria polymorpha* root rot can occur in urban areas
ENVIRONMENTAL FACTORS: Not tolerant of wet or flooded soil conditions; injured by ozone, sulfur dioxide and fluoride; sunscald to top surface of limbs exposed to direct sunlight; ice glazing of trunk causes damage
PRUNING: Minimal; stake or train to desired height and form; maintain leaf cover over top of limbs that are exposed to direct sun

ADDITIONAL NOTES

USES: Specimen, accent near walkway, deck or patio, rock garden plantings, trained on arbor or trellis and trained into topiary form
URBAN USES: Injured by air pollutants, but useful where space is limited and aesthetic effects are desired
SUBSTITUTIONS: Weeping *Prunus* cultivars, weeping *Malus* cultivars, *Acer palmatum* cultivars, *Cercis canadensis var. texensis* 'Traveller' PP 8640, *Wisteria frutescens* 'Amethyst Falls'
COMMENTS: This cultivar has a unique, interesting form with a showy Spring flower display. It is a great tree to use as a specimen.
OTHER CULTIVARS: 'Traveller' PP 8640 - smaller, weeping plant form, smaller, glossy, dark green leaves, similar flower color, much more heat tolerant, not prone to sunscald on bark

Cercis canadensis 'Forest Pansy'
Forest Pansy Redbud Tree
USDA Hardiness Zones: 6-9

DESCRIPTION

NATIVE HABITAT: Eastern North America; cultivar of nursery origin
PLANT TYPE: Deciduous, broadleaf, small Spring flowering tree
MATURE SIZE: 20-25' tall by 15-20' wide
FORM/SHAPE: Upright, rounded; can be multi-stemmed
BARK: Smooth; dark reddish brown; becomes reddish gray to black and develops plates and furrows with age
FLOWER: Light pinkish lavender; blooms in early Spring before leaves emerge; attracts insects
FRUIT: Green; changes to brownish black; 1-3" flat bean-like pod; persistent
FOLIAGE: Alternate, simple, entire, broad-ovate to heart-shaped; leaves emerge as scarlet-purple and turn bronze-green with age; turns yellow to greenish brown in Fall

LANDSCAPE CHARACTERISTICS

GROWTH RATE: Moderate   **DROUGHT TOLERANCE:** Moderate   **SALT TOLERANCE:** Low
SOIL REQUIREMENTS: Well-drained, moist, fertile, humus rich, well-limed, sandy, clay or loam soil; not tolerant of water-logged soil, short duration flooding or compacted soil
LIGHT REQUIREMENTS: Part shade to full sun; flowers best in full sun
PEST PROBLEMS: Texas leafcutter ants, mites, redheaded Ash borer, treehopper, caterpillars, scales, ambrosia beetles, black twig borer, whitefly, mealybugs, Oleander scale, white Peach scale and Oak weevil
DISEASE PROBLEMS: Anthracnose, downy mildew, *Nectria*, root rot, canker, leaf spot, *Verticillium* wilt and wetwood; virus-like disorders cause decline of Redbuds; *Xylaria polymorpha* root rot can occur in urban areas
ENVIRONMENTAL FACTORS: Not tolerant of wet or flooded soil conditions; injured by ozone, sulfur dioxide and fluoride
PRUNING: Prune for stronger structure; to remove low hanging limbs, to reduce the spread, to thin out over crowded and shaded inner limbs

ADDITIONAL NOTES

USES: Small Spring flowering tree, accent tree with burgundy-red foliage, residential lawn tree, small shade tree and use with other small landscape plants
URBAN USES: Injured by urban air pollution; can replace Dogwoods with similar plant form; not good for streetscapes but does well in medians
SUBSTITUTIONS: *Cornus* species and cultivars, *Lagerstroemia, Malus* cultivars, *Prunus* cultivars, *Stryrax japonica* and cultivars
COMMENTS: 'Forest Pansy' Redbud combines early Spring flowering with dramatic, large, burgundy-red, heart-shaped leaves to give a beautiful accent to residential landscapes. It is adaptable to most soil and landscape uses.
OTHER CULTIVARS: 'Silver Cloud' - variegated leaves with creamy white spackling, light lavender flowers, slow growing; 'Alba' - white flowers, same growth as species, may be several cultivars known as 'Alba'

Cercis chinensis 'Avondale'
Avondale Redbud Tree
USDA Hardiness Zones: 6-9

DESCRIPTION

NATIVE HABITAT: China; cultivar of garden origin
PLANT TYPE: Deciduous, broadleaf, small Spring flowering tree
MATURE SIZE: 10-20' tall by 8-10' wide
FORM/SHAPE: Upright, vase to rounded tree
BARK: Smooth; tannish gray; matures to dark gray with shallow fissures, ridges and plates
FLOWER: Deep rose-purple flowers, abundant blooming in Spring before leaves emerge; attracts insects
FRUIT: Reddish green color ripens to brown; 3-5" long, bean-like pod, very heavy fruit production
FOLIAGE: Alternate, simple, entire, broad-ovate to heart-shaped; dark green leaves turn yellow-green to yellow-brown in Fall

LANDSCAPE CHARACTERISTICS

GROWTH RATE: Slow to Moderate   **DROUGHT TOLERANCE:** Moderate   **SALT TOLERANCE:** Low
SOIL REQUIREMENTS: Well-drained, moist, fertile, humus rich, well-limed, sandy, clay or loam soil; not tolerant of water-logged soil, short duration flooding or compacted soil
LIGHT REQUIREMENTS: Part shade to full sun; flowers best in full sun
PEST PROBLEMS: Texas leafcutter ants, mites, redheaded Ash borer, treehoppers, caterpillars, scales, ambrosia beetles, black twig borer, whitefly, mealybugs, Oleander scale, white Peach scale and Oak weevil
DISEASE PROBLEMS: Anthracnose, downy mildew, *Nectria*, root rot, canker, leaf spot, *Verticillium* wilt and wetwood; virus-like disorders cause decline of Redbuds; *Xylaria polymorpha* root rot can occur in urban areas
ENVIRONMENTAL FACTORS: Not tolerant of wet or flooded soil conditions; injured by ozone, sulfur dioxide and fluoride
PRUNING: Prune for stronger structure, to remove low hanging limbs, to reduce the spread, to thin out over crowded and shaded inner limbs

ADDITIONAL NOTES

USES: Specimen, residential street tree, patio or deck planting, small Spring flowering tree, accent tree used with flowers and shrubs
URBAN USES: Injured by urban air pollution
SUBSTITUTIONS: *Cercis canadensis* cultivars, *Cercis canadensis var. texensis* cultivars, *Malus* cultivars, *Lagerstroemia* cultivars, *Styrax japonica* 'Pink Chimes', *Cornus* cultivars
COMMENTS: 'Avondale' is a small growing, well-branched, upright tree with a spreading habit. The flowers are four times larger than that of *Cercis canadensis* flowers with the stems covered completely by flowers. The tree produces many seed pods. It is a Duncan and Davies introduction.
OTHER CULTIVARS: 'Alba' - white flowers, plant form similar to species, several clones in the horticulture trade; 'Donald Egolf' - small growing tree, heavy production of deep magenta-pink blooms, no seed or pod production

Cercis reniformis 'Oklahoma'
Oklahoma Redbud Tree
USDA Hardiness Zones: 6-9

DESCRIPTION

NATIVE HABITAT: Oklahoma, Texas, New Mexico to Northeastern Mexico; cultivar of garden origin
PLANT TYPE: Deciduous, broadleaf, small Spring flowering tree
MATURE SIZE: 20-25' tall by 15-20' wide
FORM/SHAPE: Upright, irregular, slightly vase-shaped
BARK: Smooth; light brown when young becomes gray-brown to black with age
FLOWER: Rosy purple; blooms in early Spring before leaves emerge; attracts insects
FRUIT: Dark purple; 1-3" long, flat bean-like pod; persistent
FOLIAGE: Alternate, simple, heart-shaped, 2-4" long; glossy, dark green leaves turn yellow in Fall

LANDSCAPE CHARACTERISTICS

GROWTH RATE: Moderate to Fast   **DROUGHT TOLERANCE:** High   **SALT TOLERANCE:** Low
SOIL REQUIREMENTS: Well-drained, moist, fertile, humus rich, well-limed, sandy, clay or loam soil; not tolerant of water-logged soil, short duration flooding or compacted soil
LIGHT REQUIREMENTS: Part shade to full sun; flowers best in full sun
PEST PROBLEMS: Texas leafcutter ants, mites, redheaded Ash borer, treehoppers, caterpillars, scales, ambrosia beetles, black twig borer, whitefly, mealybugs, Oleander scale, white Peach scale and Oak weevil
DISEASE PROBLEMS: Anthracnose, downy mildew, *Nectria*, root rot, canker, leaf spot, *Verticillium* wilt and wetwood; virus-like disorders cause decline of Redbuds; *Xylaria polymorpha* root rot can occur in urban areas
ENVIRONMENTAL FACTORS: Not tolerant of wet or flooded soil conditions; injured by ozone, sulfur dioxide and fluoride
PRUNING: Prune for stronger structure, to remove low hanging limbs, to reduce the spread, to thin out over crowded and shaded inner limbs

ADDITIONAL NOTES

USES: Small specimen tree, deck or patio accent, small, Spring flowering tree for residential plantings, lawn tree, small shade tree and use in combination with small landscape plants
URBAN USES: Tolerates dry soil and heat stress; not tolerant of wet soil or heavy shade
SUBSTITUTIONS: *Cornus* species and cultivars, *Lagerstroemia* cultivars, *Malus* cultivars, *Prunus* cultivars, *Styrax japonica* and cultivars
COMMENTS: 'Oklahoma' is a compact, upright, vase-shaped tree with dark, rosy purple flowers. It is more adaptable to hotter, dryer sites than *Cercis canadensis*. *Cercis reniformis* is known botanically as *Cercis canadensis var. texensis*.
OTHER CULTIVARS: 'Traveller' PP 8640 - smaller, weeping plant form, smaller, glossy, dark green leaves, lavender flower color, much more heat tolerant, not prone to sunscald on bark; 'Texas White' - white flowers, glossy, dark green leaves

Chionanthus retusus
Chinese Fringetree
USDA Hardiness Zones: 6-9

DESCRIPTION

NATIVE HABITAT: China
PLANT TYPE: Deciduous, broadleaf, small flowering tree; dioecious (occurring as male or female plants)
MATURE SIZE: 25-35' tall by 25-35' wide
FORM/SHAPE: Upright, rounded and spreading
BARK: Smooth; grayish with lenticels; develops furrows and ridges; gray-black bark as plant ages
FLOWER: White, strap-like petals; light fragrance; very showy; blooms April to May; attracts insects
FRUIT: Oval-shaped; 1/2"; blue; fleshy; appears on female plants when flowers are pollinated; attracts birds, insects and animals
FOLIAGE: Opposite, simple, entire, rounded to obovate shaped; dark green leaves turn dull yellow-brown in Fall

LANDSCAPE CHARACTERISTICS

GROWTH RATE: Slow to Moderate   **DROUGHT TOLERANCE:** Moderate   **SALT TOLERANCE:** Low
SOIL REQUIREMENTS: Moist, well-drained, sandy, loam or clay soil; very adaptable to a wide range of moisture, pH and fertility conditions; mulch to keep roots cool and moist
LIGHT REQUIREMENTS: Sun to part shade; requires bright sun for good flowering
PEST PROBLEMS: Plants are not problematic; mites, caterpillars, rose scale and aphids have been reported
DISEASE PROBLEMS: Canker, dieback, gall, powdery mildew and Olive knot (gall)
ENVIRONMENTAL FACTORS: Very adaptable to soils and climatic conditions over its hardiness range
PRUNING: After flowering, prune for shape and structure; remove low limbs as needed for pedestrian circulation

ADDITIONAL NOTES

USES: Specimen tree, small shade tree or in combination with other plants; a good substitute for *Cornus* and *Prunus*
URBAN USES: Plant needs further evaluation to determine adaptability in varying urban environments
SUBSTITUTIONS: *Lagerstroemia* cultivars, *Styrax japonica* and cultivars, *Pyrus* cultivars, *Malus* cultivars
COMMENTS: *Chionanthus retusus* is in the Olive family and related to the Southeastern United States native *Chionanthus virginicus*. It is an elegant and impressive season long performer and more pest and disease free than *Chionanthus virginicus*.
OTHER CULTIVARS: Many plants grown from seed show a wide range of plant forms; 'China Snow'- atypical of species, has rounded leaves with stiff arching plant form, needs training and pruning to develop a good multi-trunk or standard tree form, very pest and disease free cultivar

Chionanthus virginicus
White Fringetree or Grancy Gray-beard
USDA Hardiness Zones: 5-9

DESCRIPTION

NATIVE HABITAT: Eastern United States
PLANT TYPE: Deciduous, broadleaf, small flowering tree; dioecious (occurring as male or female plants)
MATURE SIZE: 8-15' tall by 6-10' wide
FORM/SHAPE: Upright, open
BARK: Smooth; greenish brown young stems; gray older stems; some furrows and ridges develop on the lower trunk area
FLOWER: White, strap-like petals; very showy, blooms in April to May; attracts insects
FRUIT: Oval-shaped; 1/2"; blue; fleshy; appears on female plants when flowers are pollinated; attracts birds, insects and animals
FOLIAGE: Opposite, simple, entire, narrow, elliptical shape; medium green leaves turn dull, yellow-brown in Fall

LANDSCAPE CHARACTERISTICS

GROWTH RATE: Slow   **DROUGHT TOLERANCE:** Moderate   **SALT TOLERANCE:** Low
SOIL REQUIREMENTS: Moist, well-drained, sandy, loam or clay soil; very adaptable to a wide range of moisture, pH and fertility conditions; mulch to keep roots cool and moist
LIGHT REQUIREMENTS: Sun to part shade; requires bright sun for good flowering
PEST PROBLEMS: Plants are not problematic, mites, caterpillars, Rose scale and aphids have been reported
DISEASE PROBLEMS: Canker, dieback, gall, powdery mildew and Olive knot (gall)
ENVIRONMENTAL FACTORS: Shows good adaptability to soils and climatic conditions over its hardiness range; plants grown from seed show individual differences to environmental stresses; very adaptable to wet and dry soil
PRUNING: Prune after flowering to maintain tree form; plants grown from seed are more shrub-like and vary in quality and shape

ADDITIONAL NOTES

USES: Large shrub or small tree, borders, flowers make nice focal point, naturalized areas; female plants have showy fruit clusters in Fall
URBAN USES: Very adaptable but not commonly used except in naturalized and residential plantings
SUBSTITUTIONS: *Chionanthus retusus* 'China Snow', white or fuchsia flowered *Loropetalum*, *Lagerstroemia* cultivars, *Osmanthus americanus*
COMMENTS: Some cultivars are being selected, but are difficult to produce from cuttings. Seed produced plants have variable plant form. For mass plantings, seed produced plants are best because male and female plants are needed to produce fruit.
OTHER CULTIVARS: 'Emerald Knight' - dark green foliage

Cladrastis kentukea (syn. lutea)
American Yellowwood
USDA Hardiness Zones: 3-8

DESCRIPTION

NATIVE HABITAT: Mid-Appalachian region where limestone soils occur naturally

PLANT TYPE: Deciduous, broadleaf, large Spring flowering tree

MATURE SIZE: 40-50' tall by 20-50' wide

FORM/SHAPE: Upright, rounded and irregular

BARK: Smooth; brown-gray; younger stems are light brown; turns darker brown-gray when mature

FLOWER: White in 6-12" panicles; blooms late Spring; attracts insects; light pink flower form exists

FRUIT: 3-5" brown bean-like pod

FOLIAGE: Alternate, odd-pinnately compound with seven to eleven leaflets; light to medium green leaves turn yellowish green to clear yellow in Fall

LANDSCAPE CHARACTERISTICS

GROWTH RATE: Slow to Moderate   **DROUGHT TOLERANCE:** Moderate   **SALT TOLERANCE:** Low

SOIL REQUIREMENTS: Well-drained, clay, sandy or loam soil; not tolerant of wet or flooded soil

LIGHT REQUIREMENTS: Full sun

PEST PROBLEMS: Commonly free of pest, but mites, caterpillars, borers and scales can affect young trees

DISEASE PROBLEMS: Canker, dieback, root rot and butt rot

ENVIRONMENTAL FACTORS: Not tolerant of wet or flooded soil; tolerant of high pH limestone soil

PRUNING: Prune after flowering for good structure

ADDITIONAL NOTES

USES: Specimen tree, shade tree or accent tree

URBAN USES: Very adaptable to dry, high pH soil sites, but soil must be well-drained

SUBSTITUTIONS: *Chionanthus retusus*, *Lagerstroemia* cultivars, *Cladrastis sinensis* (Chinese species with pink tinged, white, slightly fragrant flowers)

COMMENTS: American Yellowwood should be used more often in residential plantings as well as commercial landscapes.

OTHER CULTIVARS: 'Perkins Pink' - soft pink flower form, growth habit similar to species

Cornus florida
Dogwood
USDA Hardiness Zones: 5-9

DESCRIPTION

NATIVE HABITAT: Eastern United States
PLANT TYPE: Deciduous, broadleaf, small Spring flowering tree
MATURE SIZE: 20-30' tall by 20-25' wide
FORM/SHAPE: Upright, rounded and spreading; often multi-stemmed
BARK: Smooth; stems reddish color when young; older bark becomes a dark brownish gray with ridges of small, uniform plates and furrows
FLOWER: White; four showy bracts; yellowish green center cluster of true flowers; blooms March to April; attracts insects
FRUIT: Red clusters of drupes; 1/2" in diameter; very attractive and decorative; attracts small animals and birds
FOLIAGE: Opposite, simple, ovate to oval shape; medium green leaves turn red to purple in Fall

LANDSCAPE CHARACTERISTICS

GROWTH RATE: Moderate   **DROUGHT TOLERANCE:** Low to Moderate   **SALT TOLERANCE:** Low
SOIL REQUIREMENTS: Well-drained, moist, fertile, humus rich, slightly acidic soil with adequate lime to supply calcium and magnesium for optimal growth
LIGHT REQUIREMENTS: Light shade to full sun; can adapt to full sun with irrigation
PEST PROBLEMS: Two-spotted mites, Dogwood borer, Dogwood midges, borers, aphids, leaf miner, Japanese weevil, caterpillars, ambrosia beetles, mealybugs, whitefly, scales, twig girdlers and white Peach scale
DISEASE PROBLEMS: *Discula*, anthracnose, Dogwood canker, leaf scorch, Oak root rot, *Septoria*, *Phytophthora* root rot, nematodes, crown canker, flower and leaf blight and powdery mildew
ENVIRONMENTAL FACTORS: Very shallow rooted; damaged by soil compaction; not tolerant of wet or flooded soil; injured by drought; trees decline and die from deep planting or heavy mulching
PRUNING: Pruning minimal; low limb removal or removal of crowded limb structure; remove rootstock suckers on grafted or budded trees

ADDITIONAL NOTES

USES: Specimen, naturalizing, mass planted with other shade trees and as an accent Spring flowering tree with other companion plants
URBAN USES: Not the best choice, but can adapt if soils are adequately prepared to ensure proper drainage in irrigated planting sites
SUBSTITUTIONS: *Cornus kousa*, *Cornus* (Rutgers hybrids), *Lagerstroemia* cultivars, *Malus* cultivars, *Prunus* cultivars, *Pyrus* cultivars, *Styrax japonica* and cultivars
COMMENTS: Dogwood is widely planted as a small flowering tree in residential landscapes, but it has problems with *Discula*, anthracnose, powdery mildew and ambrosia beetles. *Cornus florida* and its cultivars are becoming less desirable for landscape plantings.
OTHER CULTIVARS: 'Comco #1' PP 10,166 Cherokee Brave - dark pink flowers, good resistance to powdery mildew; 'Cherokee Princess' - white flower, compact growth habit; 'Jean's Appalachian Snow' PP 13,099 - white flower, compact plant form; powdery mildew resistant, 'Karen's Appalachian Blush' PP 13,165- pale blush flower color, powdery mildew resistant

Cornus florida 'Cherokee Princess'
Cherokee Princess Dogwood
USDA Hardiness Zones: 5-9

DESCRIPTION

NATIVE HABITAT: Eastern United States; cultivar of nursery origin

PLANT TYPE: Deciduous, broadleaf, small Spring flowering tree

MATURE SIZE: 20-25' tall by 25' wide

FORM/SHAPE: Upright, spreading, horizontal habit

BARK: Smooth, stems reddish color when young; older bark becomes a dark brownish gray with ridges of small, uniform plates and furrows

FLOWER: White; four showy bracts; yellowish green center cluster of true flowers; blooms March to April; attracts insects

FRUIT: Red clusters of drupes; 1/2" in diameter; very attractive and decorative; attracts small animals and birds

FOLIAGE: Opposite, simple, ovate to oval shape; medium green leaves turn red to purple in Fall

LANDSCAPE CHARACTERISTICS

GROWTH RATE: Moderate   **DROUGHT TOLERANCE:** Moderate   **SALT TOLERANCE:** Low

SOIL REQUIREMENTS: Well-drained, moist, fertile, humus rich, slightly acidic soil with adequate lime to supply calcium and magnesium for optimal growth

LIGHT REQUIREMENTS: Light shade to full sun; can adapt to full sun with irrigation

PEST PROBLEMS: Two-spotted mites, Dogwood borer, Dogwood midges, borers, aphids, leaf miner, Japanese weevil, caterpillars, ambrosia beetles, mealybugs, whitefly, scales, twig girdler and white Peach scale

DISEASE PROBLEMS: *Discula*, anthracnose, Dogwood canker, leaf scorch, Oak root rot, *Septoria*, *Phytophthora* root rot, nematodes, crown canker, flower and leaf blight; shows resistance to powdery mildew

ENVIRONMENTAL FACTORS: Very shallow rooted; damaged by soil compaction; not tolerant of wet or flooded soil; injured by drought; trees decline and die from deep planting or heavy mulching

PRUNING: Pruning minimal; low limb removal or removal of crowded limb structure; remove rootstock suckers on grafted or budded trees

ADDITIONAL NOTES

USES: Specimen, naturalizing, mass planted with shade trees and as an accent Spring flowering tree with other companion plants

URBAN USES: Not the best choice, but can adapt if soil is adequately prepared to ensure proper drainage in irrigated planting sites

SUBSTITUTIONS: *Cornus kousa*, *Cornus* (Rutgers hybrids), *Lagerstroemia* cultivars, *Malus* cultivars, *Prunus* cultivars, *Pyrus* cultivars, *Styrax japonica* and cultivars

COMMENTS: Cherokee Princess has shown good tolerance to powdery mildew, but good pest and disease control is needed for longevity and aesthetics in the landscape.

OTHER CULTIVARS: 'Cloud 9' - white flower, compact growth habit; 'Jean's Appalachian Snow' PP 13,099 - white flower, compact plant form, powdery mildew resistant; 'Karen's Appalachian Blush' PP 13,165 - pale blush flower, powdery mildew resistant

Cornus florida rubra 'Comco #1' PP 10,166
Cherokee Brave Dogwood
USDA Hardiness Zones: 5-9

DESCRIPTION

NATIVE HABITAT: Eastern United States; cultivar of nursery origin
PLANT TYPE: Deciduous, broadleaf, small Spring flowering tree
MATURE SIZE: 25-30' tall by 25-30' wide
FORM/SHAPE: Upright and rounded
BARK: Smooth, stems reddish color when young; older bark becomes a dark brownish gray with ridges of small, uniform plates and furrows
FLOWER: Dark, rosy pink; four showy bracts; yellowish green center cluster of true flowers; blooms March to April; attracts insects
FRUIT: Red clusters of drupes; 1/2" in diameter; very attractive and decorative; attracts small animals and birds
FOLIAGE: Opposite, simple, ovate to oval shape; medium green leaves turn red to purple in Fall

LANDSCAPE CHARACTERISTICS

GROWTH RATE: Moderate to Fast   **DROUGHT TOLERANCE:** Moderate   **SALT TOLERANCE:** Low
SOIL REQUIREMENTS: Well-drained, moist, fertile, humus rich, slightly acidic soil with adequate lime to supply calcium and magnesium for optimal growth
LIGHT REQUIREMENTS: Light shade to full sun; can adapt to full sun with irrigation
PEST PROBLEMS: Two-spotted mites, Dogwood borer, Dogwood midges, borers, aphids, leaf miner, Japanese weevil, caterpillars, ambrosia beetles, mealybugs, whitefly, scales, twig girdler and white Peach scale
DISEASE PROBLEMS: *Discula*, anthracnose, Dogwood canker, leaf scorch, Oak root rot, *Septoria*, *Phytophthora* root rot, nematodes, crown canker, flower and leaf blight; shows resistance to powdery mildew
ENVIRONMENTAL FACTORS: Very shallow rooted; damaged by soil compaction; not tolerant of wet or flooded soil; injured by drought; trees decline and die from deep planting or heavy mulching
PRUNING: Pruning minimal; low limb removal or removal of crowded limb structure; remove rootstock suckers on grafted or budded trees

ADDITIONAL NOTES

USES: Specimen, naturalizing, mass planted with shade trees and as an accent Spring flowering tree with other companion plants
URBAN USES: Not the best choice, but can adapt if soil is adequately prepared to ensure proper drainage in irrigated planting sites
SUBSTITUTIONS: *Cornus kousa*, *Cornus* (Rutgers hybrids), *Lagerstroemia* cultivars, *Malus* cultivars, *Prunus* cultivars, *Pyrus* cultivars, *Styrax japonica* and cultivars
COMMENTS: Cherokee Brave has shown good tolerance to powdery mildew, but good pest and disease control is needed for longevity and aesthetics in the landscape.
OTHER CULTIVARS: 'Cherokee Princess' - white flower, compact growth habit; 'Jean's Appalachian Snow' PP 13,099 - white flower, compact plant form; powdery mildew resistant; 'Karen's Appalachian Blush' PP 13,165 - pale blush flower, powdery mildew resistant

Cornus kousa
Chinese Dogwood
USDA Hardiness Zones: 5-8

DESCRIPTION

NATIVE HABITAT: China, Japan and Korea
PLANT TYPE: Deciduous, broadleaf, small Spring flowering tree
MATURE SIZE: 15-25' tall by 15-25' wide
FORM/SHAPE: Upright, vase-shaped; horizontal and spreads with age
BARK: Smooth, grayish brown; mature bark flakes and peels with exfoliated bark patches on the trunk; very attractive
FLOWER: Light green, matures to white; four white bracts; blooms in late Spring with leaves; attracts insects
FRUIT: Reddish pink drupe fused in clusters; 1/2" in diameter; forms a round ball 3/4 - 1 1/4" in diameter; very showy; attracts insects and animals; reportedly eaten in China and other Asian countries
FOLIAGE: Opposite, simple, ovate-elliptical, waxy; sometimes pubescent underside; dark green turns scarlet-purple in Fall

LANDSCAPE CHARACTERISTICS

GROWTH RATE: Slow to Moderate   **DROUGHT TOLERANCE:** Low   **SALT TOLERANCE:** Low
SOIL REQUIREMENTS: Moist, fertile, well-drained, humus rich soil; prefers slightly acidic soil; mulch to keep roots cool and maintain moisture; lime to maintain adequate calcium and magnesium levels
LIGHT REQUIREMENTS: Full sun to light shade; flowers better in slightly sunnier locations
PEST PROBLEMS: Good pest tolerance but can be affected by two-spotted mites, Dogwood borer, Dogwood midges, aphids, leaf miner, caterpillars, ambrosia beetles, mealybugs, whitefly, scales, twig girdler and white Peach scale
DISEASE PROBLEMS: Good disease tolerance, but can be affected by Dogwood canker, Oak root rot, flower blight, *Phytophthora* root rot and root knot nematode
ENVIRONMENTAL FACTORS: Very shallow rooted; damaged by soil compaction; not tolerant of wet or flooded soil; injured by drought; trees decline and die from deep planting or heavy mulching
PRUNING: Pruning minimal; low limb removal or removal of crowded limb structure is acceptable; remove rootstock suckers on grafted or budded trees

ADDITIONAL NOTES

USES: Foundation, border plantings, specimen, group planting with other trees or shrubs or as an accent tree grown as single trunk or multi-trunk form
URBAN USES: Adaptable to urban and residential planting where *Cornus florida* has failed; choose light shade and well-drained soils that are adequately irrigated
SUBSTITUTIONS: *Cornus florida, Cornus* (Rutgers hybrid series), *Styrax japonica* and cultivars, *Malus* cultivars, *Prunus* cultivars
COMMENTS: Seedling trees have varying flower shape, plant form and adaptability in landscape settings. Many cultivars are grown and should be used for more uniform plant shape, flower and landscape adaptability.
OTHER CULTIVARS: 'Blue Shadow' - dark green leaves with blue sheen and white flowers, excellent Fall color and heat tolerance; 'Summer Stars' - vigorous growth, robust, dark green foliage, Fall color reddish purple, white flowers last into Summer, more drought tolerant than species; 'Schmred' PP 9283 Heart Throb® - dark pink flowers, compact plant habit

Crataegus phaenopyrum
Washington Hawthorn

USDA Hardiness Zones: 4-9

DESCRIPTION

NATIVE HABITAT: Eastern United States
PLANT TYPE: Deciduous, broadleaf, small Spring flowering tree
MATURE SIZE: 20-30' tall by 20-30' wide
FORM/SHAPE: Upright, rounded
BARK: Smooth; dark grayish brown bark when young; gray bark with very shallow fissures and small plates when mature
FLOWER: White; slightly fragrant; blooms in Spring; attracts insects
FRUIT: Bright red pome; 1/4-1/3"; appears in Fall and Winter
FOLIAGE: Alternate, simple, ovate-elliptical, shallow-lobed; medium green leaves turn reddish-purple in Fall

LANDSCAPE CHARACTERISTICS

GROWTH RATE: Moderate   **DROUGHT TOLERANCE:** Moderate   **SALT TOLERANCE:** Moderate
SOIL REQUIREMENTS: Tolerant of most well-drained soils; lime application is beneficial
LIGHT REQUIREMENTS: Full sun for best flower, fruit production, and dense growth habit
PEST PROBLEMS: Elm leaf beetle, leaf miner, Hawthorn leafminer, sawfly, leafroller, caterpillars, forest tent caterpillar, mites, eriophyd mites, skeletonizer, periodic cicada, shothole borer, lacebug, mealybugs, Apple aphids, white Apple leafhopper and Hawthorn lacebug
DISEASE PROBLEMS: Quince rust on fruit, leaf spot, blights, Cedar Apple rust, mildews, fireblight, wood rot, butt rot, *Nectria* and tobacco ring spot virus
ENVIRONMENTAL FACTORS: Not tolerant of water-logged and compacted soil; moderate tolerance of air pollutants
PRUNING: Prune to develop strong structure; remove thorny lower limbs to avoid hazards to pedestrian traffic

ADDITIONAL NOTES

USES: Specimen, border plantings, lawn areas, group plantings, screening and naturalizing
URBAN USES: Good tree for residential plantings as well as commercial plantings, but stems have sharp thorns; do not use in areas with pedestrian traffic or on playgrounds; tolerates soils that are only moist from time to time and tolerates air pollutants
SUBSTITUTIONS: *Chionanthus retusus, Malus* cultivars, *Prunus* cultivars, *Styrax japonica* and cultivars, *Crataegus viridus*
COMMENTS: Washington Hawthorne is a native, small flowering tree with abundant shiny red fruit held in tight clusters (cymes). Fruit persists through the Winter offering food for birds and other wildlife. Thorns are a problem in high traffic areas and low branches should be pruned to avoid hazards.
OTHER CULTIVARS: 'Fastigiata' - columnar plant form, small fruit

Crataegus viridis 'Winter King'
Winter King Hawthorn or Green Hawthorn
USDA Hardiness Zones: 4-9

DESCRIPTION

NATIVE HABITAT: Eastern United States; cultivar of nursery origin
PLANT TYPE: Deciduous, broadleaf, small Spring flowering tree
MATURE SIZE: 20-30' tall by 20-30' wide
FORM/SHAPE: Upright, smooth outline, rounded, vase-shaped
BARK: Smooth; gray-green glaucous stems when young; grayish black with shallow fissures and small plates when mature; exfoliated plates show cinnamon-brown bark beneath
FLOWER: White; small round clusters (corymbs); blooms in Spring; attracts insects
FRUIT: Orange and fleshy; 1/2" round; attracts birds and insects
FOLIAGE: Alternate, simple, ovate and serrate; medium, glossy green leaves turn yellow-orange to red or purple in Fall

LANDSCAPE CHARACTERISTICS

GROWTH RATE: Moderate   **DROUGHT TOLERANCE:** Moderate to High   **SALT TOLERANCE:** Moderate
SOIL REQUIREMENTS: Well-drained, moist, fertile, humus rich, sandy, clay or loam soil; can tolerate occasionally wet soils
LIGHT REQUIREMENTS: Full sun for best flower, fruit production, and dense growth habit
PEST PROBLEMS: Elm leaf beetle, leaf miner, Hawthorn leafminer, sawfly, leafroller, caterpillars, forest tent caterpillar, mites, eriophyd mites, skeletonizer, periodic cicada, shothole borer, lacebug, mealybugs, Apple aphids, white Apple leafhopper and Hawthorn lacebug
DISEASE PROBLEMS: Quince rust on fruit, leaf spot, blights, Cedar Apple rust, mildews, fireblight, wood rot, butt rot, *Nectria* and tobacco ring spot virus
ENVIRONMENTAL FACTORS: Not tolerant of water-logged soil; moderate tolerance of air pollutants; can tolerate short duration of soil saturation, but the water must drain freely from root zone
PRUNING: Prune for strong structure; remove low limbs to avoid hazards to people from the thorns on the stems

ADDITIONAL NOTES

USES: Specimen, border plantings, lawn areas, group plantings, screening and naturalizing
URBAN USES: Good tree for residential plantings as well as commercial plantings, but stems have sharp thorns; do not use in areas with pedestrian traffic or on playgrounds; tolerates soil that is only moist from time to time; tolerates air pollutants
SUBSTITUTIONS: *Chionanthus retusus, Malus* cultivars, *Prunus* cultivars, *Styrax japonica* and cultivars, *Crataegus phaenopyrum*
COMMENTS: Winter King Hawthorn is a native, small flowering tree with an abundant shiny red fruit held in tight clusters. The fruit persists through Winter offering food for birds and other wildlife. Thorns are a problem in high traffic areas, and low branches should be pruned to avoid hazards.
OTHER CULTIVARS: No known commercial cultivars are presently grown

Fagus grandifolia
American Beech
USDA Hardiness Zones: 3-8

DESCRIPTION

NATIVE HABITAT: Eastern North America
PLANT TYPE: Deciduous, broadleaf, large tree
MATURE SIZE: 50-80' tall by 40-70' wide
FORM/SHAPE: Upright; dense, rounded dome
BARK: Smooth; young stems brown with zig-zag pattern; old stems are smooth and gray with darker mottling
FLOWER: Inconspicuous; late Winter to Spring
FRUIT: Brown, triangular, edible nut with dehiscent husk; fruit and husks make messy litter
FOLIAGE: Alternate; simple; ovate; distinct veins on surface; serrate margins; medium to dark green leaves turn golden brown to bronze in Winter; many leaves hang on limbs throughout Winter, considered an attractive feature by some

LANDSCAPE CHARACTERISTICS

GROWTH RATE: Slow to Moderate   **DROUGHT TOLERANCE:** Low   **SALT TOLERANCE:** Low
SOIL REQUIREMENTS: Well-drained, moist, fertile, humus rich soil; tolerant of somewhat heavy soil with adequate organic matter and good water drainage
LIGHT REQUIREMENTS: Full sun to light shade
PEST PROBLEMS: Skeletonizer, Pear thrips, caterpillars, gypsy moth, Oak weevil, locust, leaf miner, galling insects, mites, Chestnut and Beech borer, Beech lacebug, leafhopper
DISEASE PROBLEMS: Butt rot, bleeding bark canker, leaf spot, *Hypoxylon*, *Nectria*, powdery mildew, root rot, Winter sunscald and wood decay
ENVIRONMENTAL FACTORS: Not tolerant of water-logged soil or prolonged drought; adequate tolerance to sulfur dioxide air pollutants, squirrels and sapsucker birds damage bark
PRUNING: Selectively prune for good structure; maintain central leader if needed when young and allow for multi-leader crown when older

ADDITIONAL NOTES

USES: Lawn specimen, shade tree, naturalizing and wildlife food tree; not a good selection for small gardens
URBAN USES: Limited urban use; site and soil selection critical for good survival and growth
SUBSTITUTIONS: *Fagus sylvatica* species and cultivars, *Quercus* species and cultivars, *Zelkova* cultivars, *Carpinus* species and cultivars, *Betula* cultivars
COMMENTS: A beautiful large tree not used enough in large landscape design. *Fagus grandifolia* demands proper soil conditions and transplants poorly. It needs a high oxygen content in the soil and requires ideal drainage. Moisture must always be available to the plant roots. There is limited availability of ball and burlapped plants.
OTHER CULTIVARS: No known commercial cultivars are presently offered, but avid plant collectors are making selections with unique plant form and foliage; several botanical forms may be recognized as superior throughout the diverse geographical distribution of the common American Beech

Fraxinus americana 'Junginger'
Autumn Purple® White Ash
USDA Hardiness Zones: 4-9

DESCRIPTION

NATIVE HABITAT: Eastern North America; cultivar of nursery origin
PLANT TYPE: Deciduous, broadleaf, large tree
MATURE SIZE: 35-40' tall by 20-25' wide
FORM/SHAPE: Upright, dense, rounded
BARK: Smooth; gray when young; matures to grayish brown; narrow, corky, diamond-shaped ridges and furrows
FLOWER: Very small with shades of green, purple and black; inconspicuous; blooms mid-to-late April
FRUIT: Seedless male cultivar
FOLIAGE: Opposite, pinnately compound; smaller leaf than species; dark, glabrous green in Summer; Fall color begins as orange-yellow and turns to purplish mahogany

LANDSCAPE CHARACTERISTICS

GROWTH RATE: Fast   **DROUGHT TOLERANCE:** Low to Moderate   **SALT TOLERANCE:** Moderate
SOIL REQUIREMENTS: Best in deep, moist, well-drained soil; mulch to keep roots cooler in full sun
LIGHT REQUIREMENTS: Full sun to part shade; more dense in full sun
PEST PROBLEMS: Emerald Ash borer, Japanese weevil, Pear thrips, Ash plant bug, caterpillars, Eastern tent caterpillar, forest tent caterpillar, mites, leaf miner, Lilac borer, roundheaded Apple tree borer, lacebug, Ash sawfly, *Pittosporum* scales and gall midge
DISEASE PROBLEMS: Ash dieback, Ash yellows, anthracnose, leaf spot, rusts, *Verticillium* wilt, wood rot, Ash decline and dieback due to prolonged drought stress
ENVIRONMENTAL FACTORS: Very adaptable to landscape stress conditions; susceptible to late and early season freezes and frosts; tolerant of ozone and sulfur dioxide air pollutants; not tolerant of prolonged drought
PRUNING: Prune to maintain central leader when tree is young and to reduce co-dominant leaders

ADDITIONAL NOTES

USES: Lawn tree, specimen, shade tree and streetscapes
URBAN USES: Tolerant of adverse air quality and soil extremes
SUBSTITUTIONS: Other *Fraxinus* species and cultivars, Chinese Pistache, *Robinia*, *Quercus* species
COMMENTS: *Fraxinus* are commonly used in the Central and Northern United States, but the introduction of emerald Ash borer has caused major changes in its use. Autumn Purple® White Ash is tolerant of ozone pollution.
OTHER CULTIVARS: Autumn Applause® - seedless; small oval crown with purple Fall color; 'Empire' - columnar form with straight, strong central leader dominance; 'Tures' Windy City ᵀᴹ - seedless; resists frost cracking problem of trunk and good central leader development

Fraxinus pennsylvanica 'Oconee'
Georgia Gem® Green Ash
USDA Hardiness Zones: 6-9

DESCRIPTION

NATIVE HABITAT: Eastern North America; Southern selection
PLANT TYPE: Deciduous, broadleaf, large tree
MATURE SIZE: 40-50' tall by 25-35' wide
FORM/SHAPE: Upright, oval crown
BARK: Smooth; gray-brown to gray; narrow, corky, diamond-shaped ridges and furrows
FLOWER: Inconspicuous; blooms mid-to-late April
FRUIT: Seedless male cultivar
FOLIAGE: Opposite, pinnately compound, five to eleven leaflets; glossy, dark green leaves turn yellow in Fall

LANDSCAPE CHARACTERISTICS

GROWTH RATE: Fast   **DROUGHT TOLERANCE:** Moderate to High   **SALT TOLERANCE:** Moderate
SOIL REQUIREMENTS: Well-drained, moist soil; does best in deep soil
LIGHT REQUIREMENTS: Full sun to part shade; more dense in full sun
PEST PROBLEMS: Emerald Ash borer, Japanese weevil, Pear thrips, Ash plant bug, caterpillars, Eastern tent caterpillar, forest tent caterpillar, mites, leaf miner, Lilac borer, roundheaded Apple tree borer, lacebug, Ash sawfly, *Pittosporum* scales and gall midge
DISEASE PROBLEMS: Ash dieback, Ash yellows, anthracnose, leaf spot, rusts, *Verticillium* wilt, wood rot, Ash decline and dieback due to prolonged drought stress
ENVIRONMENTAL FACTORS: Very adaptable to landscape stress conditions; susceptable to late and early season freezes and frosts; tolerant of ozone, sulfur dioxide and air pollutants
PRUNING: Prune to maintain central leader when tree is young and to reduce co-dominant leaders

ADDITIONAL NOTES

USES: Streetscapes, lawns, specimen and shade tree
URBAN USES: Tolerant of adverse air quality and soil extremes
SUBSTITUTIONS: Other *Fraxinus* species and cultivars, Chinese Pistache, *Robinia, Quercus* species
COMMENTS: Georgia Gem® is widely planted due to its high adaptability to urban landscapes having varying air quality and soil extremes. It has been affected by the introduction of the emerald Ash borer which is present in almost all regions.
OTHER CULTIVARS: 'Johnson' PP 9,136 Leprechaun™ - dwarf to medium height, 18' tall by 16' wide; 'Marshall' - dark green foliage, male cultivar, broad, oval shape; 'Rugby' Prairie Spire® - seedless, narrow, pyramidal, very hardy to USDA Hardiness Zone 3; Urbanite® - seedless; large, broad pyramidal

Fraxinus pennsylvanica 'Patmore'
Patmore Green Ash
USDA Hardiness Zones: 2-8

DESCRIPTION

NATIVE HABITAT: Eastern North America; cultivar of nursery origin
PLANT TYPE: Deciduous, broadleaf, large tree
MATURE SIZE: 40-45' tall by 30-35' wide
FORM/SHAPE: Upright, dense, pyramidal; more uniform than species or other cultivars
BARK: Smooth; grayish tan when young; matures from grayish brown to blackish gray; narrow, corky, diamond shaped ridges and furrows
FLOWER: Purplish black flower; inconspicuous; blooms late Spring to early Summer
FRUIT: Seedless male cultivar
FOLIAGE: Opposite, pinnately compound, five to nine leaflets; glossy, dark, green leaves, turn bright yellow in Fall; holds Fall color longer than species

LANDSCAPE CHARACTERISTICS

GROWTH RATE: Fast   **DROUGHT TOLERANCE:** Moderate   **SALT TOLERANCE:** Moderate
SOIL REQUIREMENTS: Moist, well-drained, soil; highly tolerant of short duration flooding
LIGHT REQUIREMENTS: Full sun to part shade; more dense in full sun
PEST PROBLEMS: Emerald Ash borer, Japanese weevil, Pear thrips, Ash plant bug, caterpillars, Eastern tent caterpillar, forest tent caterpillar, mites, leaf miner, Lilac borer, roundheaded Apple tree borer, lacebug, Ash sawfly, *Pittosporum* scales and gall midge
DISEASE PROBLEMS: Ash dieback, Ash yellows, anthracnose, leaf spot, rusts, *Verticillium* wilt, wood rot, Ash decline and dieback due to prolonged drought stress
ENVIRONMENTAL FACTORS: Very adaptable to landscape stress conditions; susceptible to late and early season freezes and frosts; tolerant of ozone and sulfur dioxide air pollutants; not tolerant of prolonged drought
PRUNING: Prune to maintain central leader when tree is young and to reduce co-dominant leaders

ADDITIONAL NOTES

USES: Lawn tree, specimen, shade tree and streetscapes
URBAN USES: Tolerant of adverse air quality and soil extremes
SUBSTITUTIONS: Other *Fraxinus* species and cultivars, Chinese Pistache, *Robinia*, *Quercus* species
COMMENTS: 'Patmore' is highly adaptable to adverse urban conditions, however, the emerald Ash borer has limited the areas where *Fraxinus* can be planted.
OTHER CULTIVARS: Autumn Applause® - seedless; small, oval crown with purple Fall color; 'Empire' - columnar form with straight, strong central leader dominance; 'Tures' Windy City ™ - seedless; resists frost cracking problem of trunk and good central leader development

Fraxinus pennsylvanica 'Urbanite' PP 6,215
Urbanite® Green Ash
USDA Hardiness Zones: 5-8

DESCRIPTION

NATIVE HABITAT: Eastern North America; cultivar of nursery origin
PLANT TYPE: Deciduous, broadleaf, large tree
MATURE SIZE: 50-60' tall by 35-45' wide
FORM/SHAPE: Broadly pyramidal crown; spreads with age
BARK: Smooth; grayish brown when young; has furrows and corky, diamond-shaped ridges with age; thicker bark than species; resists trunk sunscald
FLOWER: Yellowish green; inconspicuous; blooms in Spring
FRUIT: Seedless male cultivar
FOLIAGE: Opposite, pinnately compound; five to nine leaflets; glossy, dark green leaves turn deep bronze to purple in Fall

LANDSCAPE CHARACTERISTICS

GROWTH RATE: Moderate to Fast   **DROUGHT TOLERANCE:** Moderate   **SALT TOLERANCE:** Moderate
SOIL REQUIREMENTS: Moist, well-drained soil; highly tolerant of short duration flooding
LIGHT REQUIREMENTS: Full sun to part shade; more dense in full sun
PEST PROBLEMS: Emerald Ash borer, Japanese weevil, Pear thrips, Ash plant bug, caterpillars, Eastern tent caterpillar, forest tent caterpillar, mites, leaf miner, Lilac borer, roundheaded Apple tree borer, lacebug, Ash sawfly, *Pittosporum* scales and gall midge
DISEASE PROBLEMS: Ash dieback, Ash yellows, anthracnose, leaf spot, rusts, *Verticillium* wilt and wood rot
ENVIRONMENTAL FACTORS: Very adaptable to landscape stress conditions; susceptible to late and early season freezes and frosts; tolerant of ozone and sulfur dioxide air pollutants; not tolerant of prolonged drought
PRUNING: Prune to maintain central leader when tree is young and to reduce co-dominant leaders

ADDITIONAL NOTES

USES: Parks, golf courses, specimen in large areas or as a street tree
URBAN USES: Tolerant of adverse air quality and soil extremes
SUBSTITUTIONS: Other *Fraxinus* species and cultivars, Chinese Pistache, *Robinia*, *Quercus* species
COMMENTS: Urbanite® is widely planted due to its high adaptability to urban landscapes with varying air quality and soil extremes. It has been affected by the introduction of the emerald Ash borer which is present in almost all regions. Urbanite® Ash's bark thickens as the tree matures which creates more resistance to trunk sunscald than the species and other cultivars.
OTHER CULTIVARS: 'Johnson' PP 9,136 Leprechaun™ - dwarf to medium height, 18' tall by 16' wide; 'Marshall' - dark green foliage, male cultivar, broad oval shape; 'Rugby' Prairie Spire® - seedless, narrowly pyramidal, very hardy to USDA Hardiness Zone 3

Ginkgo biloba
Ginkgo Tree
USDA Hardiness Zones: 4-8

DESCRIPTION

NATIVE HABITAT: China
PLANT TYPE: Deciduous, coniferous, large tree
MATURE SIZE: 40-60' tall by 30-50' wide
FORM/SHAPE: Upright, somewhat irregular
BARK: Smooth; yellowish gray-brown young stems; older bark dark gray with furrows and ridges
FLOWER: Greenish; inconspicuous; blooms in Spring
FRUIT: Orange; fleshy covered seed; very foul odor on female plant
FOLIAGE: Alternate, simple, fan-shaped with wavy margins; bright green leaves turn a very showy bright yellow in Fall; one of the first trees to change color in Fall

LANDSCAPE CHARACTERISTICS

GROWTH RATE: Slow to Moderate   **DROUGHT TOLERANCE:** Moderate to High   **SALT TOLERANCE:** Low
SOIL REQUIREMENTS: Prefers moist, well-drained, light soil; plant is somewhat adaptable to soil that is occasionally wet, but excess water must freely drain off
LIGHT REQUIREMENTS: Full sun to light shade
PEST PROBLEMS: American Plum borer, Grape mealybugs and other trunk feeding insects
DISEASE PROBLEMS: Anthracnose, *Glomerella* stem dieback, nematode, *Oxyporus, Pestalotiopsis* and root rot
ENVIRONMENTAL FACTORS: Avoid wet compacted soil sites; not tolerant of salt from roadway or sidewalk de-icing; girdling roots develop when root extension is restricted
PRUNING: Keep a central leader when young; lack of root pruning can result in circling roots in containers; prune for good structure and root development; each tree and cultivar may develop different tree crown structures

ADDITIONAL NOTES

USES: Lawn specimen, garden borders, focal point in Fall and avenue street tree
URBAN USES: Adaptable to many soil and climatic zones; tolerant of moderate air pollution if soil is well-drained; relatively free of pest and disease problems when well-maintained
SUBSTITUTIONS: *Aspen, Pseudolarix, Larix* and *Quercus* species, *Acer saccharum* species and cultivars, *Cladrastis* species
COMMENTS: No other tree has the dramatic effect of the *Ginkgo*. Few colors surpass the beauty of its golden yellow Fall foliage. To avoid the messy fruit, choose a male cultivar. If a seedling is chosen, it may not produce fruit or flower for many years. Male cultivars are grafted onto seedling rootstocks, so make certain the grafted cultivar is maintained by removing any rootstock suckers. Since rooted cuttings are now produced, this problem is reduced.
OTHER CULTIVARS: 'Autumn Gold' - male cultivar, slow growth; Golden Globe® PP 12,765 - male cultivar with broad, round crown, bright golden yellow Fall foliage color, strong grower in Southern regions; 'Princeton Sentry' - broad, columnar male cultivar

Gleditsia triacanthos var. inermis 'Shademaster'
Shademaster® Honeylocust
USDA Hardiness Zones: 4-8

DESCRIPTION

NATIVE HABITAT: Eastern North America; cultivar of nursery origin
PLANT TYPE: Deciduous, broadleaf, large tree
MATURE SIZE: 30-50' tall by 20-30' wide
FORM/SHAPE: Upright, very open with a thin crown
BARK: Smooth; young stems are greenish; older bark is gray-brown with deep, narrow furrows
FLOWER: Green racemes; inconspicuous; blooms in Spring
FRUIT: Fruitless cultivar
FOLIAGE: Alternate, pinnate or bipinnately compound; medium to dark green leaves turn yellowish brown in Fall

LANDSCAPE CHARACTERISTICS

GROWTH RATE: Moderate to Fast   **DROUGHT TOLERANCE:** Moderate to High   **SALT TOLERANCE:** Moderate to High
SOIL REQUIREMENTS: Prefers moist, well-drained, loamy soil; tolerant of a wide range of soil types, pH ranges and fertility levels
LIGHT REQUIREMENTS: Full sun to part shade
PEST PROBLEMS: Whitefly, periodic cicada, twig pruner, bagworm, Mimosa webworm, leafhopper, caterpillars, Honeylocust spider mites, Honeylocust plant bug, twig gindler, Grape mealybugs, gall midges, Honeylocust borer, Hickory borer and aphids
DISEASE PROBLEMS: Anthracnose, canker, powdery mildew, bark rot, butt rot, *Glomerella* stem dieback, *Nectria* canker, root rot, tar spot, wood decay and witches broom
ENVIRONMENTAL FACTORS: Moderately tolerant of water-logged soil; hot, dry urban areas and hot, humid conditions result in chronic insect and disease problems
PRUNING: Prune to maintain central leader when young; prune out limbs with acute limb to trunk angles that result in embedded bark and weak limb crotch attachments to the main trunk

ADDITIONAL NOTES

USES: Good choice when a background showing through foliage is desired; naturalizing, borders, medians, street tree, planter boxes and urban plantings
URBAN USES: Moderate to high tolerance of urban air pollution; adaptable to many soil types and light shade; small leaves not a litter problem; insect pests and trunk diseases limit utilization
SUBSTITUTIONS: *Lagerstroemia* cultivars, *Fraxinus* cultivars, *Cladrastis* species
COMMENTS: Shademaster® Honeylocust has vase-shaped form with ascending branches holding limbs out of line of sight in traffic areas, thereby reducing the need to prune.
OTHER CULTIVARS: 'Moraine' - wide, vase-shaped with rounded top, fine texture, golden Fall color; Halka® - wide oval crown, rapid growth, heavy caliper, yellow Fall color

Gleditsia triacanthos var. inermis 'Skycole'
Skyline® Honeylocust
USDA Hardiness Zones: 4-8a

DESCRIPTION

NATIVE HABITAT: Eastern North America; cultivar of nursery origin

PLANT TYPE: Deciduous, broadleaf, large tree

MATURE SIZE: 50-70' tall by 35-50' wide

FORM/SHAPE: Upright, symmetrical, slightly rounded canopy

BARK: Smooth; greenish gray young stems; older bark is gray-brown with deep, narrow, scaly furrows and ridges

FLOWER: Yellow; fragrant; inconspicuous; blooms in Spring

FRUIT: Fruitless cultivar

FOLIAGE: Alternate, bipinnately compound or pinnately compound; medium green leaves turn coppery yellow in Fall

LANDSCAPE CHARACTERISTICS

GROWTH RATE: Fast   **DROUGHT TOLERANCE:** High   **SALT TOLERANCE:** High

SOIL REQUIREMENTS: Prefers moist, well-drained, sandy, clay or loamy soil; tolerant of occasionally wet soil

LIGHT REQUIREMENTS: Best in full sun; tolerates part shade

PEST PROBLEMS: Whitefly, periodic cicada, twig pruner, bagworm, Mimosa webworm, boring insects, leafhopper, pod gall, caterpillars, Honeylocust spider mites, Honeylocust lacebug, twig gindler, Hickory borer, Grape mealybugs, leaf miner

DISEASE PROBLEMS: Anthracnose, canker, leaf spot, powdery mildew, bark rot, butt rot, *Glomerella* stem dieback, *Nectria* canker, root rot, tar spot, wood decay and witches broom

ENVIRONMENTAL FACTORS: Moderately tolerant of water-logged soil; hot, dry urban areas and hot, humid conditions result in chronic insect and disease problems

PRUNING: Prune to maintain central leader when young; prune out limbs with acute limb to trunk angles that result in embedded bark and weak limb crotch attachments to the main trunk

ADDITIONAL NOTES

USES: Large parking lot islands, lawn specimens, naturalized border, median tree, street tree, planter boxes and urban plantings

URBAN USES: Moderate to high tolerance of urban air pollution; adaptable to many soil types and light shade; small leaves not a litter problem; insect pests and trunk diseases limit utilization

SUBSTITUTIONS: *Lagerstroemia* cultivars, *Fraxinus* cultivars, *Cladrastis* species

COMMENTS: The broad pyramidal form and ascending, spreading branch habit of the Skyline® Honeylocust has good branch-to-trunk angles. It is well-suited to withstand environmental stresses.

OTHER CULTIVARS: True Shade® - broad oval crown, fast growth, heavy caliper, 45 degree branch to trunk angle; Imperial® - round crown, fast growth, compact, wide branch angle, resists storm damage

Koelreuteria paniculata
Goldenrain Tree
USDA Hardiness Zones: 5-9

DESCRIPTION

NATIVE HABITAT: China, Japan, and Korea
PLANT TYPE: Deciduous, broadleaf, small tree
MATURE SIZE: 20-30' tall by 20-25' wide
FORM/SHAPE: Upright, rounded, irregular
BARK: Smooth; light brown to gray-brown; older bark has shallow furrows
FLOWER: Yellow; 6-12" long; upright panicles; blooms in Summer; attracts insects
FRUIT: Three valved capsules; 1-1 1/2" long; yellowish turning brown when mature
FOLIAGE: Alternate, pinnately compound, 8-16" long, coarsely and irregularly serrate; dark to bright green leaves turn yellow in Fall

LANDSCAPE CHARACTERISTICS

GROWTH RATE: Moderate to Fast   **DROUGHT TOLERANCE:** Moderate to High   **SALT TOLERANCE:** Moderate to High
SOIL REQUIREMENTS: Adaptable to a wide range of well-drained soils; tolerant of high pH
LIGHT REQUIREMENTS: Sun to part shade; flower and plant form best in full sun
PEST PROBLEMS: Ambrosia beetles, Japanese weevil, white Peach scale, aphids, spider mites, Cranberry rootworm and black twig borer
DISEASE PROBLEMS: Canker, dieback, *Nectria*, *Verticillium* wilt and leaf spot
ENVIRONMENTAL FACTORS: Moderately tolerant of air pollutants; tolerant of high salt levels
PRUNING: Not necessary, but can improve structure and density

ADDITIONAL NOTES

USES: Specimen tree, small shade tree, group plantings, medians and avenues
URBAN USES: Tree is very adaptable to varying soils, moisture levels, air pollutants, and high salt levels; fast growth rate makes it desirable for urban applications
SUBSTITUTIONS: *Lagerstroemia* cultivars, *Malus* cultivars, *Cercis* species and cultivars, *Cornus* cultivars, *Acer palmatum* cultivars
COMMENTS: Goldenrain Tree is a tough, adaptable tree with few problems. It exhibits a Summer show of flowers with a fast growth rate. Most trees planted are seedlings. Seed capsules can become very messy and flowers attract insects.
OTHER CULTIVARS: 'Fastigiata' - narrow with upright, fastigiated limbs, limited flower production; 'September Gold' - similar plant form, flowers in September to October

Lagerstroemia indica 'Catawba'
Catawba Crape Myrtle
USDA Hardiness Zones: 6b-9

DESCRIPTION

NATIVE HABITAT: Species native to China and Korea; cultivar developed by Dr. Donald Egolf at U.S. National Arboretum
PLANT TYPE: Deciduous, broadleaf, small to medium size Summer flowering tree
MATURE SIZE: 12-18' tall by 10-12' wide
FORM/SHAPE: Upright, vase-shaped; often a multi-trunk tree
BARK: Smooth; tannish gray to silvery gray; exfoliating bark
FLOWER: Dark purple; blooms early to late Summer; attracts insects
FRUIT: Oval to round, dry, brown capsule; persistent
FOLIAGE: Opposite, simple, obtuse to elliptical, 1-2" long; dark green Summer leaves turn yellow, orange, or red in Fall

LANDSCAPE CHARACTERISTICS

GROWTH RATE: Moderate   **DROUGHT TOLERANCE:** Moderate to High   **SALT TOLERANCE:** Low to Moderate
SOIL REQUIREMENTS: Well-drained, moist, clay, loam or sandy soil; needs adequate lime and fertility
LIGHT REQUIREMENTS: Full sun for best growth and bloom
PEST PROBLEMS: Aphids, *Camellia* mining scale, leaf-footed bug, ambrosia beetles, Japanese beetle, caterpillars and spider mites
DISEASE PROBLEMS: Dieback, canker, *Rhizoctonia* blight, leaf spot, root rot, wood rot, Oak root rot; good tolerance of powdery mildew
ENVIRONMENTAL FACTORS: Frost injury to top growth, bark splitting from cold temperatures, ice and wind storms cause breakage and splitting; do not prune or over fertilize in late Summer as this favors freeze injury and bark splitting
PRUNING: Prune in late Winter to Spring; should not be pruned in late Summer; plant can be grown as a single-stem or multi-stem form; prune to remove low limbs and crossing branches; pruning will not induce flowering and may even delay flower production

ADDITIONAL NOTES

USES: Medium size flowering tree, shade tree, planters, parking lot islands, specimen, flowering accent tree and for Winter stem interest
URBAN USES: Very adaptable to urban growing sites; moderately tolerant of air pollutants, compacted soil, crowded growing conditions and severe pruning
SUBSTITUTIONS: *Vitex agnus-castus* 'Shoal Creek', *Vitex agnus-castus* 'Carolina Blue'
COMMENTS: 'Catawba' is a medium-sized, tough *Lagerstroemia* having the darkest purple flower color, silvery gray bark, and good powdery mildew resistance. 'Catawba' has a long bloom season and a moderate growth rate .
OTHER CULTIVARS: 'Conestoga' - bicolor, medium to light lavender flower color, silvery gray bark, open arching form, 12-18' tall; 'Powhatan' - light lavender flower color, silver gray bark, upright vase shape, 18' tall; 'Wichita' - light magenta flower color, dark russet brown bark color

Lagerstroemia indica 'Whit II' PP 10,296
Dynamite® Crape Myrtle
USDA Hardiness Zones: 6-9

DESCRIPTION

NATIVE HABITAT: Species native to China and Korea; cultivar of nursery origin

PLANT TYPE: Deciduous, broadleaf, small to medium size Summer flowering tree

MATURE SIZE: 15-20' tall by 8-10' wide

FORM/SHAPE: Upright, broad, vase-shaped, often a multi-trunk tree

BARK: Smooth; tan to gray; exfoliating bark

FLOWER: Crimson buds open to cherry red flowers; some flowers may exhibit white to pink color due to shade or weather conditions; blooms late Spring to Summer; attracts insects

FRUIT: Oval to round, dry, brown capsule; persistent

FOLIAGE: Opposite, simple, obtuse to elliptical, 1-2" long; new foliage emerges reddish burgundy matures to dark green in Summer; leaves turn yellow, orange, or red in Fall

LANDSCAPE CHARACTERISTICS

GROWTH RATE: Slow to Moderate   **DROUGHT TOLERANCE:** Moderate to High   **SALT TOLERANCE:** Low to Moderate

SOIL REQUIREMENTS: Well-drained, moist, clay, loam or sandy soil; needs adequate lime and fertility

LIGHT REQUIREMENTS: Full sun for best growth and bloom

PEST PROBLEMS: Aphids, *Camellia* mining scale, leaf-footed bug, ambrosia beetles, Japanese beetle, caterpillars and spider mites

DISEASE PROBLEMS: Dieback, canker, *Rhizoctonia* blight, leaf spot, root rot, wood rot, Oak root rot; good tolerance of powdery mildew

ENVIRONMENTAL FACTORS: Frost injury to top growth, bark splitting from cold temperatures, ice and wind storms cause breakage and splitting; do not prune or over fertilize in late Summer as this favors freeze injury and bark splitting

PRUNING: Prune in late Winter to Spring; should not be pruned in late Summer; plant can be grown as a single-stem or multi-stem form; prune to remove low limbs and crossing branches; pruning will not induce flowering and may even delay flower production

ADDITIONAL NOTES

USES: Small flowering tree, shade tree, planters, parking lot islands, specimen, flowering accent tree, and for Winter stem interest

URBAN USES: Very adaptable to urban growing sites; moderately tolerant of air pollutants, compacted soil, crowded growing conditions and severe pruning

SUBSTITUTIONS: *Lagerstroemia (i. x fauriei)* 'Arapaho', *Lagerstroemia (i. x fauriei)* 'Tonto', *Malus* cultivars, or *Cercis* cultivars

COMMENTS: *Lagerstroemia* is a standard for southern landscapes. Dynamite® displays a bright, red color for that "show stopping" landscape design.

OTHER CULTIVARS: 'Whit III' PP 10,319 Pink Velour® - pink flower color, small tree, wide vase form; 'Powhatan' - light lavender flower color, silver-gray bark, upright vase shape, 18' tall; 'Whit VII' PP 14,975 Siren Red® - brilliant, dark fiery red flower color, small tree, vase-shaped plant form

Lagerstroemia (i. x fauriei) 'Muskogee'
Muskogee Crape Myrtle
USDA Hardiness Zones: 6b-10a

DESCRIPTION

NATIVE HABITAT: A hybrid between two species native to China, Japan and Korea; cultivar developed by Dr. Donald Egolf at the U.S. National Arboretum

PLANT TYPE: Deciduous, broadleaf, large Summer flowering tree

MATURE SIZE: 20-30' tall by 15-25' wide

FORM/SHAPE: Vase-shaped, often multi-trunk tree

BARK: Smooth; tannish gray and chalky; exfoliating bark

FLOWER: Pinkish lavender bloom; blooms early to late Summer; attracts insects

FRUIT: Oval to round, dry, brown capsule; persistent

FOLIAGE: Opposite, simple, oblanceolate to elliptical, 2-4" long; dark green Summer leaves turn yellow, orange or red in Fall

LANDSCAPE CHARACTERISTICS

GROWTH RATE: Moderate to Fast   **DROUGHT TOLERANCE:** Moderate to High   **SALT TOLERANCE:** Low to Moderate

SOIL REQUIREMENTS: Well-drained, moist, clay, loam or sandy soil; needs adequate lime and fertility

LIGHT REQUIREMENTS: Full sun for best growth and bloom

PEST PROBLEMS: Aphids, *Camellia* mining scale, leaf-footed bug, ambrosia beetles, Japanese beetle, caterpillars and spider mites

DISEASE PROBLEMS: Dieback, canker, *Rhizoctonia* blight, leaf spot, root rot, wood rot, Oak root rot; good tolerance of powdery mildew

ENVIRONMENTAL FACTORS: Frost injury to top growth, bark splitting from cold temperatures, ice and wind storms cause breakage and splitting; do not prune or over fertilize in late Summer as this favors freeze injury and bark splitting

PRUNING: Prune in late Winter to Spring; should not be pruned in late Summer; plant can be grown as a single-stem or multi-stem form; prune to remove low limbs and crossing branches; pruning will not induce flowering and may even delay flower production

ADDITIONAL NOTES

USES: Large flowering tree, shade tree, planters, parking lot islands, specimen, flowering accent tree and for Winter stem interest

URBAN USES: Very adaptable to urban growing sites; moderately tolerant of air pollutants, compacted soil, crowded growing conditions and severe pruning

SUBSTITUTIONS: *Lagerstroemia indica* 'Powhatan', *Malus* cultivars, or *Cercis* cultivars

COMMENTS: This is a large, tough, hybrid Crape Myrtle with lavender flowers, tannish gray exfoliating bark, powdery mildew resistance and few insect problems. 'Muskogee' has an early and long blooming season as well as a fast growth rate.

OTHER CULTIVARS: 'Catawba' - small to medium broad vase-shaped, purple flowering, good powdery mildew resistance; 'Powhatan' -small to medium, broad vase-shaped, soft purple flower, good powdery mildew resistance; 'Yuma' - small, narrow, vase-shaped, light lavender flower, good powdery mildew resistance

Lagerstroemia (i. x fauriei) 'Natchez'
Natchez Crape Myrtle
USDA Hardiness Zones: 7-9

DESCRIPTION

NATIVE HABITAT: A hybrid between two species native to China, Japan and Korea; cultivar developed by Dr. Donald Egolf at the U.S. National Arboretum
PLANT TYPE: Deciduous, broadleaf, large Summer flowering tree
MATURE SIZE: 20-30' tall by 15-25' wide
FORM/SHAPE: Broad, tall, vase-shaped; often a mult-trunk tree
BARK: Smooth; tannish gray; exfoliates to reveal cinnamon bark
FLOWER: White; blooms early to late Summer; attracts insects
FRUIT: Oval to round, dry, brown capsule; persistent
FOLIAGE: Opposite, simple, obtuse to elliptical, 2-4" long; dark green Summer leaves turn yellow, orange, or red in Fall

LANDSCAPE CHARACTERISTICS

GROWTH RATE: Moderate to Fast   **DROUGHT TOLERANCE:** Moderate to High   **SALT TOLERANCE:** Low to Moderate
SOIL REQUIREMENTS: Well-drained, moist, clay, loam or sandy soil; needs adequate lime and fertility
LIGHT REQUIREMENTS: Full sun for best growth and bloom
PEST PROBLEMS: Aphids, *Camellia* mining scale, leaf-footed bug, ambrosia beetles, Japanese beetle, caterpillars and spider mites
DISEASE PROBLEMS: Dieback, canker, *Rhizoctonia* blight, leaf spot, root rot, wood rot, Oak root rot; very resistant of powdery mildew
ENVIRONMENTAL FACTORS: Frost injury to top growth, bark splitting from cold temperatures, ice and wind storms cause breakage and splitting; do not prune or over fertilize in late Summer as this favors freeze injury and bark splitting
PRUNING: Prune in late Winter to Spring; should not be pruned in late Summer; plant can be grown as a single-stem or multi-stem form; prune to remove low limbs and crossing branches; pruning will not induce flowering and may even delay flower production

ADDITIONAL NOTES

USES: Large flowering tree, shade tree, planters, parking lot islands, specimen, flowering accent tree and for Winter stem interest
URBAN USES: Very adaptable to urban growing sites; moderately tolerant of air pollutants, compacted soil, crowded growing conditions and severe pruning
SUBSTITUTIONS: *Lagerstroemia (i. x fauriei)* 'Acoma', *Lagerstroemia indica* 'Byers White', *Styrax japonica* species and cultivars, *Chionanthus retusus* 'China Snow', *Malus* cultivars, *Lagerstroemia fauriei* 'Townhouse' and 'Fantasy', *Lagerstroemia (i. x fauriei)* 'Sarah's Favorite', or *Loropetalum chinensis*
COMMENTS: 'Natchez' is a large, tough, hybrid *Lagerstroemia* with white flowers, cinnamon brown exfoliating bark, very good powdery mildew resistance, free of aphids and bothered by few other insect pests. 'Natchez' has an early and long blooming season and a moderate to fast growth rate. This is the most commonly used cultivar, but is too large for some locations. The hybrid cultivar 'Acoma' should be used in sites with limited space.
OTHER CULTIVARS: 'Acoma' - white flower color, silvery gray to tannish gray bark, low spreading to broad vase-shaped, 9-12' tall, resistant to powdery mildew and insects; High Cotton™ - white flowers, light cinnamon brown bark, tall upright vase-shaped, 25-30' tall, resistant to powdery mildew, dark green foliage, late and long bloom season

Lagerstroemia (i. x fauriei) 'Tuscarora'
Tuscarora Crape Myrtle
USDA Hardiness Zones: 7-9

DESCRIPTION

NATIVE HABITAT: A hybrid between two species native to China, Japan and Korea; cultivar developed by Dr. Donald Egolf at the U.S. National Arboretum

PLANT TYPE: Deciduous, broadleaf, medium size Summer flowering tree

MATURE SIZE: 15-20' tall by 10-12' wide

FORM/SHAPE: Broad, vase-shaped; often a mult-trunk tree

BARK: Smooth; light brown; exfoliating bark

FLOWER: Dark, coral pink; blooms early to late Summer; attracts insects

FRUIT: Oval to round, dry, brown capsule; persistent

FOLIAGE: Opposite, simple, obtuse to elliptical, 2-4" long; dark green Summer leaves turn yellow, orange, or red in Fall

LANDSCAPE CHARACTERISTICS

GROWTH RATE: Moderate   **DROUGHT TOLERANCE:** Moderate to High   **SALT TOLERANCE:** Low to Moderate

SOIL REQUIREMENTS: Well-drained, moist, clay, loam or sandy soil; needs adequate lime and fertility

LIGHT REQUIREMENTS: Full sun for best growth and bloom

PEST PROBLEMS: Aphids, *Camellia* mining scale, leaf-footed bug, ambrosia beetles, Japanese beetle, caterpillars and spider mites

DISEASE PROBLEMS: Dieback, canker, *Rhizoctonia* blight, leaf spot, root rot, wood rot, Oak root rot; good tolerance of powdery mildew

ENVIRONMENTAL FACTORS: Frost injury to top growth, bark splitting from cold temperatures, ice and wind storms cause breakage and splitting; do not prune or over fertilize in late Summer as this favors freeze injury and bark splitting

PRUNING: Prune in late Winter to Spring; should not be pruned in late Summer; plant can be grown as a single-stem or multi-stem form; prune to remove low limbs and crossing branches; pruning will not induce flowering and may even delay flower production

ADDITIONAL NOTES

USES: Medium size flowering tree, shade tree, planters, parking lot islands, specimen, flowering accent tree and for Winter stem interest

URBAN USES: Very adaptable to urban growing sites; moderately tolerant of air pollutants, compacted soil, crowded growing conditions and severe pruning

SUBSTITUTIONS: *Lagerstroemia (i. x fauriei)* 'Arapaho', *Lagerstroemia (i. x fauriei)* 'Comanche', or *Lagerstroemia indica* 'Cherokee'

COMMENTS: This is a medium size, hybrid *Lagerstroemia* with dark coral-pink flower color, light brown exfoliating bark, powdery mildew resistance and few insect problems. 'Tuscarora' has an early and long bloom season as well as a moderate growth rate.

OTHER CULTIVARS: 'Arapaho' - dark red flower color, light tan bark, powdery mildew resistance, upright vase-shaped, 20-25' tall; 'Comanche' - dark coral-pink flower color, light sandalwood colored bark, upright globose form, 12-15' tall

Lagerstroemia indica 'Carolina Beauty'
Carolina Beauty Crape Myrtle

USDA Hardiness Zones: 6b-9

MATURE SIZE: 20-30' tall by 12-15' wide
BARK: Smooth; gray-brown exfoliating bark
FLOWER: Dark watermelon-red; blooms early to late Summer; attracts insects
SUBSTITUTIONS: *Lagerstroemia (i. x fauriei)* 'Arapaho', *Lagerstroemia indica* 'Cherokee'
COMMENTS: 'Carolina Beauty' is a large, tough *Lagerstroemia indica* with dark red watermelon flowers and gray-brown bark. It is susceptible to powdery mildew. Heavy aphid infestation can cause a severe, sooty mold problem.

Lagerstroemia indica 'Potomac'
Potomac Crape Myrtle

USDA Hardiness Zones: 6b-9

MATURE SIZE: 16-18' tall by 10-12' wide
BARK: Smooth; tannish gray; exfoliates to reveal silver-gray bark
FLOWER: Clear, medium pink; blooms early to late Summer; attracts insects
SUBSTITUTIONS: *Lagerstroemia (i. x fauriei)* 'Osage', *Lagerstroemia (i. x fauriei)* 'Miami', *Lagerstroemia indica* 'Seminole', *Styrax japonica* 'Pink Chimes' or *Loropetalum chinensis rubrum* 'Blush'
COMMENTS: 'Potomac' is a medium size, tough *Lagerstroemia* with clear, medium pink flowers and silvery gray exfoliating bark. It also has good powdery mildew resistance, a long bloom season and a moderate growth rate.

Lagerstroemia indica 'Whit III' PP 10,319
Pink Velour® Crape Myrtle

USDA Hardiness Zones: 6b-9

MATURE SIZE: 8-10' tall by 8-10' wide
BARK: Smooth; tannish gray; exfoliates to reveal tan bark
FLOWER: Crimson buds open to bright pink; blooms late Spring to Summer; attracts insects
SUBSTITUTIONS: *Lagerstroemia (i. x fauriei)* 'Sioux' and 'Hopi', *Malus* cultivars, *Cercis* cultivars and *Loropetalum* cultivars
COMMENTS: *Lagerstroemia* is a standard for southern landscapes. Pink Velour® may be one of the best choices, for its burgundy-wine foliage that matures to a dark purple-green. It has a bright pink flower color and a compact size useful in landscape design.

CRAPE MYRTLE CULTIVARS

Lagerstroemia indica 'Whit IV' PP 11,342
Red Rocket® Crape Myrtle

USDA Hardiness Zones: 6b-9

MATURE SIZE: 10-15' tall by 10-15' wide
BARK: Smooth; tan to light brown-gray; exfoliates to reveal brown-gray bark
FLOWER: Cherry red; blooms late Spring to early Summer; attracts insects
SUBSTITUTIONS: *Lagerstroemia indica* 'Centennial Spirit', *Malus* cultivars, *Prunus* cultivars and *Loropetalum* cultivars
COMMENTS: Red Rocket® exhibits beautiful foliage and flower color in the Summer landscape, making it a valuable asset to combine with other flowers and shrubs.

Lagerstroemia (i. x fauriei) 'Biloxi'
Biloxi Crape Myrtle

USDA Hardiness Zones: 7-9

MATURE SIZE: 20-24' tall by 12-15' wide
BARK: Smooth; brownish gray; exfoliates to reveal dark brown bark
FLOWER: Pale pink; blooms early to late Summer; attracts insects
SUBSTITUTIONS: *Lagerstroemia indica* 'Potomac', *Lagerstroemia (i. x fauriei)* 'Osage', *Lagerstroemia (i. x fauriei)* 'Hopi', *Lagerstroemia (i. x fauriei)* 'Choctaw'
COMMENTS: This is a large, tough hybrid *Lagerstroemia* with pale pink flowers, dark brown exfoliating bark, powdery mildew resistance and few insect probelms. 'Biloxi' has a long bloom season and fast growth rate.

Lagerstroemia (i. x fauriei) 'Choctaw'
Choctaw Crape Myrtle

USDA Hardiness Zones: 7-9

MATURE SIZE: 20-24' tall by 15-18' wide
BARK: Smooth; brownish gray; exfoliates to reveal mottled, light cinnamon-brown bark
FLOWER: Clear, bright pink; blooms early to late Summer; attracts insects
SUBSTITUTIONS: *Lagerstroemia (i. x fauriei)* 'Caddo', *Lagerstroemia (i. x fauriei)* 'Comanche', *Lagerstroemia (i. x fauriei)* 'Pecos', *Lagerstroemia (i. x fauriei)* 'Miami'
COMMENTS: 'Choctaw' is a large, tough, hybrid *Lagerstroemia* with clear, bright pink flowers and mottled light cinnamon-brown exfoliating bark. It also has powdery mildew resistance and few insect problems. 'Choctaw' has a long bloom season and fast growth rate.

Lagerstroemia fauriei 'Fantasy'
Fantasy Crape Myrtle

USDA Hardiness Zones: 7b-9

MATURE SIZE: 30-50' tall by 20-30' wide
BARK: Smooth; tanned gray; exfoliates to reveal combinations of cinnamon and reddish-brown bark
FLOWER: White; blooms late Spring to early Summer; attracts insects
SUBSTITUTIONS: *Lagerstroemia* hybrid cultivars 'Natchez' and 'Acoma', *Lagerstroemia indica* 'Byers White', *Malus* cultivars, *Prunus* cultivars and *Cercis* cultivars
COMMENTS: 'Fantasy' is resistant to powdery mildew. Introduced in the 1950's by Dr. John Creech, former director of the U.S. National Arboretum. The cultivar was named by Dr. J.C. Raulston of the J.C. Raulston Arboretum in Raleigh, North Carolina.

Lagerstroemia (i. x fauriei) 'Miami'
Miami Crape Myrtle

USDA Hardiness Zones: 7-9

MATURE SIZE: 15-20' tall by 12-15' wide
BARK: Smooth; maroon; exfoliates to reveal mottled, dark chestnut-brown bark
FLOWER: Dark pink; blooms early to late Summer; attracts insects
SUBSTITUTIONS: *Lagerstroemia (i. x fauriei)* 'Wichita', *Lagerstroemia (i. x fauriei)* 'Lipan'
COMMENTS: 'Miami' has dark pink flowers, mottled, exfoliating cinnamon-maroon to chestnut-brown bark and good powdery mildew resistance.

Lagerstroemia (i. x fauriei) 'Sarah's Favorite'
Sarah's Favorite Crape Myrtle

USDA Hardiness Zones: 7-9

MATURE SIZE: 20-30' tall by 12-15' wide
BARK: Smooth; tannish gray; exfoliates to reveal cinnamon-brown bark
FLOWER: White; blooms early to late Summer; attracts insects
SUBSTITUTIONS: *Lagerstroemia (i. x fauriei)* 'Natchez', *Lagerstroemia (i. x fauriei)* 'Acoma', *Styrax japonica* cultivars, *Chionanthus retusus* 'China Snow', *Loropetalum chinensis*, *Malus* cultivars, *Lagerstroemia fauriei* 'Kiowa'
COMMENTS: This is a large, tough hybrid *Lagerstroemia* with white flowers, cinnamon-brown exfoliating bark and powdery mildew resistance. It has an upright, vase-shaped form that is more narrow than 'Natchez' but with a similar height and growth rate.

CRAPE MYRTLE CULTIVARS

Lagerstroemia (i. x fauriei) 'Sioux'
Sioux Crape Myrtle

USDA Hardiness Zones: 7-9

MATURE SIZE: 15-20' tall by 10-12' wide
BARK: Smooth; medium gray-brown; exfoliates to reveal chesnut-brown bark
FLOWER: Medium, dark pink; blooms late Spring to early Summer; attracts insects
SUBSTITUTIONS: *Lagerstroemia (i. x fauriei)* 'Pecos', *Lagerstroemia (i. x fauriei)* 'Osage', *Lagerstroemia indica* 'Potomac', *Styrax japonica* 'Pink Chimes', and *Loropetalum chinensis rubrum* 'Blush'
COMMENTS: 'Sioux' is one of the best Summer foliaged Crape Myrtles with showy beautiful flowers that are vibrant and long-lived. 'Sioux' also has superb Fall color and interesting Winter bark. It is very mildew resistant.

Lagerstroemia (i. x fauriei) 'Tonto'
Tonto Crape Myrtle

USDA Hardiness Zones: 7-9

MATURE SIZE: 8-10' tall by 8-10' wide
BARK: Smooth; cream to taupe, gray-brown; exfoliates to reveal tan bark
FLOWER: Fuchsia red to maroon; blooms early to late Summer; attracts insects
SUBSTITUTIONS: *Lagerstroemia indica* 'Cherokee', *Lagerstroemia (i.x fauriei)* 'Caddo', *Lagerstroemia (i. x fauriei)* 'Pecos', *Lagerstroemia (i.x fauriei)* 'Zuni' and *Lagerstroemia (i.x fauriei)* 'Arapaho'
COMMENTS: 'Tonto' is a good Crape Myrtle choice with a true red bloom color. It is a great specimen choice where a small tree is needed. It grows much smaller than other Crape Myrtle varieties.

Lagerstroemia (i. x fauriei) 'Tuskegee'
Tuskegee Crape Myrtle

USDA Hardiness Zones: 7-9

MATURE SIZE: 15-20' tall by 12-15' wide
BARK: Smooth; light grayish tan; exfoliates to reveal tan bark
FLOWER: Dark pink to red; blooms early to late Summer; attracts insects
SUBSTITUTIONS: *Lagerstroemia indica* 'Cherokee', *Lagerstroemia indica* 'Seminole', *Lagerstroemia (i.) x fauriei* 'Tuscarora', *Lagerstroemia (i. x fauriei)* 'Arapaho' and *Lagerstroemia (i. x fauriei)* 'Sioux'
COMMENTS: This is a medium size, hybrid *Lagerstroemia* with a dark pink to red flower color, light gray-tan exfoliating bark, powdery mildew resistance and few insect problems. It has an early and long bloom season and a fast growth rate.

Liquidambar styraciflua
Sweetgum
USDA Hardiness Zones: 5b-10a

DESCRIPTION

NATIVE HABITAT: Throughout Eastern United States to Texas, Oklahoma, Mexico and Central America
PLANT TYPE: Deciduous, broadleaf, large tree
MATURE SIZE: 60-75' tall by 35-50' wide
FORM/SHAPE: Pyramidal, symmetrical canopy with a straight trunk
BARK: Smooth; pale gray; twigs are brown-green with some corky outgrowth; bark matures to dark gray with many rough, vertically woven ridges and furrows
FLOWER: Male flower in terminal clusters are green with a brown tinge; female flowers are in green capsular fruit, turns reddish tan to brown in Fall
FRUIT: Hard, spiny gumballs; emerge green and turns reddish tan to brown in Fall; 1-1 3/4" diameter; hazard in pedestrian or lawn areas; considered a nuisance and messy
FOLIAGE: Alternate, five to seven-lobed, coarse, star-shaped leaf with partially serrated margins; green to glossy green leaves turn yellow-green, yellow, orange, red to purple-red in Fall

LANDSCAPE CHARACTERISTICS

GROWTH RATE: Fast   **DROUGHT TOLERANCE:** Low to Moderate   **SALT TOLERANCE:** Low
SOIL REQUIREMENTS: Well-drained, moist soil but tolerant of many soil types, fertility and pH levels; tolerant of wet soil and short duration flooding once established
LIGHT REQUIREMENTS: Full sun to part shade
PEST PROBLEMS: Ambrosia beetles, leafcutting ants, Oak weevil, thrips, caterpillars, forest tent caterpillar, twig pruner, black twig borer, whitefly, Sweetgum scale, cottony cushion scale, aphids and mites
DISEASE PROBLEMS: Canker, *Cercospora* leaf spot, *Nectria*, bleeding canker, butt rot, *Cylindrocladium*, dieback, *Fusarium* root rot, *Ganoderma*, *Oxyporus* and *Phytophthora*
ENVIRONMENTAL FACTORS: Drought stress promotes stem canker and dieback diseases; deep planting causes root death from low oxygen in the soil; moderate tolerance to air pollutants; moderate tolerance to water-logged soil
PRUNING: Minimal pruning needed; prune to remove low hanging limbs, co-dominant leaders and rootstock suckers on budded or grafted cultivars

ADDITIONAL NOTES

USES: Parking lot islands, reclamation plantings, residential street tree and naturalizing
URBAN USES: Moderate tolerance to water-logged soil and urban air pollutants; shallow root development may cause problems with sidewalks and other paved surfaces;messy gumballs are considered a hazard in pedestrian areas
SUBSTITUTIONS: *Acer rubrum* cultivars, *Acer barbatum*, *Nyssa*, *Quercus* species and cultivars, *Magnolia virginiana* or *Ginkgo* cultivars
COMMENTS: Selected cultivars are grafted or budded to seedling root stock which may vary in their ability to tolerate deep planting or water-logged soil. Sweetgum is a fast growing tree and needs adequate soil moisture during drought stress conditions. Dieback, canker or ambrosia beetles may become problematic.
OTHER CULTIVARS: 'Cherokee' - foliage typical of species, columnar, upright, growth habit and compact; 'Moraine' - fast growth, round, upright, rounded form, species, glossy, dark green Summer foliage, red to purple Fall color, very cold hardy; 'Palo Alto' - uniform, moderate growth rate, Summer foliage to yellow-orange and red Fall color; 'Variegata' - *syn.* 'Aurea' - typical growth and form, variegated leaves with golden yellow splotches

Liquidambar styraciflua 'Rotundiloba'
Rotundiloba Sweetgum
USDA Hardiness Zones: 6-10a

DESCRIPTION

NATIVE HABITAT: Throughout Eastern United States to Texas, Oklahoma, Mexico and Central America; Southern selection
PLANT TYPE: Deciduous, broadleaf, large tree
MATURE SIZE: 30-50' tall by 15-20' wide
FORM/SHAPE: Upright, narrow, irregular outline
BARK: Smooth; pale gray; twigs are brown-green with some corky outgrowth; bark matures to dark gray with many rough, vertically woven ridges and furrows
FLOWER: Male flower in terminal clusters are green with a brown tinge; female flowers are in green capsular fruit, turns reddish tan to brown in Fall
FRUIT: Fruitless
FOLIAGE: Alternate, unique leaves have rounded lobes, shorter than species with entire thickened margins, wavy texture; dark glossy green top surface, olive to light green on underside of leaves; turning yellow to purple in Fall, no outstanding Fall color

LANDSCAPE CHARACTERISTICS

GROWTH RATE: Moderate   **DROUGHT TOLERANCE:** Low to Moderate   **SALT TOLERANCE:** Low
SOIL REQUIREMENTS: Well-drained, moist soil but tolerant of many soil types, fertility and pH levels; tolerant of wet soil and short duration flooding once established
LIGHT REQUIREMENTS: Full sun to part shade
PEST PROBLEMS: Ambrosia beetles, leafcutting ants, Oak weevil, thrips, caterpillars, forest tent caterpillar, twig pruner, black twig borer, whitefly, Sweetgum scale, cottony cushion scale, aphids and mites
DISEASE PROBLEMS: Canker, *Cercospora* leaf spot, *Nectria*, bleeding canker, butt rot, *Cylindrocladium*, dieback, *Fusarium* root rot, *Ganoderma*, *Oxyporus* and *Phytophthora*
ENVIRONMENTAL FACTORS: Drought stress promotes stem canker and dieback diseases; deep planting causes root death from low oxygen in the soil; moderate tolerance to air pollutants; moderate tolerance to water-logged soils
PRUNING: Minimal pruning needed; prune to remove low hanging limbs, co-dominant leaders and rootstock suckers on budded or grafted cultivars

ADDITIONAL NOTES

USES: Parking lot islands, reclamation plantings, residential street tree and naturalizing
URBAN USES: Moderate tolerance to water-logged soil and urban air pollutants; shallow root development may cause problems with sidewalks and other paved surfaces
SUBSTITUTIONS: *Acer rubrum* cultivars, *Acer barbatum*, *Nyssa*, *Quercus* species and cultivars, *Magnolia virginiana* or *Ginkgo* cultivars
COMMENTS: Selected cultivars are grafted or budded to seedling root stock which may vary in their ability to tolerate deep planting or water-logged soil. Sweetgum is a fast growing tree and needs adequate soil moisture during drought stress conditions. Dieback, canker or ambrosia beetles may become problematic.
OTHER CULTIVARS: 'Cherokee' - foliage typical of species, columnar, upright, growth habit and compact; 'Moraine' - fast growth, round, upright, rounded form, species, glossy, dark green Summer foliage, red to purple Fall color, very cold hardy; 'Palo Alto' - uniform, moderate growth rate, Summer foliage to yellow-orange and red Fall color; 'Variegata' - *syn.* 'Aurea' - typical growth and form, variegated leaves with golden yellow splotches

Liquidambar styraciflua 'Slender Silhouette'
Columnar or Slender Silhouette Sweetgum
USDA Hardiness Zones: 6-9

DESCRIPTION

NATIVE HABITAT: Throughout Eastern United States to Texas, Oklahoma, Mexico and Central America; native woodland selection
PLANT TYPE: Deciduous, broadleaf, narrow, large tree
MATURE SIZE: 30-40' tall by 7' wide
FORM/SHAPE: Narrow, columnar canopy
BARK: Smooth; whitish gray; twigs are brown-green with some corky outgrowths; bark matures to dark gray with many rough, vertically woven ridges and furrows
FLOWER: Cultivar reported not to form flower structures
FRUIT: Reported to be fruitless, but fruiting could develop as tree matures
FOLIAGE: Alternate, five to seven-lobed, coarse, star-shaped leaf with partially serrated margin; green to glossy, green leaves turn yellow, orange to reddish purple in Fall

LANDSCAPE CHARACTERISTICS

GROWTH RATE: Moderate to Fast　　**DROUGHT TOLERANCE:** Low to Moderate　　**SALT TOLERANCE:** Low
SOIL REQUIREMENTS: Well-drained, moist soil but tolerant of many soil types, fertility and pH levels; tolerant of wet soil and short duration flooding once established
LIGHT REQUIREMENTS: Full sun to part shade
PEST PROBLEMS: Ambrosia beetles, leafcutting ants, Oak weevil, thrips, caterpillars, forest tent caterpillar, twig pruner, black twig borer, whitefly, Sweetgum scale, cottony cushion scale, aphids and mites
DISEASE PROBLEMS: Canker, *Cercospora* leaf spot, *Nectria*, bleeding canker, butt rot, *Cylindrocladium*, dieback, *Fusarium* root rot, *Ganoderma*, *Oxyporus* and *Phytophthora*
ENVIRONMENTAL FACTORS: Drought stress promotes stem canker and dieback diseases; deep planting causes root death from low oxygen in the soil; moderate tolerance to air pollutants; moderate tolerance to water-logged soil
PRUNING: Minimal pruning needed; prune to remove low hanging limbs, co-dominant leaders and rootstock suckers on budded or grafted cultivars; best to prune in Winter

ADDITIONAL NOTES

USES: Accent plant, specimen, streetscapes, columnades; can be used to frame landscape or architectural features
URBAN USES: A Sweetgum cultivar that is unique in urban applications; tight crown form makes it a good choice for areas with limited space; moderately tolerant of water-logged soil and air pollutants
SUBSTITUTIONS: Columnar *Acer rubrum* cultivars, columnar *Acer saccharum* cultivars, columnar *Acer buergerianum* cultivars, *Thuja occidentalis* 'Degroot's Spire', *Styrax japonica* Snowcone® or columnar *Ginkgo* cultivar
COMMENTS: This Sweetgum has an extremely tight crown which makes it a good choice for tight spaces and makes it a desirable plant for urban and residential applications.
OTHER CULTIVARS: 'Cherokee' - foliage typical of species, columnar, upright, growth habit and compact; 'Moraine' - fast growth, round, upright, rounded form, species, glossy, dark green Summer foliage, red to purple Fall color, very cold hardy; 'Palo Alto' - uniform, moderate growth rate, Summer foliage to yellow-orange and red Fall color; 'Variegata' - *syn.* 'Aurea' - typical growth and form, variegated leaves with golden yellow splotches

Liriodendron tulipifera
Tulip Poplar or Tulip Tree
USDA Hardiness Zones: 5-9a

DESCRIPTION

NATIVE HABITAT: Eastern and Southern United States
PLANT TYPE: Deciduous, broadleaf, large tree
MATURE SIZE: 80-100' tall by 30-50' wide
FORM/SHAPE: Symmetrically oval crown
BARK: Smooth; brownish green twigs and trunk when young; matures to whitish gray; develops deep fissures and large ridges and plates; bark is easily damaged
FLOWER: Greenish yellow; fragrant flowers in shoot terminals; blooms in late Spring after leaf expansion is complete
FRUIT: Hard, woody cone; collection of scale-like fruit
FOLIAGE: Alternate, simple, broad spatulate with four to six lobes, upper lobe forms a "V" to truncate shape; green to dark green leaves turn a showy yellow to yellow-brown in Fall

LANDSCAPE CHARACTERISTICS

GROWTH RATE: Fast   **DROUGHT TOLERANCE:** Low to Moderate   **SALT TOLERANCE:** Low
SOIL REQUIREMENTS: Well-drained, moist, fertile, humus rich, slightly acidic soil; benefits from well-limed soil
LIGHT REQUIREMENTS: Full sun to part shade; best in full sun
PEST PROBLEMS: Ambrosia beetles, Yellow Poplar weevil, Oak weevil, Tulip Tree leafminer, caterpillars, mites, Magnolia spider mites, flatheaded Apple tree borer, Columbian timber beetle, tree cricket, aphids, Tulip Tree aphid, scales, oyster shell scale and Tulip Tree scale
DISEASE PROBLEMS: Anthracnose, bark rot, butt rot, canker, *Cylindrocladium*, tar spot, dieback, *Fusarium*, *Ganoderma*, *Glomerella, Hypoxylon*, leaf spot, *Nectria*, nematodes, *Phomopsis, Phytophthora*, powdery mildew, *Verticillium* wilt, sap streak and wetwood
ENVIRONMENTAL FACTORS: Not tolerant of water-logged soil or prolonged drought; suffers from Spring frost injury and lighting strikes; limb damage caused by strong wind, snow or ice; large surface roots and can blow over in heavy wind
PRUNING: Prune to remove low limbs, maintain single leader and remove storm damaged limbs (which reduces wood invading fungi)

ADDITIONAL NOTES

USES: Large specimen tree, lawn shade tree, street tree if given enough space and distance from paved areas, naturalizing and remediation of wetland areas
URBAN USES: Not tolerant of air pollutants, compacted or water-logged soil or severe drought stress; large, fast growing trees need large space to develop
SUBSTITUTIONS: *Quercus* species and cultivars, *Acer rubrum* cultivars, deciduous *Magnolia* species, *Liquidambar* species and cultivars, *Nyssa* species, *Platanus* species and cultivars
COMMENTS: The Tulip Poplar is a large, fast growing tree that needs a large growing area with ample space for root growth. It produces filtered shade that allows shade-tolerant grass species to grow beneath the tree canopy. The soil should be well-drained and fertile. The Tulip Poplar is not tolerant of soil compaction or water-logged soil. Large leaves, hard, woody cones and twig shedding can form litter for pedestrian areas.
OTHER CULTIVARS: 'Aureomarginatum' - yellow-green to golden yellow color, wide margin to the leaf, light yellow-green leaf in shade; 'Fastigiatum' - narrowly pyramidal, upright branching, 50-60' tall by 15-20' wide

Magnolia stellata
Star Magnolia
USDA Hardiness Zones: 4-8

DESCRIPTION

NATIVE HABITAT: Japan

PLANT TYPE: Deciduous, broadleaf, small flowering tree

MATURE SIZE: 15-18' tall by 10-14' wide

FORM/SHAPE: Rounded, symmetrical canopy, often multi-stemmed and tree formed

BARK: Smooth; whitish gray; normally grown with multiple trunks

FLOWER: White, star-shaped flower; 3-4" in diameter; very showy and fragrant; blooms in Spring; attracts insects

FRUIT: Elongated, dry, hard, brown cone; 1-3" long

FOLIAGE: Alternate, simple, oblong, 2-4" long; green leaves turn coppery yellow in Fall

LANDSCAPE CHARACTERISTICS

GROWTH RATE: Slow to Moderate   **DROUGHT TOLERANCE:** Moderate   **SALT TOLERANCE:** Low

SOIL REQUIREMENTS: Moist, fertile, humus rich, well-limed soil; prefers well-drained, rich and porous soil

LIGHT REQUIREMENTS: Full sun produces best growth and flower; tolerates part shade

PEST PROBLEMS: Oleander scale, false Oleander scale, spider mites, Tulip tree scale, black twig borer and leaf miner

DISEASE PROBLEMS: Leaf spot, blights, canker, stem canker, root rot, *Verticillium* wilt and wetwood

ENVIRONMENTAL FACTORS: No serious problems; needs adequate soil moisture and fertility for optimal growth and aesthetics; adaptable to less desirable environmental conditions; spreading root system makes trees difficult to preserve on construction sites; late frost can damage blooms

PRUNING: Little pruning required; can be limbed up to create a multi-trunk tree formed specimen; can be heavily pruned in Spring after flowering to maintain size without reducing next year's flowering; pruning will strengthen limb structure

ADDITIONAL NOTES

USES: Container or planter, small lawn tree, specimen and accent near a deck or patio

URBAN USES: Shows no significant problem in urban planting sites

SUBSTITUTIONS: *Magnolia kobus x stellata* 'Centennial', *Magnolia x loebneri* 'Merrill', *Malus* cultivars, *Pyrus* cultivars, *Prunus* cultivars

COMMENTS: This tree's flowers are not as cold sensitive as Saucer Magnolia. Star Magnolia makes a nice specimen or multi-stemmed tree valued for its early Spring bloom.

OTHER CULTIVARS: *M. kobus x stellata* 'Centennial' - large, pinkish white blooms, heavy flowering, pyramidal bush habit, 10-12' tall by 6-8' wide; *M. x loebneri* 'Merrill' - large, white petals with blushed, rosy-purple, semi-double blooms; large, upright, dome-shaped small tree, 20-25' tall by 10-15' wide

Magnolia x soulangiana
Saucer Magnolia
USDA Hardiness Zones: 5-9a

DESCRIPTION

NATIVE HABITAT: Hybrid origin from France and Japan
PLANT TYPE: Deciduous, broadleaf, small flowering tree
MATURE SIZE: 20-25' tall by 20-30' wide
FORM/SHAPE: Rounded, upright with an open canopy, often multi-stemmed
BARK: Thin; light gray; nice Winter interest
FLOWER: Spectacular pink or white; very showy; blooms in Spring or late Winter; frost can damage bloom; attracts insects
FRUIT: Elongated, dry, hard, woody cone; red with pinkish red berries; can be showy
FOLIAGE: Alternate, simple, oblong, 4-8" long; green leaves turn yellow in Fall; showy Fall color; leaf litter can be messy

LANDSCAPE CHARACTERISTICS

GROWTH RATE: Moderate to Fast   **DROUGHT TOLERANCE:** Moderate   **SALT TOLERANCE:** Low
SOIL REQUIREMENTS: Moist, fertile, humus rich, well-limed soil; prefers well-drained, rich and porous soil
LIGHT REQUIREMENTS: Full sun produces best growth and flower; tolerates part shade
PEST PROBLEMS: Oleander scale, false Oleander scale, spider mites, Tulip tree scale, black twig borer and leaf miner
DISEASE PROBLEMS: Leaf spot, blights, cankers, stem canker, root rot, *Verticillium* wilt and wetwood
ENVIRONMENTAL FACTORS: No serious problems; needs adequate soil moisture and fertility for optimal growth and aesthetics; adaptable to less desirable environmental conditions; spreading root system makes trees difficult to preserve on construction sites; late frost can damage blooms
PRUNING: Little pruning required; limb up to allow pedestrian or vehicular circulation; best to prune and train the plants when they are young, older plant wounds may not close well; can be limbed up to create multi-trunk tree formed specimen

ADDITIONAL NOTES

USES: Container or planter, espaliered, specimen and accent near a deck or patio
URBAN USES: Adaptable to most soil types, but moderately tolerant of limestone soil and has good air pollution tolerance
SUBSTITUTIONS: *Magnolia* cultivars of the *soulangiana* type, *Magnolia stellata* and hybrid cultivars, *Malus* cultivars, *Pyrus* cultivars, *Prunus* cultivars
COMMENTS: Saucer Magnolia is a good specimen plant that displays an early Spring bloom that may be damaged by late frosts. *Magnolia x soulangiana* is a hybrid group with many known cultivars. Some seedling cultivars are grown and may exhibit variable plant shape, flower color and form.
OTHER CULTIVARS: 'Alexandrina' - large, upright growing, free-flowering, erect, white flowers that flush purple; 'Rustica Rubra' - vigorous growth, cup-shaped, rosy red flowers

Malus 'Prairifire'
Prairifire Crabapple
USDA Hardiness Zones: 4-8a

DESCRIPTION

NATIVE HABITAT: Hybrid selection
PLANT TYPE: Deciduous, broadleaf, small flowering tree
MATURE SIZE: 20' tall by 20' wide
FORM/SHAPE: Rounded crown
BARK: Smooth; burgundy-gray when young; slate gray when mature
FLOWER: Dark, pinkish red; blooms in Spring
FRUIT: Red-purple fruit; small pomes in clusters; 1/2" or smaller
FOLIAGE: Alternate, simple, serrate; burgundy-red leaves age to reddish green in Summer and turn yellow in Fall

LANDSCAPE CHARACTERISTICS

GROWTH RATE: Moderate   **DROUGHT TOLERANCE:** Moderate   **SALT TOLERANCE:** Low
SOIL REQUIREMENTS: Well-drained, clay, loam or sandy soil; adaptable to varying soil conditions; prefers well-limed soil
LIGHT REQUIREMENTS: Full sun
PEST PROBLEMS: Pear thrips, Japanese beetle, Dogwood borer, caterpillars, green fruit worm, gypsy moth, Eastern tent caterpillar, spider mites, aphids, roundheaded Apple tree borer, flatheaded Apple tree borer, Apple leafhopper, scales and mealybugs
DISEASE PROBLEMS: Good resistance to Apple scab, Cedar Apple rust, powdery mildew, and fireblight; can have problems with anthracnose, stem canker, dieback, *Nectria* stem canker, Oak root rot and other root rot diseases
ENVIRONMENTAL FACTORS: Not tolerant of wet, compacted soil; needs well-limed soil to avoid growth and nutritional problems
PRUNING: Prune to remove water sprout growth; to shape, open plant center to light; should be pruned before June; blooms on old fruiting spurs and previous season's growth

ADDITIONAL NOTES

USES: Specimen planting, accent near a patio or deck, espaliered and along a streetscape to add Spring color
URBAN USES: Tree performs well in urban settings, especially when used in mixed plantings
SUBSTITUTIONS: *Malus* cultivars, *Lagerstroemia* cultivars, *Cornus* cultivars, *Prunus* cultivars, *Pyrus* cultivars
COMMENTS: The disease resistant Crabapple cultivar, 'Prairifire', is a good, small tree and is used in many different landscape applications. It is an attractive plant during the three weeks in Spring when the tree is in full bloom, and is also attractive during the Summer months. The flowers and fruit attract insects, birds and other animals.
OTHER CULTIVARS: Many *Malus* cultivars are available; important to choose disease resistant cultivars such as: 'Indian Summer' - rose-red flowers, small, red fruit; 'Strawberry Parfait' - pink flowers, heavy bloomer

Malus x 'Sutyzam'
Sugar Tyme® Crabapple
USDA Hardiness Zones: 4-8

DESCRIPTION

NATIVE HABITAT: Hybrid selection
PLANT TYPE: Deciduous, broadleaf, small flowering tree
MATURE SIZE: 15-20' tall by 10' wide
FORM/SHAPE: Oval, upright
BARK: Smooth; burgundy-gray when young; slate-gray to white when mature
FLOWER: Pale pink buds open to a white flower; blooms in Spring
FRUIT: Small pome in clusters; red to red-orange; heavy fruiting variety
FOLIAGE: Alternate, simple, serrate; dark green leaves turn yellow in Fall

LANDSCAPE CHARACTERISTICS

GROWTH RATE: Moderate   **DROUGHT TOLERANCE:** Moderate   **SALT TOLERANCE:** Low
SOIL REQUIREMENTS: Well-drained, clay, loam or sandy soil; adaptable to varying soil conditions; prefers well-limed soil
LIGHT REQUIREMENTS: Full sun
PEST PROBLEMS: Pear thrips, Japanese beetle, Dogwood borer, caterpillars, green fruit worm, gypsy moth, Eastern tent caterpillar, spider mites, aphids, roundheaded Apple tree borer, flatheaded Apple tree borer, Apple leafhopper, scales and mealybugs
DISEASE PROBLEMS: Good resistance to Apple scab, Cedar Apple rust and powdery mildew; can have problems with anthracnose, stem canker, dieback, *Nectria* stem canker, fireblight, Oak root rot and other root rot diseases
ENVIRONMENTAL FACTORS: Not tolerant of wetm compacted soil; needs well-limed soil to avoid growth and nutritional problems
PRUNING: Prune to remove water sprout growth; to shape, open plant center to light; should be pruned before June; blooms on old fruiting spurs and previous season's growth

ADDITIONAL NOTES

USES: Specimen planting, accent near a patio or deck, espaliered and along a streetscape to add Spring color
URBAN USES: Tree performs well in urban settings, especially when used in mixed plantings
SUBSTITUTIONS: *Malus* cultivars, *Lagerstroemia* cultivars, *Cornus* cultivars, *Prunus* cultivars, *Pyrus* cultivars
COMMENTS: The disease resistant Crabapple cultivar, Sugar Tyme® is a heavy fruiting Crabapple with a stunning flower display. It can be considered messy in some urban applications because of profuse fruiting. The flowers and fruit attract insects, birds and other animals.
OTHER CULTIVARS: Many *Malus* cultivars are available; it is important to choose disease resistant cultivars such as: 'Adirondack' - white flower, small, red fruit; 'Jewelberry' - whitish, pink edged flower, red 1/2" fruit; 'Professor Sprenger'- pink bud, white flower, orange-red fruit; 'Sargent' - fragrant, white flower, dark red fruit

Malus x 'Zumi'
Zumi Crabapple
USDA Hardiness Zones: 4-7

DESCRIPTION

NATIVE HABITAT: Hybrid selection introduced by Charles Sargent around 1890
PLANT TYPE: Deciduous, broadleaf, small flowering tree
MATURE SIZE: 20' tall by 15-20' wide
FORM/SHAPE: Pyramidal, becomes rounded with age
BARK: Smooth; gray-brown
FLOWER: Pale pink buds open to a white flower; blooms in Spring
FRUIT: Red; 3/8" diameter; globose pome
FOLIAGE: Alternate, simple, serrate; ovate to broad lanceolate leaves, rarely lobed, sparsely pubescent; dark green leaves have a satin sheen that turn yellow to yellow-green in Fall

LANDSCAPE CHARACTERISTICS

GROWTH RATE: Moderate **DROUGHT TOLERANCE:** Moderate **SALT TOLERANCE:** Low
SOIL REQUIREMENTS: Well-drained, clay, loam or sandy soil; adaptable to varying soil conditions; prefers well-limed soil
LIGHT REQUIREMENTS: Full sun
PEST PROBLEMS: Pear thrips, Japanese beetle, Dogwood borer, caterpillars, green fruit worm, gypsy moth, Eastern tent caterpillar, spider mites, aphids, roundheaded Apple tree borer, flatheaded Apple tree borer, Apple leaf hopper, scales and mealybugs
DISEASE PROBLEMS: Good resistance to Apple scab, Cedar Apple rust and powdery mildew; can have problems with anthracnose, stem canker, dieback, *Nectria* stem canker, fireblight, Oak root rot and other root rot diseases
ENVIRONMENTAL FACTORS: Not tolerant of wet, compacted soil; needs well-limed soil to avoid growth and nutritional problems
PRUNING: Prune to remove water sprout growth; to shape, open plant center to light; should be pruned before June; blooms on old fruiting spurs and previous season's growth

ADDITIONAL NOTES

USES: Specimen planting, accent near a patio or deck, espaliered and along a streetscape to add Spring color
URBAN USES: Moderately tolerant to air pollutants and other urban environmental stresses
SUBSTITUTIONS: *Malus* cultivars, *Lagerstroemia* cultivars, *Cornus* cultivars, *Prunus* cultivars, *Pyrus* cultivars
COMMENTS: This old and time tested cultivar shows good tolerance to *Malus* disease and pest problems. The plant is adaptable to a wide range of climatic conditions. All *Malus* grow best and show less disease and growth problems when soil is well-limed. The flowers and fruit attract insects, birds and other animals.
OTHER CULTIVARS: Many *Malus* cultivars are available; it is important to choose disease resistant cultivars such as: 'Adirondack' - white flower, small red fruit; 'Jewelberry' - whitish, pink edged flower, red 1/2" fruit; 'Professor Sprenger'- pink bud, white flower, orange-red fruit; 'Sargent' - white fragrant flower, dark red fruit

Metasequoia glyptostroboides
Dawn Redwood
USDA Hardiness Zones: 5-8

DESCRIPTION

NATIVE HABITAT: China
PLANT TYPE: Deciduous, coniferous, large tree
MATURE SIZE: 70-90' tall by 15-25' wide
FORM/SHAPE: Pyramidal, symmetrical canopy
BARK: Rough; orange-red to brown; buttress-like root flare at base of trunk
FLOWER: Inconspicuous; late Winter to Spring
FRUIT: Elongated; small round, brown cones 1 1/2" wide by 1" long; cones do not attract wildlife
FOLIAGE: Needle-like, less than 2" long; green foliage turns orange to yellow in Fall

LANDSCAPE CHARACTERISTICS

GROWTH RATE: Fast   **DROUGHT TOLERANCE:** Moderate   **SALT TOLERANCE:** Low
SOIL REQUIREMENTS: Do not plant in soil with a high PH; prefers acidic, well-drained clay, loam, or sandy soil; one of the best trees for wet soil sites
LIGHT REQUIREMENTS: Full sun; tolerant of part shade
PEST PROBLEMS: Relatively pest free
DISEASE PROBLEMS: Cankers on stems
ENVIRONMENTAL FACTORS: Tree has large buttress trunk and large roots at soil surface which can lift sidewalks, highway surfaces and foundations
PRUNING: Trees self-prune and lose small limbs in strong wind; lower branches may need to be removed in some urban settings

ADDITIONAL NOTES

USES: Specimen in large lawn areas, buffer plantings and median strip plantings; good plant for wet soil sites around ponds or other water features
URBAN USES: Good tolerance to ozone and sulfur dioxide air pollution
SUBSTITUTIONS: *Taxodium* species
COMMENTS: The Dawn Redwood looks like an evergreen tree because of the needle-like leaves, but it is actually deciduous. This tree should be planted for its unique ornamental look and winter interest.
OTHER CULTIVARS: 'National' - grows to 85' tall; 'Sheradon Spire' - narrow, pyramidal form; 'Ogon' bright, golden yellow foliage, fast growing

Nyssa sylvatica
Black Gum
USDA Hardiness Zones: 4b-9

DESCRIPTION

NATIVE HABITAT: Michigan, Texas and Eastern United States
PLANT TYPE: Deciduous, broadleaf, large tree
MATURE SIZE: 65-75' tall by 25-35' wide
FORM/SHAPE: Symmetrical canopy; oval to pyramidal
BARK: Smooth; gray when young; matures to grayish black with deep fissures, ridges and plates
FLOWER: White; inconspicuous; blooms in Spring
FRUIT: Small; oval-shaped; blue; attracts birds
FOLIAGE: Alternate, simple, entire; green leaves with brilliant and showy red or deep purple color in Fall

LANDSCAPE CHARACTERISTICS

GROWTH RATE: Slow to Moderate   **DROUGHT TOLERANCE:** High   **SALT TOLERANCE:** Low
SOIL REQUIREMENTS: Moist, well-drained, slightly acidic, clay, loam, or sandy soil
LIGHT REQUIREMENTS: Full sun to part shade
PEST PROBLEMS: Scales, forest tent caterpillar, Tupelo leafminer, eriophyid mites and Eastern tent caterpillar
DISEASE PROBLEMS: Branch cankers, leaf spot, leaf blotch, *Fusarium, Hypoxylon, Nectria* and root rot
ENVIRONMENTAL FACTORS: Ice glazing; tolerates intermittent flooding during dormant season; fruit litter can be messy in some urban settings
PRUNING: Minimal pruning required; lower limbs may need to be removed for vehicular or pedestrian clearance

ADDITIONAL NOTES

USES: Shade tree or specimen, large parking lot islands, buffer strips and median plantings
URBAN USES: Moderate tolerance to sulfur dioxide air pollution; fruit attracts wildlife and can be messy in some urban settings
SUBSTITUTIONS: *Acer* species and cultivars, *Quercus* species and cultivars, *Lagerstroemia* cultivars
COMMENTS: Black Gum is a nice tree that should be used more often. It exhibits good structure in the garden and has a beautiful Fall color.
OTHER CULTIVARS: A few cultivars have been selected but are not commonly available

Oxydendrum arboreum
Sourwood
USDA Hardiness Zones: 5-9

DESCRIPTION

NATIVE HABITAT: Eastern United States
PLANT TYPE: Deciduous, broadleaf, medium size tree
MATURE SIZE: 40-60' tall by 25-30' wide
FORM/SHAPE: Irregular, oval, pyramidal crown; spreading habit with drooping branches
BARK: Smooth; reddish gray bark when young; becomes whitish gray with deep fissures and ridges in older trees
FLOWER: White; terminal clusters of racemes with bell-shaped flowers; blooms in late Summer
FRUIT: Brown oval-shaped capsule; small; inconspicuous; persistant
FOLIAGE: Alternate, simple, or slightly doubly serrate, entire; dark green, lustrous leaves appear to hang or weep; turn a striking red and orange color in Fall; very showy

LANDSCAPE CHARACTERISTICS

GROWTH RATE: Slow to Moderate   **DROUGHT TOLERANCE:** Moderate   **SALT TOLERANCE:** Moderate
SOIL REQUIREMENTS: Prefers slightly acidic, humus rich, loam soil; also grows in well-drained clay or sandy soil
LIGHT REQUIREMENTS: Part shade; will grow in full sun in cooler regions
PEST PROBLEMS: *Rhododendron* stem borer, Azalea stem borer, Dogwood twig borer, mites and forest webworms
DISEASE PROBLEMS: Canker, leaf spot, *Nectria* canker, drought injury and root rot
ENVIRONMENTAL FACTORS: Not tolerant of excessively wet or dry soil; needs acidic soil and excellent drainage
PRUNING: Minimum pruning required

ADDITIONAL NOTES

USES: Specimen or small tree, naturalizing and in combination with other woodland plants
URBAN USES: No proven urban tolerance; limb up if used along streets; not recommended for median plantings
SUBSTITUTIONS: *Lagerstroemia* cultivars, *Cornus kousa*, *Nyssa*, *Amelanchier* cultivars
COMMENTS: Sourwood is a very attractive tree for specimen use. It has beautiful and showy Fall color.
OTHER CULTIVARS: A few rare cultivars are grown by avid plant collectors; all commercial plants are seedlings

Pistacia chinensis
Chinese Pistache
USDA Hardiness Zones: 6b-9

DESCRIPTION

NATIVE HABITAT: Central and Western China
PLANT TYPE: Deciduous, broadleaf, large tree
MATURE SIZE: 25-35' tall (up to 60' tall) by 25-35' wide
FORM/SHAPE: Vase-shaped, oval, rounded to irregular crown shape
BARK: Gray-brown that peels to expose salmon-red bark underneath; showy and attractive
FLOWER: Shades of red, yellow and brown (dioecious); blooms in Spring
FRUIT: Bright red fruit ripens to a dark blue color
FOLIAGE: Alternate; even, pinnately compound leaves; lustrous, dark green leaves turn shades of orange and red in Fall; in warmer zones, Fall color is not as brilliant; each plant may vary in Fall color

LANDSCAPE CHARACTERISTICS

GROWTH RATE: Moderate   **DROUGHT TOLERANCE:** High   **SALT TOLERANCE:** Low
SOIL REQUIREMENTS: Moderately fertile and well-drained soil, but grows in all soil types that are well-drained
LIGHT REQUIREMENTS: Full sun to part shade; best in full sun
PEST PROBLEMS: Oleander scale, California red scale and leaf-footed bug
DISEASE PROBLEMS: *Verticillium* wilt, root rot, canker and dieback
ENVIRONMENTAL FACTORS: Some other plants may not grow well as understory plantings in the root zone of Chinese Pistache; from seed, Chinese Pistache will show variation in Fall foliage color, branch habit and timing of new growth in Spring
PRUNING: Prune to establish shape when young; tree looks open and leggy when young unless pruned properly

ADDITIONAL NOTES

USES: Outstanding specimen, shade or street tree
URBAN USES: Great plant for urban areas as a street or median tree
SUBSTITUTIONS: *Lagerstroemia* cultivars or *Chionanthus retusus*
COMMENTS: Chinese Pistache is a tough, drought tolerant tree useful in planting sites where poor soil conditions and limited irrigation prohibit the use of other trees. Fall foliage color can be dramatic.
OTHER CULTIVARS: Poor asexual reproduction of tree has limited commercial development of cultivars

Platanus occidentalis
Sycamore
USDA Hardiness Zones: 4b-9

DESCRIPTION

NATIVE HABITAT: Eastern United States
PLANT TYPE: Deciduous, broadleaf, large tree
MATURE SIZE: 75-90' tall by 50-70' wide
FORM/SHAPE: Pyramidal in youth, but develops a spreading, rounded, irregular crown
BARK: Smooth; olive to light gray, quickly develops mottled bark patches of creamy white and olive, gray-green
FLOWER: Male flowers reddish brown held in ball-like heads; female flowers brownish yellow to green held in ball-like heads; inconspicuous; blooms in Spring
FRUIT: Fruit formed in ball-like heads (Sycamore ball); fruit can be hazardous in lawn and pedestrian areas
FOLIAGE: Alternate, simple, truncate to palmately lobed, large leaf; light green leaves turn yellowish to brown in Fall; Fall color is not showy

LANDSCAPE CHARACTERISTICS

GROWTH RATE: Fast   **DROUGHT TOLERANCE:** High   **SALT TOLERANCE:** Moderate
SOIL REQUIREMENTS: Well-drained, slightly alkaline to acidic, clay, loam or sandy soil; tolerant of infrequent flooding
LIGHT REQUIREMENTS: Full sun; young trees tolerate some shade
PEST PROBLEMS: Mealybugs, aphids, mites, bagworm, Sycamore lacebug, borers, leafhopper, scales; caterpillars, black twig borer, whitefly, Sycamore scale, ambrosia beetles, cottony Maple scale, Plum borer, plant bug, Oak weevil, Columbian timber borer, bark aphids, leaf miner and Japanese beetle
DISEASE PROBLEMS: *Ganoderma*, *Hypoxylon*, *Oxyporus*, root rot, wood decay, butt rot, dieback, anthracnose, powdery mildew, canker, drought damage, Winter stem crack damage and wood rot
ENVIRONMENTAL FACTORS: Messy large leaves and fruit (Sycamore balls); late frost damage; Winter freeze can cause trunk cracks; drought damage; leaf and bacterial leaf scorch
PRUNING: Prune to maintain central leader when plant is young and acute limb angles that cause embedded bark to form a weak limb to trunk union

ADDITIONAL NOTES

USES: Large parking lot islands, buffer plantings, median strips, screen plantings, shade tree, reclamation plantings, and as a street tree
URBAN USES: Shows good adaptability to urban soil conditions; shallow roots are problems for sidewalks and paved areas; tolerant to air pollutants; drought stress can reduce aesthetic quality
SUBSTITUTIONS: *Platanus x acerifolia* 'Yarwood', *Quercus* species, *Acer rubrum* cultivars, or *Acer saccharum* cultivars
COMMENTS: Sycamore is best suited for soil that is moist and does not completely dry out. This tree grows in places that appear unsuitable for plant growth. It is not the best tree for residential lawns because large leaves create a litter problem and tree roots can release a substance that can kill newly planted grass and reduce the growth of other plants in the root zone area. This characteristic is known as allelopathy. Drought and dry Summer heat can cause leaf scorch and early leaf drop.
OTHER CULTIVARS: 'Columbia' - deeply lobed, green foliage, strong, broad pyramidal form, good resistance to anthracnose, a U.S. National Arboretum release, crosses made by Dr. Frank Santamour, Jr.; 'Liberty' - broad, shallowy lobed green foliage, strong pyramidal form when young, good resistance to anthracnose, a U.S. National Arboretum release, crosses made by Dr. Frank Santamour, Jr.

Platanus x acerifolia 'Bloodgood'
Bloodgood London Planetree
USDA Hardiness Zones: 5-9a

DESCRIPTION

NATIVE HABITAT: Hybrid origin between *Platanus occidentalis* and *Platanus orientalis*
PLANT TYPE: Deciduous, broadleaf, large tree
MATURE SIZE: 50-60' tall by 30-40' wide
FORM/SHAPE: Rounded, spreading, pyramidal with a dense crown
BARK: Smooth; olive to light gray, quickly develops mottled bark patches of creamy white and olive, gray-green
FLOWER: Male flowers are reddish brown held in ball-like heads; female flowers are brownish yellow to green held in ball-like heads; inconspicuous; blooms in Spring
FRUIT: Fruit formed in ball-like heads (Sycamore ball); fruit can be hazardous in lawn and pedestrian areas
FOLIAGE: Alternate, simple, truncate to palmately lobed, large leaf; light green leaves turn yellowish to brown in Fall; Fall color is not showy

LANDSCAPE CHARACTERISTICS

GROWTH RATE: Fast   **DROUGHT TOLERANCE:** High   **SALT TOLERANCE:** Moderate
SOIL REQUIREMENTS: Well-drained, slightly alkaline to acidic, clay, loam or sandy soil; tolerant of infrequent flooding
LIGHT REQUIREMENTS: Full sun; young trees tolerate some shade
PEST PROBLEMS: Mealybugs, aphids, mites, bagworm, Sycamore lacebug, borers, leafhopper, scales, caterpillars, black twig borer, whitefly, Sycamore scale, ambrosia beetles, cottony Maple scale, Plum borer, plant bug, Oak weevil, Columbian timber borer, bark aphids, leaf miner and Japanese beetle
DISEASE PROBLEMS: *Ganoderma*, *Hypoxylon*, *Oxyporus*, root rot, wood decay, butt rot, dieback, anthracnose, powdery mildew, canker, drought damage, Winter stem crack damage and wood rot
ENVIRONMENTAL FACTORS: Messy large leaves and fruit (Sycamore balls); late frost damage; Winter freeze can cause trunk cracks; drought damage; leaf and bacterial leaf scorch
PRUNING: Prune to maintain central leader when tree is young and acute limb angles that cause embedded bark to form a weak limb to trunk union

ADDITIONAL NOTES

USES: Large parking lot islands, buffer plantings or residential street tree
URBAN USES: Shows good adaptability to urban soil conditions; shallow roots are problems for sidewalks and paved areas; tolerant to some air pollutants; drought stress can reduce aesthetic quality
SUBSTITUTIONS: *Platanus x acerifolia* 'Yarwood', *Quercus* species, *Acer rubrum* cultivars or *Acer saccharum* cultivars
COMMENTS: 'Bloodgood' is affected by diseases such as anthracnose and powdery mildew. 'Bloodgood' is not tolerant to ozone and some air pollutants. Drought and dry Summer heat can cause early Fall coloration.
OTHER CULTIVARS: 'Columbia' - U.S. National Arboretum selection, exhibits good resistance to anthracnose

Platanus x acerifolia 'Yarwood'
Yarwood London Planetree
USDA Hardiness Zones: 6-9a

DESCRIPTION

NATIVE HABITAT: Hybrid origin between *Platanus occidentalis* and *Platanus orientalis*

PLANT TYPE: Deciduous, broadleaf, large tree

MATURE SIZE: 50-60' tall by 30-40' wide

FORM/SHAPE: Broad, pyramidal to dome-shaped

BARK: Smooth; olive to light gray, quickly develops mottled bark patches of creamy white and olive, gray-green

FLOWER: Male flowers are reddish brown held in ball-like heads; female flowers are brownish yellow to green held in ball-like heads; inconspicuous; blooms in Spring

FRUIT: Fruit formed in ball-like heads (Sycamore ball); fruit can be hazardous in lawn and pedestrian areas

FOLIAGE: Alternate, simple, truncate to palmately lobed, large leaf; light green leaves turn yellowish to brown in Fall; Fall color is not showy

LANDSCAPE CHARACTERISTICS

GROWTH RATE: Fast   **DROUGHT TOLERANCE:** Moderate to High   **SALT TOLERANCE:** Moderate

SOIL REQUIREMENTS: Well-drained, slightly alkaline to acidic, clay, loam or sandy soil; tolerant of infrequent flooding

LIGHT REQUIREMENTS: Full sun; young trees tolerate some shade

PEST PROBLEMS: Mealybugs, aphids, mites, bagworm, Sycamore lacebug, borers, leafhopper, scales, caterpillars, black twig borer, whitefly, Sycamore scale, ambrosia beetles, cottony Maple scale, Plum borer, plant bug, Oak weevil, Columbian timber borer, bark aphids, leaf miner and Japanese beetle

DISEASE PROBLEMS: *Ganoderma, Hypoxylon, Oxyporus*, root rot, wood decay, butt rot, dieback, anthracnose, powdery mildew, canker, drought damage, Winter stem crack damage and wood rot

ENVIRONMENTAL FACTORS: Messy large leaves and fruit (Sycamore balls); late frost damage; Winter freeze can cause trunk cracks; drought damage; leaf and bacterial leaf scorch

PRUNING: Prune to maintain central leader when plant is young and acute limb angles that cause embedded bark to form a weak limb to trunk union

ADDITIONAL NOTES

USES: Large parking lots, large lawn tree, buffer strips, street tree or tree medians

URBAN USES: Shows good adaptability to urban soil conditions; shallow roots are problems for sidewalks and paved areas; tolerant to some air pollutants; drought stress can reduce aesthetic quality

SUBSTITUTIONS: *Platanus x acerifolia* 'Columbia' and 'Liberty', *Pyrus* cultivars, *Quercus* species and cultivars, *Acer rubrum* cultivars, *Acer saccharum* cultivars, *Acer barbatum* or *Zelkova* cultivars

COMMENTS: 'Yarwood' is a University of California at Berkeley selection that shows good resistance to powdery mildew and anthracnose in the upper Southern Piedmont regions of the United States.

OTHER CULTIVARS: 'Columbia' - deeply lobed, green foliage, strong, broad pyramidal form, good resistance to anthracnose, a U.S. National Arboretum release, crosses made by Dr. Frank Santamour, Jr.; 'Liberty' - broad, shallowy lobed green foliage, strong pyramidal form when young, good resistance to anthracnose, a U.S. National Arboretum release, crosses made by Dr. Frank Santamour, Jr.

Prunus cerasifera 'Thundercloud'
Thundercloud Plum

USDA Hardiness Zones: 5-8a

DESCRIPTION

NATIVE HABITAT: Southeastern Europe and Southwestern Asia Minor; cultivar of nursery origin
PLANT TYPE: Deciduous, broadleaf, small flowering tree
MATURE SIZE: 15-25' tall by 15-25' wide
FORM/SHAPE: Broad, vase-shaped when young; matures to a symmetrical, rounded dome
BARK: Smooth; dark purplish brown with transverse lenticels when young; older trunks become rough with shallow furrows and a brownish black color; ridges form small plates
FLOWER: Soft pink; blooms late Winter before leaves emerge; attracts insects
FRUIT: Small, 1" round, reddish purple drupe (Cherry-sized plum); fruit ripens in late Summer; attracts insects and animals; can create litter
FOLIAGE: Alternate, simple, serrate leaf margin; broad obovate to oblanceolate; leaf emerges burgundy-red and matures to dark purple; maintains purple color through Fall; older leaves show yellowish red color before shedding

LANDSCAPE CHARACTERISTICS

GROWTH RATE: Moderate to Fast   **DROUGHT TOLERANCE:** Moderate   **SALT TOLERANCE:** Low to Moderate
SOIL REQUIREMENTS: Well-drained, moist, fertile, humus rich, slightly acidic but well-limed soil
LIGHT REQUIREMENTS: Full sun
PEST PROBLEMS: Peach tree borer, Dogwood borer, ambrosia beetles, white fringed beetle, Pear thrips, caterpillars, leafroller, Eastern tent caterpillar, treehopper, leaf miner, spider mites, eriophyid mites, sawfly, skeletonizer, Japanese beetle, Plum borer, shothole borer, Apple leafhopper, terrapin scale, white Peach scale and *Euonymus* scale
DISEASE PROBLEMS: *Alternaria*, leaf spot, black knot, blight, canker, collar rot, *Cylindrocladium*, *Ganoderma*, leaf blister, *Nectria, Phomopsis, Phytophthora,* powdery mildew, *Taphrina, Verticillium* wilt, Oak root rot, *Pseudomonas,* crown gall and virus disorder
ENVIRONMENTAL FACTORS: Not tolerant of water-logged soil; may be short-lived with lack of pest and disease control and poor plant nutrition; dropped fruit can be messy and a nuisance
PRUNING: Prune to limb up tree for maintenance, storm damage, dead interior limbs and root suckers on grafted trees

ADDITIONAL NOTES

USES: Accent or specimen tree, planters, small ornamental flowering foliage tree and small shade tree
URBAN USES: Very adaptable to the soil and space limitations of urban areas; moderately tolerant of air pollutants; can be a short-lived plant due to disease and pests
SUBSTITUTIONS: *Loropetalum chinense rubrum* cultivars, red foliaged *Acer palmatum* cultivars, red foliaged *Malus* cultivars, purple leaf Smoke bush, red foliaged *Lagerstroemia* cultivars, *Acer platanoides* 'Crimson King'
COMMENTS: The 'Thundercloud' is highly ornamental with a strong effect. It needs plenty of space and to be planted with other green trees to soften the strong color effect. Unfortunately, it has a short life span in the Southern United States due to disease, pest and nutrition problems.
OTHER CULTIVARS: 'Newport' - cold hardy, smaller compact plant form, similar foliage color; 'Krauter Vesuvius' - similar foliage color, smaller, more upright limb habit, heat tolerant

Prunus serrulata 'Kwanzan'
Kwanzan Cherry
USDA Hardiness Zones: 5b-9a

DESCRIPTION

NATIVE HABITAT: Japan; in cultivation for possibly centuries and believed to be a hybrid of several species or other cultivars

PLANT TYPE: Deciduous, broadleaf, small flowering tree

MATURE SIZE: 15-25' tall by 15-25' wide

FORM/SHAPE: Broad, vase-shaped when young; matures to a symmetrical, rounded dome

BARK: Smooth; chestnut-brown with large, corky lenticel lines

FLOWER: Double pink bloom, very showy; blooms in late Spring with foliage

FRUIT: Sterile, produces no fruit

FOLIAGE: Alternate, simple, serrate leaf margin, ovate to oblanceolate leaves; green Summer leaves turn copper, orange or yellow in Fall

LANDSCAPE CHARACTERISTICS

GROWTH RATE: Moderate   **DROUGHT TOLERANCE:** Moderate   **SALT TOLERANCE:** Low

SOIL REQUIREMENTS: Well-drained, moist, fertile, humus rich, slightly acidic but well-limed soil

LIGHT REQUIREMENTS: Full sun

PEST PROBLEMS: Peach tree borer, Dogwood borer, ambrosia beetles, white fringed beetle, Pear thrips, caterpillars, leafroller, Eastern tent caterpillar, treehopper, leaf miner, spider mites, eriophyid mites, sawfly, skeletonizer, Japanese beetle, Plum borer, shothole borer, Apple leafhopper, terrapin scale, white Peach scale and *Euonymus* scale

DISEASE PROBLEMS: *Alternaria*, leaf spot, black knot, blight, canker, collar rot, *Cylindrocladium, Ganoderma,* leaf blister, *Nectria, Phomopsis, Phytophthora,* powdery mildew, *Taphrina, Verticillium* wilt, Oak root rot, *Pseudomonas,* crown gall and virus disorder

ENVIRONMENTAL FACTORS: Not tolerant of wet compacted soil; may be short-lived with lack of pest and disease control and poor plant nutrition

PRUNING: Prune to limb up tree for maintenance, storm damage, dead interior limbs and root suckers on grafted trees

ADDITIONAL NOTES

USES: Bonsai, container, large parking lot islands, buffer strips, medians, specimen or in residential landscapes

URBAN USES: Not good for urban sites or exposed streetscapes

SUBSTITUTIONS: *Lagerstroemia* cultivars, *Malus* cultivars or *Loropetalum* cultivars

COMMENTS: 'Kwanzan' is a short-lived tree due to disease and insect problems. It is, however, a glorious Spring flowering tree, well worth planting and maintaining to prevent disease and insect problems.

OTHER CULTIVARS: 'Mount Fuji' - spreading plant form with large double white flowers; 'Royal Burgundy' - purple foliaged form of 'Kwanzan'

Prunus subhirtella 'Autumnalis Rosea'
Pink Autumn Flowering Cherry
USDA Hardiness Zones: 5-8

DESCRIPTION

NATIVE HABITAT: Japan (probably a hybrid selection)
PLANT TYPE: Deciduous, broadleaf, small flowering tree
MATURE SIZE: 25-35' tall by 25-35' wide
FORM/SHAPE: Symmetrical canopy; can potentially grow to a width greater than its height; vase-shaped when young
BARK: Smooth; brown
FLOWER: Semi-double bloom; pink bud fully opens to a white flower; blooms in early Spring and may bloom again in Fall if warm weather permits
FRUIT: Small, black drupes; attracts birds and bees
FOLIAGE: Alternate, simple, serrate leaf margin, ovate to oblanceolate leaves; dark green leaves turn yellow and bronze in Fall

LANDSCAPE CHARACTERISTICS

GROWTH RATE: Fast   **DROUGHT TOLERANCE:** Moderate   **SALT TOLERANCE:** Low
SOIL REQUIREMENTS: Well-drained, moist, fertile, humus rich, slightly acidic but well-limed soil
LIGHT REQUIREMENTS: Full sun
PEST PROBLEMS: Peach tree borer, Dogwood borer, ambrosia beetles, white fringed beetle, Pear thrips, caterpillars, leafroller, Eastern tent caterpillar, treehopper, leaf miner, spider mites, eriophyid mites, sawfly, skeletonizer, Japanese beetle, Plum borer, shothole borer, Apple leafhopper, terrapin scale, white Peach scale and *Euonymus* scale
DISEASE PROBLEMS: *Alternaria*, leaf spot, black knot, blight, canker, collar rot, *Cylindrocladium*, *Ganoderma*, leaf blister, *Nectria, Phomopsis, Phytophthora,* powdery mildew, *Taphrina*, *Verticillium* wilt, Oak root rot, *Pseudomonas*, crown gall and virus disorder
ENVIRONMENTAL FACTORS: Not tolerant of wet compacted soil; may be short-lived with lack of pest and disease control and poor plant nutrition
PRUNING: Prune to thin canopy for better light and air filtration into the crown, create a stronger limb structure, and remove root suckers on grafted trees

ADDITIONAL NOTES

USES: Buffer strips, highway medians, near deck or patio, shade tree and as a specimen
URBAN USES: No proven urban tolerance, but works well as a street tree or in median plantings
SUBSTITUTIONS: *Malus* cultivars, *Lagerstroemia* cultivars, *Cercis* species and cultivars
COMMENTS: Pink Autumn Flowering Cherry should be grown on its own roots for best long-term survival. When it is started on Peach seedling rootstock it will be very prone to problems. The growth rate of this tree will slow as the plant matures.
OTHER CULTIVARS: 'Autumnalis' - same plant habit, pink flower bud, flower opens white

Prunus x 'Okame'
Okame Cherry
USDA Hardiness Zones: 6b-9

DESCRIPTION

NATIVE HABITAT: Bred in England by Collingwood Ingram
PLANT TYPE: Deciduous, broadleaf, small flowering tree
MATURE SIZE: 15-20' tall by 15-20' wide
FORM/SHAPE: Oval, upright, symmetrical crown
BARK: Smooth; reddish brown when young; matures to smooth, grayish brown
FLOWER: Pink, very showy; blooms late Winter to early Spring; attracts bees and insects
FRUIT: Small, round, fleshy; purple-black; infrequently produced
FOLIAGE: Alternate, simple, doubly serrate, ovate leaves; green Summer leaves turn copper, orange, red and yellow in Fall

LANDSCAPE CHARACTERISTICS

GROWTH RATE: Moderate   **DROUGHT TOLERANCE:** Moderate   **SALT TOLERANCE:** Low to Moderate
SOIL REQUIREMENTS: Well-drained, moist, fertile, humus rich, slightly acidic but well-limed soil
LIGHT REQUIREMENTS: Full sun
PEST PROBLEMS: Peach tree borer, Dogwood borer, ambrosia beetles, white fringed beetle, Pear thrips, caterpillars, leafroller, Eastern tent caterpillar, treehopper, leaf miner, spider mites, eriophyid mites, sawfly, skeletonizer, Japanese beetle, Plum borer, shothole borer, Apple leafhopper, terrapin scale, white Peach scale and *Euonymus* scale
DISEASE PROBLEMS: *Alternaria*, leaf spot, black knot, blight, canker, collar rot, *Cylindrocladium*, *Ganoderma*, leaf blister, *Nectria, Phomopsis, Phytophthora,* powdery mildew, *Taphrina*, *Verticillium* wilt, Oak root rot, *Pseudomonas*, crown gall and virus disorder
ENVIRONMENTAL FACTORS: Not tolerant of wet compacted soil; may be short-lived with lack of pest and disease control and poor plant nutrition
PRUNING: Prune to limb up tree for maintenance, storm damage, dead interior limbs, and root suckers on grafted trees

ADDITIONAL NOTES

USES: Container and planters, buffer strips, near decks or patios, avenue planting and in combination with other plants
URBAN USES: No proven urban tolerance, but works well as a street tree or in median plantings
SUBSTITUTIONS: *Malus* cultivars, *Lagerstroemia* cultivars, *Cercis* species and cultivars
COMMENTS: 'Okame' Cherry should be grown on its own roots. Its root system is more adaptable to soil and planting site problems than seedling Peach and most Cherry species commonly used as rootstock. 'Okame' has good tolerance to common Cherry pests and diseases.
OTHER CULTIVARS: Many cultivars and species exists: 'Snow Goose' - upright, vase-shaped, wide spreading when mature, pure white single flowers, good foliar disease resistance; 'First Lady' - upright, broad columnar form, vibrant rose-pink flowers, similar to Okame in other aspects, introduced by U.S. National Arboretum

Prunus x yedoensis
Yoshino Cherry
USDA Hardiness Zones: 5b-8a

DESCRIPTION

NATIVE HABITAT: Japan; cultivar of garden origin
PLANT TYPE: Deciduous, broadleaf, large flowering tree
MATURE SIZE: 35-45' tall by 30-40' wide
FORM/SHAPE: Symmetrical canopy; round to vase-shaped, upright and horizontal branching
BARK: Smooth; grayish brown marked with prominent lenticels; matures to gray and blackish gray with large, corky lenticel lines
FLOWER: Pale pink to white; very showy; blooms in Spring; attracts insects
FRUIT: Small, black drupes; attracts birds and bees
FOLIAGE: Alternate, simple, doubly serrate, oblong leaves; green Summer leaves turn yellow to orange in Fall

LANDSCAPE CHARACTERISTICS

GROWTH RATE: Moderate to Fast   **DROUGHT TOLERANCE:** Moderate   **SALT TOLERANCE:** Moderate
SOIL REQUIREMENTS: Well-drained, moist, fertile, humus rich, slightly acidic but well-limed soil
LIGHT REQUIREMENTS: Full sun
PEST PROBLEMS: Peach tree borer, Dogwood borer, ambrosia beetles, white fringed beetle, Pear thrips, caterpillars, leafroller, Eastern tent caterpillar, treehopper, leaf miner, spider mites, eriophyid mites, sawfly, skeletonizer, Japanese beetle, Plum borer, shothole borer, Apple leafhopper, terrapin scale, white Peach scale and *Euonymus* scale
DISEASE PROBLEMS: *Alternaria*, leaf spot, black knot, blight, canker, collar rot, *Cylindrocladium*, *Ganoderma*, leaf blister, *Nectria, Phomopsis, Phytophthora,* powdery mildew, *Taphrina, Verticillium* wilt, Oak root rot, *Pseudomonas*, crown gall and virus disorder
ENVIRONMENTAL FACTORS: Not tolerant of wet, compacted soil; may be short-lived with lack of pest and disease control and poor plant nutrition
PRUNING: Prune to limb up tree for maintenance, storm damage, dead interior limbs, and root suckers on grafted trees

ADDITIONAL NOTES

USES: Buffer strips, shade tree, along walks, over patios or decks, avenue plantings and in combination with other plants
URBAN USES: No proven tolerance in urban areas; not a good street tree or parking lot tree choice because of disease and drought sensitivity
SUBSTITUTIONS: *Malus* cultivars, *Lagerstroemia* cultivars, *Cercis* species and cultivars
COMMENTS: The Yoshino Cherry is a relatively short-lived tree. As with all *Prunus* species, Yoshino has many pest and disease problems, but has shown good tolerance to these problems with a moderate amount of pest prevention.
OTHER CULTIVARS: 'Akebono' - pure pink flowers; 'Shidare Yoshino'- irregularly, pendulous branches

Pyrus calleryana 'Bradford'
Bradford Pear
USDA Hardiness Zones: 5-9a

DESCRIPTION

NATIVE HABITAT: China; cultivar developed in United States
PLANT TYPE: Deciduous, broadleaf, medium size flowering tree
MATURE SIZE: 30-40' tall by 30-40' wide
FORM/SHAPE: Symmetrical canopy, oval, rounded, dense crown
BARK: Smooth; dark gray to black; small ridges and plates when mature
FLOWER: Clusters of greenish white buds open white; very showy; blooms from late Winter to early Spring; attracts insects
FRUIT: Small pome fruit; 1/2-5/8" diameter; rusty, golden tan when mature; attracts birds and animals
FOLIAGE: Alternate, simple, broadly ovate with finely serrated leaf margin; green to glossy, dark green leaves; turn a showy reddish to purple color in Fall

LANDSCAPE CHARACTERISTICS

GROWTH RATE: Moderate to Fast   **DROUGHT TOLERANCE:** Moderate to High   **SALT TOLERANCE:** Moderate to High
SOIL REQUIREMENTS: Well-drained, moist, fertile, slightly acidic soil should be well-limed; very adaptable to varying soil types and pH levels
LIGHT REQUIREMENTS: Full sun; tolerates part shade but will reduce flowering
PEST PROBLEMS: Ambrosia beetles, aphids, mites, leafroller, tent caterpillar, mealybugs, Dogwood borer, Pear root aphid, cottony cushion scale, oyster scale, Pear plant bug, cottony Maple scale and Pear thrips
DISEASE PROBLEMS: *Alternaria*, anthracnose, canker, *Ganoderma, Hypoxylon*, leaf spot, *Nectria*, root rot, rust, scab, Pear decline (transmitted by Pear psylla); trees show early red to purple leaf coloring; slow growth and early leaf drop; problems common in Western growing areas and trees from Pear orchard regions; good resistance to fireblight
ENVIRONMENTAL FACTORS: Trees develop co-dominant leaders when topped as young trees resulting in limbs growing close together to form weak limb to trunk unions; trees split and blow apart in wind and ice storms
PRUNING: Pruning is critical to develop a strong limb and trunk structure; maintain central leader in tree

ADDITIONAL NOTES

USES: Container or above ground planters, parking lot, lawn trees, screening, shade, specimen, and where root or crown growth is restricted
URBAN USES: Good for urban areas; great as a street tree or in median plantings; good for urban areas where conditions are poor and roots have restricted growing area
SUBSTITUTIONS: *Lagerstroemia* cultivars, *Malus* cultivars, *Chionanthus retusus*
COMMENTS: Bradford Pear has an inferior branching habit with vertical limbs and embedded bark. Dense crowns and long branches make it susceptible to wind and ice damage. Proper and corrective limb and crown pruning will greatly reduce breakage problems. Many cultivars are grown with better limb structure, but most have other problems such as fireblight which will weaken limbs and trunks and lead to wind or ice breakage. The fragrance of the flowers may also be offensive.
OTHER CULTIVARS: 'Glen's Form' Callery Pear - more compact, with early corrective pruning, has very good limb structure; 'Holmford' - has good branching and good disease resistance; 'Capital' - narrow, columnar form, red-purple Fall color, released by U.S. National Arboretum, cross made by Dr. Frank Santamour Jr.; 'Redspire' - pyramidal, dense form, red-purple Fall color

Pyrus calleryana 'Glen's Form'
Chanticleer® Pear
USDA Hardiness Zones: 5-9a

DESCRIPTION

NATIVE HABITAT: Cultivar developed in United States
PLANT TYPE: Deciduous, broadleaf, medium size flowering tree
MATURE SIZE: 30-40' tall by 15-18' wide
FORM/SHAPE: Upright, narrow, pyramidal crown
BARK: Smooth; dark gray to black; shallow furrows and ridges form small angular plates when mature
FLOWER: Clusters of soft pink buds open white; very showy; blooms from late Winter to early Spring; attracts insects
FRUIT: Small pome fruit; 1/2-5/8" diameter; rusty, golden tan when mature; attracts birds and animals
FOLIAGE: Alternate, simple, broadly ovate with finely serrated leaf margin; green to glossy, dark green leaves turn a showy reddish to purple color in Fall

LANDSCAPE CHARACTERISTICS

GROWTH RATE: Moderate to Fast   **DROUGHT TOLERANCE:** Moderate to High   **SALT TOLERANCE:** Moderate to High
SOIL REQUIREMENTS: Well-drained, moist, fertile, slightly acidic soil should be well-limed; very adaptable to varying soil types and pH levels
LIGHT REQUIREMENTS: Full sun; tolerates part shade but will reduce flowering
PEST PROBLEMS: Ambrosia beetles, aphids, mites, leafroller, tent caterpillar, mealybugs, Dogwood borer, Pear root aphid, cottony cushion scale, oyster scale, Pear plant bug, cottony Maple scale and Pear thrips
DISEASE PROBLEMS: *Alternaria*, anthracnose, canker, *Ganoderma, Hypoxylon*, leaf spot, *Nectria*, root rot, rust, scab, Pear decline (transmitted by Pear psylla); trees show early red to purple leaf coloring; slow growth and early leaf drop; problems common in Western growing areas and trees from Pear orchard regions; good resistance to fireblight
ENVIRONMENTAL FACTORS: Trees develop co-dominant leaders when topped as young trees resulting in limbs growing close together to form weak limb to trunk unions; trees split and blow apart in wind and ice storms
PRUNING: Pruning is critical to develop a strong limb and trunk structure; maintain central leader in tree

ADDITIONAL NOTES

USES: Container or above ground planters, parking lot, lawn trees, screening, shade, specimen, and where root or crown growth is restricted
URBAN USES: Good for urban areas; great as a street tree or in median plantings; good for urban areas where conditions are poor and roots have restricted growing area
SUBSTITUTIONS: *Lagerstroemia* cultivars, *Acer rubrum* cultivars, *Quercus* cultivars and species, *Malus* cultivars, *Prunus* cultivars, *Chionanthus retusus*
COMMENTS: 'Glen's Form' is a beautiful, narrow, pyramidal, tough and adaptable tree with compact growth, beautiful flowering and Fall color. The Fall color is variable from year to year and from region to region.
OTHER CULTIVARS: 'Capital' - narrow, columnar form, red-purple Fall color, released by U.S. National Arboretum, cross made by Dr. Frank Santamour Jr.; 'Redspire' - pyramidal, dense form, red-purple Fall color

Quercus acutissima
Sawtooth Oak

USDA Hardiness Zones: 5b-9a

DESCRIPTION

NATIVE HABITAT: China, Japan and Korea
PLANT TYPE: Deciduous, broadleaf, large tree
MATURE SIZE: 35-50' tall by 35-50' wide
FORM/SHAPE: Broad, rounded dome
BARK: Smooth; ash gray when young; matures to dark gray with deep fissures and corky ridges
FLOWER: Gray-green to tan male catkin; yellow-green to tan female flower matures to brown acorn; blooms in late Winter to early Spring
FRUIT: Large, brown acorn, 1-1 1/4"; abundantly produced in large quantities; attracts animals
FOLIAGE: Alternate, simple, long oblanceolate; 4-8" long by 1 1/2-2 1/2" wide leaves; strongly serrated to dentate margins; dull to glossy yellow-green leaves mature to green; turns dull yellow to brownish tan color in Fall, leaves gradually shed, but most remain on the tree through late Winter

LANDSCAPE CHARACTERISTICS

GROWTH RATE: Fast   **DROUGHT TOLERANCE:** Moderate   **SALT TOLERANCE:** Low to Moderate
SOIL REQUIREMENTS: Well-drained, moist, fertile, humus rich, slightly acidic soil; adaptable to many soil types except alkaline or water-logged soil
LIGHT REQUIREMENTS: Full sun; tolerates part shade
PEST PROBLEMS: Mites (blister, Oak, eriophyid, *Platanus*), ambrosia beetles, Texas leafcutter ants, leaf miner, Cranberry root worm, caterpillars, orange-striped Oakworm, Oak webworm, Oak skeletonizer, bud gall mite, flatheaded Apple tree borer, Red Oak and branch borer, Ash borer, broadnecked root borer, spittlebug, Oak lacebug, leafhopper, aphids, scales, golden and red cottony cushion scales
DISEASE PROBLEMS: Anthracnose, Oak root rot, bleeding canker, canker rot, *Endothia*, *Ganoderma*, *Hypoxylon*, leaf blight, *Nectria*, Oak wilt, powdery mildew, root rot, *Phytophthora*, *Taphrina* and xylem limiting bacteria
ENVIRONMENTAL FACTORS: Not tolerant of compacted, water-logged soil; heavy acorn production is messy and a hazard in public walking areas; acorns may attract deer and lead to feeding damage on other plants; high soil pH and salt spray injury to foliage may weaken and stress tree
PRUNING: Maintain central leader; remove limbs with acute branch to trunk angles and remove low hanging limbs

ADDITIONAL NOTES

USES: Shade tree, street or parking lot tree, lawn specimen and wildlife food source
URBAN USES: Adaptable to many soil types; fast growing tree; may be messy for public areas
SUBSTITUTIONS: *Quercus lyrata, Quercus nuttallii, Quercus shumardii, Quercus macrocarpa, Ulmus* species and cultivars, *Pyrus* cultivars, *Quercus rubra, Quercus velutina, Quercus muehlenbergii*
COMMENTS: Sawtooth Oak is a fast growing tree useful for temporary shade while slower growing trees develop. This Oak species supplies acorns for wildlife habitat. Heavy acorn production and clinging leaves make it a messy species in public access areas.
OTHER CULTIVARS: No known commercial cultivars are presently grown

Quercus alba
White Oak

USDA Hardiness Zones: 3b-8

DESCRIPTION

NATIVE HABITAT: From the Eastern United States coast to Minnesota down through Arkansas and into Texas
PLANT TYPE: Deciduous, broadleaf, large tree
MATURE SIZE: 60-100' tall by 60-80' wide
FORM/SHAPE: Irregular outline; rounded, pyramidal crown
BARK: Light gray; plates when young; matures to gray with deep furrows and blocky, broad ridges
FLOWER: Brown; blooms in late Winter to Spring
FRUIT: Dry, hard acorn, 1/2-1" long; mature in Fall
FOLIAGE: Alternate, simple, deeply lobed; green leaves turn brown to red to burgundy in Fall

LANDSCAPE CHARACTERISTICS

GROWTH RATE: Moderate   **DROUGHT TOLERANCE:** Moderate   **SALT TOLERANCE:** Moderate to High
SOIL REQUIREMENTS: Well-drained, slightly acidic, clay, loam or sandy soil
LIGHT REQUIREMENTS: Full sun to part shade
PEST PROBLEMS: Mites (blister, Oak, eriophyid, *Platanus*), ambrosia beetles, Texas leafcutter ants, leaf miner, Cranberry root worm, caterpillars, orange-striped Oakworm, Oak webworm, Oak skeletonizer, bud gall mite, flatheaded Apple tree borer, Red Oak and branch borer, Ash borer, broadnecked root borer, spittlebug, Oak lacebug, leafhopper, aphids, scales, golden and red cottony cushion scales
DISEASE PROBLEMS: Anthracnose, Oak root rot, bleeding canker, canker rot, *Endothia*, *Ganoderma*, *Hypoxylon*, leaf blight, *Nectria*, Oak wilt, powdery mildew, root rot, *Phytophthora*, *Taphrina* and xylem limiting bacteria
ENVIRONMENTAL FACTORS: May decline when soil becomes compacted or soil environment does not support necessary mycorrhizal growth around tree roots or when soil has low oxygen content with poor drainage
PRUNING: Maintain central leader; remove limbs with acute branch to trunk angles and remove low hanging limbs

ADDITIONAL NOTES

USES: Large parking lots, lawn tree and shade tree
URBAN USES: Good for urban areas as a street tree or in large medians; allow plenty of space for growth; can live for several hundred years; acorns may cause problems in pedestrian areas
SUBSTITUTIONS: *Quercus lyrata, Quercus macrocarpa, Quercus bicolor*
COMMENTS: A deep growing tap root makes transplanting White Oaks difficult. They transplant better when root pruned a season before being dug for planting. It is best to transplant this tree when young.
OTHER CULTIVARS: No known commercial cultivars are presently grown

Quercus coccinea
Scarlet Oak
USDA Hardiness Zones: 4-8

DESCRIPTION

NATIVE HABITAT: Eastern North America
PLANT TYPE: Deciduous, broadleaf, large tree
MATURE SIZE: 60-75' tall by 45-60' wide; some specimens reach even larger sizes
FORM/SHAPE: Rounded, pyramidal, spreading canopy
BARK: Smooth; gray when young; dark brown or black with age
FLOWER: Gray-green to tan male catkin; yellow-green to tan female flower matures to brown acorn; blooms in late Winter to early Spring
FRUIT: Hard, brown acorn, 1/2-5/8" tall by 5/8-3/4" wide
FOLIAGE: Alternate, simple, deeply lobed; green leaves turn a showy, vibrant, bright red to scarlet in Fall; vibrant and showy Fall color

LANDSCAPE CHARACTERISTICS

GROWTH RATE: Moderate   **DROUGHT TOLERANCE:** Moderate   **SALT TOLERANCE:** Moderate
SOIL REQUIREMENTS: Well-drained, moist, fertile, humus rich, slightly acidic soil; adaptable to many soil types except alkaline or water-logged soil
LIGHT REQUIREMENTS: Full sun; tolerates part shade
PEST PROBLEMS: Mites (blister, Oak, eriophyid, *Platanus*), ambrosia beetles, Texas leafcutter ants, leaf miner, Cranberry root worm, caterpillars, orange-striped Oakworm, Oak webworm, Oak skeletonizer, bud gall mite, flatheaded Apple tree borer, Red Oak and branch borer, Ash borer, broadnecked root borer, spittlebug, Oak lacebug, leafhopper, aphids, scales, golden and red cottony cushion scales
DISEASE PROBLEMS: Anthracnose, Oak root rot, bleeding canker, canker rot, *Endothia*, *Ganoderma*, *Hypoxylon*, leaf blight, *Nectria*, Oak wilt, powdery mildew, root rot, *Phytophthora*, *Taphrina* and xylem limiting bacteria
ENVIRONMENTAL FACTORS: May decline when soil becomes compacted or soil environment does not support necessary mycorrhizal growth around tree roots or when soil has low oxygen content with poor drainage
PRUNING: Maintain central leader; remove limbs with acute branch to trunk angles and remove low hanging limbs

ADDITIONAL NOTES

USES: Large parking lot islands, lawn tree, buffer strips, residential street tree or shade tree and naturalizing
URBAN USES: Good as a street or median tree where it has plenty of soil space to develop
SUBSTITUTIONS: *Quercus nuttallii* or *Quercus shumardii*
COMMENTS: The *Quercus coccinea* looks similar to *Quercus rubra,* except that the leaves are more deeply lobed. The plant is more adaptable to dry southern conditions. This tree will reseed itself in the landscape. It can be difficult to transplant with a good survival rate.
OTHER CULTIVARS: No known commercial cultivars are presently grown

Quercus laurifolia
Laurel Oak, Swamp Laurel Oak or Diamond-leaf Oak
USDA Hardiness Zones: 6b-10a

DESCRIPTION

NATIVE HABITAT: Eastern and Southern United States
PLANT TYPE: Semi-evergreen to deciduous, broadleaf, large tree
MATURE SIZE: 60-70' tall by 35-50' wide
FORM/SHAPE: Dense, broad, pyramidal to rounded dome
BARK: Smooth; olive to yellow-brown when young; glabrous; mature
bark becomes grayish brown to blackish gray; shallow fissures and ridges become rough with age
FLOWER: Olive green to tan male catkin; brown-green female flower matures to grayish brown; blooms in late Winter to Spring
FRUIT: Small, grayish brown, oval-shaped acorn, 3/8-1/2"
FOLIAGE: Alternate, simple, variably shaped, long, narrow oblanceolate to subrhombic (diamond-shaped); glossy, green to dark green leaves, old inner foliage turns yellow-brown and sheds through the Winter and abundantly at the time of new growth

LANDSCAPE CHARACTERISTICS

GROWTH RATE: Moderate   **DROUGHT TOLERANCE:** Moderate   **SALT TOLERANCE:** Low
SOIL REQUIREMENTS: Well-drained, moist, fertile, humus rich, slightly acidic to slightly alkaline soil; found growing in areas with infrequent flooding
LIGHT REQUIREMENTS: Full sun; tolerates part shade
PEST PROBLEMS: Mites (blister, Oak, eriophyid, *Platanus*), ambrosia beetles, Texas leafcutter ants, leaf miner, Cranberry root worm, caterpillars, orange-striped Oakworm, Oak webworm, Oak skeletonizer, bud gall mite, flatheaded Apple tree borer, Red Oak and branch borer, Ash borer, broadnecked root borer, spittlebug, Oak lacebug, leafhopper, aphids, scales, golden and red cottony cushion scales
DISEASE PROBLEMS: Anthracnose, Oak root rot, bleeding canker, canker rot, *Endothia*, *Ganoderma*, *Hypoxylon*, leaf blight, *Nectria*, Oak wilt, powdery mildew, root rot, *Phytophthora*, *Taphrina* and xylem limiting bacteria
ENVIRONMENTAL FACTORS: Species is not tolerant of extreme drought conditions; moderately tolerant of infrequent flooding during Winter when dormant; more deciduous in the colder region of its native range
PRUNING: Maintain central leader; remove low hanging limbs, storm damaged limbs and acute limbs that promote included bark in limb crotch and remove co-dominant leaders

ADDITIONAL NOTES

USES: Screening, specimen, near ponds or lakes or as a graceful accent plant
URBAN USES: Adaptable to moist or well-drained soil sites; moderately tolerant of air pollutants; needs large space for root system and crown development
SUBSTITUTIONS: *Quercus hemisphaerica*, *Quercus phellos* and cultivars, *Quercus virginiana* and cultivars, *Ilex myrtifolia, Ilex x attenuata* cultivars or *Betula nigra* and cultivars
COMMENTS: Laurel Oak is adaptable to soil and environments that are infrequently wet, but prefers to be planted on well-drained sites. Laurel Oak is partly evergreen in the southern and warmer regions where it is hardy enough to be used.
OTHER CULTIVARS: No known commercial cultivars are presently grown

Quercus lyrata
Overcup Oak

USDA Hardiness Zones: 6-9a

DESCRIPTION

NATIVE HABITAT: Central and Eastern United States
PLANT TYPE: Deciduous, broadleaf, large tree
MATURE SIZE: 30-40' tall by 30-40' wide
FORM/SHAPE: Rounded silhouette with large diameter branches
BARK: Rough; reddish or gray-brown; forms irregular plates with thinner scales with age
FLOWER: Brown male catkin; greenish tan, female flower; inconspicuous; blooms in Spring
FRUIT: Acorns with large, rough cup almost covering nut, acorns are ovate to flattened, 1-1 1/2" long and wide
FOLIAGE: Alternate, simple, leather; dark green leaves turn coppery brown in Fall

LANDSCAPE CHARACTERISTICS

GROWTH RATE: Moderate to Fast   **DROUGHT TOLERANCE:** Moderate   **SALT TOLERANCE:** Low to Moderate
SOIL REQUIREMENTS: Well-drained, moist, fertile, humus rich, slightly acidic to slightly alkaline soil; found growing in areas with infrequent flooding
LIGHT REQUIREMENTS: Full sun; tolerates part shade
PEST PROBLEMS: Mites (blister, Oak, eriophyid, *Platanus*), ambrosia beetles, Texas leafcutter ants, leaf miner, Cranberry root worm, caterpillars, orange-striped Oakworm, Oak webworm, Oak skeletonizer, bud gall mite, flatheaded Apple tree borer, Red Oak and branch borer, Ash borer, broadnecked root borer, spittlebug, Oak lacebug, leafhopper, aphids, scales, golden and red cottony cushion scales
DISEASE PROBLEMS: Anthracnose, Oak root rot, bleeding canker, canker rot, *Endothia*, *Ganoderma*, *Hypoxylon*, leaf blight, *Nectria*, Oak wilt, powdery mildew, root rot, *Phytophthora*, *Taphrina* and xylem limiting bacteria
ENVIRONMENTAL FACTORS: May decline when soil becomes compacted or soil environment does not support necessary mycorrhizal growth around tree roots or when soil has low oxygen content with poor drainage
PRUNING: Maintain central leader; remove low hanging limbs, storm damaged limbs and acute limbs that promote included bark in limb crotch and remove co-dominant leaders

ADDITIONAL NOTES

USES: Parking lot islands, lawn tree, buffer strips around parking lots, reclamation plantings, shade tree or residential street tree
URBAN USES: Adaptable to moist or well-drained soil sites; moderately tolerant of air pollutants; needs large space for root system and crown development
SUBSTITUTIONS: *Quercus* species, *Ginkgo* cultivars, large *Lagerstroemia* cultivars or *Ulmus* cultivars
COMMENTS: Overcup Oak is showing promise as a dependable landscape tree with some cultivar forms in development. It is tolerant of occasionally flooded soil.
OTHER CULTIVARS: 'QLFTB' PP 13,470 Highbeam® - clonal form with uniform growth

Quercus phellos
Willow Oak
USDA Hardiness Zones: 6-9

DESCRIPTION

NATIVE HABITAT: Eastern and Southern United States
PLANT TYPE: Deciduous, broadleaf, large tree
MATURE SIZE: 60-75' tall by 40-50' wide
FORM/SHAPE: Broad, pyramidal to rounded dome
BARK: Smooth; gray when young; matures to dark gray to grayish black with shallow fissures, ridges and irregular, small plates and scales
FLOWER: Olive-green to tan male catkin; brown-green female flower, matures to grayish brown acorn; blooms in late Winter to Spring; male flowers produce an abundance of pollen
FRUIT: Small, grayish brown, oval-shaped acorn, 3/8-1/2"; can cause litter problems in public access areas
FOLIAGE: Alternate, simple, linear to lanceolate; light green to dark green leaves; turns yellow in Fall

LANDSCAPE CHARACTERISTICS

GROWTH RATE: Moderate to Fast   **DROUGHT TOLERANCE:** Moderate to High   **SALT TOLERANCE:** Moderate to High
SOIL REQUIREMENTS: Well-drained, moist, fertile, humus rich, slightly acidic soil; adaptable to clay, loam and sandy soils; moderately tolerant of wet soils and infrequent flooding
LIGHT REQUIREMENTS: Full sun; tolerates part shade
PEST PROBLEMS: Mites (blister, Oak, eriophyid, *Platanus*), ambrosia beetles, Texas leafcutter ants, leaf miner, Cranberry rootworm, caterpillars, orange-striped Oakworm, Oak webworm, Oak skeletonizer, bud gall mite, flatheaded Apple tree borer, Red Oak and branch borer, Ash borer, broadnecked root borer, spittlebug, Oak lacebug, leafhopper, aphids, golden and red cottony cushion scales
DISEASE PROBLEMS: Anthracnose, Oak root rot, bleeding canker, canker rot, *Endothia*, *Ganoderma*, *Hypoxylon*, leaf blight, *Nectria*, Oak wilt, powdery mildew, root rot, *Phytophthora*, *Taphrina* and xylem limiting bacteria
ENVIRONMENTAL FACTORS: Transplant to well-drained soil for best survival; once established, will tolerate moderately wet sites and infrequent flooding; acorns can be messy in public areas; leaf bronzing from mites occurs when conditions are windy, dry and hot
PRUNING: Maintain central leader; remove low hanging limbs, storm damaged limbs and acute limbs that promote included bark in limb crotch and remove co-dominant leaders

ADDITIONAL NOTES

USES: Shade tree in parks, lining streets and boulevards, buffer strips, medians or reclamation plantings
URBAN USES: Excellent choice for streets and medians
SUBSTITUTIONS: *Quercus lyrata*, other *Quercus* species and cultivars, *Lagerstroemia* cultivars, *Zelkova* cultivars or *Ulmus* cultivars
COMMENTS: The Willow Oak is well adapted to urban conditions, but can develop chlorosis in high pH soils and root rot in confined planting areas. Avoid deep planting. The tree must have several growing seasons to establish and adapt to stressed conditions.
OTHER CULTIVARS: The following cultivars are produced on their own roots: 'QPMTF' PP 15,217 Wynstar® - fast, uniform growth, clonal form; 'QPSTA' PP 13,677 Hightower® - fast, uniform growth, clonal form

Quercus phellos 'QPMTF' PP 15,217
Wynstar® Willow Oak
USDA Hardiness Zones: 6-9

DESCRIPTION

NATIVE HABITAT: Eastern and Southern United States; culitvar of nursery origin
PLANT TYPE: Deciduous, broadleaf, large tree
MATURE SIZE: 55-65' tall by 30-45' wide
FORM/SHAPE: Broad, pyramidal to rounded dome
BARK: Smooth; gray when young; matures to dark gray to grayish black with shallow fissures, ridges and irregular, small plates and scales
FLOWER: Olive-green to tan male catkin; brown-green female flower, matures to grayish brown acorn; blooms in late Winter to Spring; male flowers produce an abundance of pollen
FRUIT: Small, grayish brown, oval-shaped acorn, 3/8-1/2"; can cause litter problems in public access areas
FOLIAGE: Alternate, simple, lanceolate to narrowly elliptic-lanceolate; new growth emerges light green and matures to dark or olive-green; russet-orange Fall color

LANDSCAPE CHARACTERISTICS

GROWTH RATE: Moderate to Fast   **DROUGHT TOLERANCE:** Moderate to High   **SALT TOLERANCE:** Moderate to High
SOIL REQUIREMENTS: Well-drained, moist, fertile, humus rich, slightly acidic soil; adaptable to clay, loam and sandy soil; moderately tolerant of wet soil and infrequent flooding
LIGHT REQUIREMENTS: Full sun; tolerates part shade
PEST PROBLEMS: Mites (blister, Oak, eriophyid, *Platanus*), ambrosia beetles, Texas leafcutter ants, leaf miner, Cranberry rootworm, caterpillars, orange-striped Oakworm, Oak webworm, Oak skeletonizer, bud gall mite, flatheaded Apple tree borer, Red Oak and branch borer, Ash borer, broadnecked root borer, spittlebug, Oak lacebug, leafhopper, aphids, golden and red cottony cushion scales
DISEASE PROBLEMS: Anthracnose, Oak root rot, bleeding canker, canker rot, *Endothia*, *Ganoderma*, *Hypoxylon*, leaf blight, *Nectria*, Oak wilt, powdery mildew, root rot, *Phytophthora*, *Taphrina* and xylem limiting bacteria
ENVIRONMENTAL FACTORS: Transplant to well drained soil for best survival; once established, will tolerate moderately wet sites and infrequent flooding; acorns can be messy in public areas; leaf bronzing from mites occurs when conditions are windy, dry and hot
PRUNING: Maintain central leader; remove low hanging limbs, storm damaged limbs and acute limbs that promote included bark in limb crotch and remove co-dominant leaders

ADDITIONAL NOTES

USES: Street tree, specimen, parking lots and highly visible public planting sites when uniformity is needed
URBAN USES: Very adaptable to well-drained clay or loam soil; adaptable and durable once established; very uniform growth; limb structure problems are minimal in comparison to seedling trees
SUBSTITUTIONS: *Quercus phellos* 'QPSTA' PP 13,677 Hightower®, *Quercus laurifolia*, *Quercus hemisphaerica*, *Ulmus* cultivars and species, *Quercus phellos* or *Zelkova* cultivars
COMMENTS: Wynstar® is very fast growing with consistent, uniform growth, a dominant central leader and pyramidal form. Trees produced on their own roots give uniform growth and development, along with a well-anchored root system. Wynstar® has better mite tolerance than others of its species.
OTHER CULTIVARS: 'QPSTA' PP 13,677 Hightower® - narrow, pyramidal form, uniform clonal growth consistent with cultivar, dense canopy, dominant central leader, yellow Fall color leaves shed cleanly from tree in Autumn

Quercus phellos 'QPSTA' PP 13,677
Hightower® Willow Oak
USDA Hardiness Zones: 6-9

DESCRIPTION

NATIVE HABITAT: Eastern and Southern United States; cultivar of nursery origin
PLANT TYPE: Deciduous, broadleaf, large tree
MATURE SIZE: 55-65' tall by 30-45' wide
FORM/SHAPE: Broad, pyramidal to rounded dome
BARK: Smooth; gray when young; matures to dark gray to grayish black with shallow fissures, ridges and irregular, small plates and scales
FLOWER: Olive-green to tan male catkin; brown-green female flower, matures to grayish brown acorn; blooms in late Winter to Spring; male flowers produce an abundance of pollen
FRUIT: Small, grayish brown, oval-shaped acorn, 3/8-1/2"; can cause litter problems in public access areas
FOLIAGE: Alternate, simple, lanceolate to narrowly elliptic-lanceolate; new growth emerges light green and matures to dark green; turns yellowish green to yellow Fall color

LANDSCAPE CHARACTERISTICS

GROWTH RATE: Moderate to Fast **DROUGHT TOLERANCE:** Moderate to High **SALT TOLERANCE:** Moderate to High
SOIL REQUIREMENTS: Well-drained, moist, fertile, humus rich, slightly acidic soil; adaptable to clay, loam and sandy soils; moderately tolerant of wet soils and infrequent flooding
LIGHT REQUIREMENTS: Full sun; tolerates part shade
PEST PROBLEMS: Mites (blister, Oak, eriophyid, *Platanus*), ambrosia beetles, Texas leafcutter ants, leaf miner, Cranberry rootworm, caterpillars, orange-striped Oakworm, Oak webworm, Oak skeletonizer, bud gall mite, flatheaded Apple tree borer, Red Oak and branch borer, Ash borer, broadnecked root borer, spittlebug, Oak lacebug, leafhopper, aphids, golden and red cottony cushion scales
DISEASE PROBLEMS: Anthracnose, Oak root rot, bleeding canker, canker rot, *Endothia*, *Ganoderma*, *Hypoxylon*, leaf blight, *Nectria*, Oak wilt, powdery mildew, root rot, *Phytophthora*, *Taphrina* and xylem limiting bacteria
ENVIRONMENTAL FACTORS: Transplant to well-drained soil for best survival; once established, will tolerate moderately wet sites and infrequent flooding; acorns can be messy in public areas; leaf bronzing from mites occurs when conditions are windy, dry and hot
PRUNING: Maintain central leader; remove low hanging limbs, storm damaged limbs and acute limbs that promote included bark in limb crotch and remove co-dominant leaders

ADDITIONAL NOTES

USES: Street tree, specimen, parking lots and highly visible public planting sites when uniformity is needed
URBAN USES: Very adaptable to well-drained clay or loam soil; adaptable and durable once established; very uniform growth; limb structure problems are minimal in comparison to seedling trees
SUBSTITUTIONS: *Quercus phellos* 'QPMTF' PP 15,217 Wynstar®, *Quercus laurifolia*, *Quercus hemisphaerica*, *Ulmus* species and cultivars, *Quercus phellos* or *Zelkova* cultivars
COMMENTS: Hightower® has a narrow, pyramidal form with a dense canopy, dominant central leader, well placed limbs and elegant form. It is consistently reproduced on its own roots. The yellow leaves of Fall are cleanly shed from tree.
OTHER CULTIVARS: 'QTMTF' PP 15,217 Wynstar® - pyramidal form, uniform, clonal growth, consistent with cultivar, vigorous growth, plant size and leaf characteristics of species, Fall foliage is russet-orange

Quercus rubra
Northern Red Oak
USDA Hardiness Zones: 5-8a

DESCRIPTION

NATIVE HABITAT: From the Eastern United States coast to Minnesota down through Arkansas and into Texas
PLANT TYPE: Deciduous, broadleaf, large tree
MATURE SIZE: 60-70' tall by 50-60' wide
FORM/SHAPE: Round, dense crown, symmetrical
BARK: Smooth; grayish brown when young; matures dark gray to blackish brown; marked with horizontal light gray lines; develops shallow, vertical fissures and rounded ridges; becomes checkered with age
FLOWER: Grayish green to tannish male catkin; yellowish brown female flower; blooms in late Winter to early Spring
FRUIT: Dry, hard, brown, oval, acorn; attracts squirrels and other small animals; messy in public access areas
FOLIAGE: Alternate, simple, oblong, eight to nine ascending lobes, sinuses between lobes extend halfway to mid rib, toothed lobes end in a bristle tip; dark green, glabrous olive-green leaves; turns yellow to brownish red in Fall; showy Fall color

LANDSCAPE CHARACTERISTICS

GROWTH RATE: Fast   **DROUGHT TOLERANCE:** Moderate to High   **SALT TOLERANCE:** High
SOIL REQUIREMENTS: Well-drained, moist, fertile, humus rich, slightly acidic soil; adaptable to many soil types except alkaline or water-logged soil
LIGHT REQUIREMENTS: Full sun; tolerates part shade
PEST PROBLEMS: Mites (blister, Oak, eriophyid, *Platanus*), ambrosia beetles, Texas leafcutter ants, leaf miner, Cranberry root worm, caterpillars, orange-striped Oakworm, Oak webworm, Oak skeletonizer, bud gall mite, flatheaded Apple tree borer, Red Oak and branch borer, Ash borer, broadnecked root borer, spittlebug, Oak lacebug, leafhopper, aphids, scales, golden and red cottony cushion scales
DISEASE PROBLEMS: Anthracnose, Oak root rot, bleeding canker, canker rot, *Endothia*, *Ganoderma*, *Hypoxylon*, leaf blight, *Nectria*, Oak wilt, powdery mildew, root rot, *Phytophthora*, *Taphrina* and xylem limiting bacteria
ENVIRONMENTAL FACTORS: Large area needed for crown development; not tolerant of wet soil or flooding; large acorns and leaves can create litter problem
PRUNING: Maintain central leader; remove limbs with acute branch to trunk angles and low hanging limbs

ADDITIONAL NOTES

USES: Large parking lot islands, lawn trees, buffer strips, median strips, large shade tree, specimen and naturalizing
URBAN USES: Good choice for urban area; tolerates air pollution, drought and moderately high salt levels; holds up well in urban environment with a low failure rate; roots can cause sidewalks to heave
SUBSTITUTIONS: *Quercus shumardii, Quercus coccinea, Quercus velutina, Quercus lyrata* and cultivars, *Quercus nuttallii* and cultivars
COMMENTS: Ball and burlap trees of Northern Red Oak are best if planted in the Spring. Container grown trees can be planted in Spring, Summer, or Fall. It has a showy Fall color and is a good choice for a street or shade tree due to its good tolerance of urban air pollution.
OTHER CULTIVARS: 'Aurea' - smaller than species, yellow new growth changing to light green in summer, has to be grown in shade to prevent sunscald of foliage; a novelty cultivar for collectors

Quercus shumardii
Shumard Oak
USDA Hardiness Zones: 5b-9

DESCRIPTION

NATIVE HABITAT: Eastern United States to Southwestern Illinois and along the Mississippi River to Louisiana and Eastern Texas
PLANT TYPE: Deciduous, broadleaf, large tree
MATURE SIZE: 55-80' tall by 50-60' wide
FORM/SHAPE: Narrow, rounded at maturity, open canopy
BARK: Smooth, gray-brown when young; gray, scaly ridges with dark fissures and tan inner bark with age
FLOWER: Gray-brown male catkin; gray-green female flower matures to gray-brown acorn; blooms in Spring
FRUIT: Acorns; 1" long by 3/4" wide
FOLIAGE: Alternate, simple, oblong; six to eight pairs of ascending lobes; dark green leaves; turns brilliant red to reddish orange in Fall

LANDSCAPE CHARACTERISTICS

GROWTH RATE: Fast **DROUGHT TOLERANCE:** High **SALT TOLERANCE:** Moderate
SOIL REQUIREMENTS: Well-drained, moist, fertile, humus rich, slightly acidic to slightly alkaline soil; found growing in areas with infrequent flooding
LIGHT REQUIREMENTS: Full sun; tolerates part shade
PEST PROBLEMS: Mites (blister, Oak, eriophyid, *Platanus*), ambrosia beetles, Texas leafcutter ants, leaf miner, Cranberry root worm, caterpillars, orange-striped Oakworm, Oak webworm, Oak skeletonizer, bud gall mite, flatheaded Apple tree borer, Red Oak and branch borer, Ash borer, broadnecked root borer, spittlebug, Oak lacebug, leafhopper, aphids, scales, golden and red cottony cushion scales
DISEASE PROBLEMS: Anthracnose, Oak root rot, bleeding canker, canker rot, *Endothia*, *Ganoderma*, *Hypoxylon*, leaf blight, *Nectria*, Oak wilt, powdery mildew, root rot, *Phytophthora*, *Taphrina* and xylem limiting bacteria
ENVIRONMENTAL FACTORS: Fruit, twigs, and foliage cause substantial litter
PRUNING: Requires pruning to develop strong structure; less pruning is needed with Shumard than with Live or Pin Oak

ADDITIONAL NOTES

USES: Large parking lots, lawn tree, buffer strips, reclamation plantings or shade tree
URBAN USES: Good for streets and medians; very adaptable to urban stresses
SUBSTITUTIONS: *Quercus coccinea, Acer saccharum, Quercus nuttallii, Lagerstroemia* cultivars or *Ulmus* cultivars
COMMENTS: This tree is successfully grown in urban areas where air pollution, poor drainage, compacted soil and drought stresses are common. The Shumard Oak has outstanding ornamental features and should be planted more often.
OTHER CULTIVARS: 'QSFTC' PP 14,424 Panache® - fast, uniform growth, clonal form

Salix babylonica
Weeping Willow
USDA Hardiness Zones: 4-9

DESCRIPTION

NATIVE HABITAT: Northeastern and Eastern United States to Southern Canada

PLANT TYPE: Deciduous, pendulous, broadleaf, dioecious, large tree

MATURE SIZE: 30-50' tall by 20-40' wide

FORM/SHAPE: Symmetrical, rounded, weeping canopy

BARK: Smooth; olive to yellow-brown; glabrous; matures to dark grayish brown or blackish gray; shallow fissures and ridges become rough with age

FLOWER: Yellow-green; inconspicuous capsules; flowers unisexual, male catkins at the same time as leaf emergence; blooms in Spring

FRUIT: Dry, hard, brown, narrowly-ovoid, sessile capsule; inconspicuous

FOLIAGE: Alternate, simple, entire, linear to lanceolate, glabrous, leaf margins unevenly spinulose-serrate, petiole are tomentose, glandular above the tip; yellowish, light green leaves above, glaucous on underside; showy, yellow Fall color

LANDSCAPE CHARACTERISTICS

GROWTH RATE: Fast   **DROUGHT TOLERANCE:** Low to Moderate   **SALT TOLERANCE:** Moderate

SOIL REQUIREMENTS: Well-drained, very moist, fertile soil; but will tolerate most soil types

LIGHT REQUIREMENTS: Full sun to part shade

PEST PROBLEMS: Scales, caterpillars, borers, aphids, gypsy moth host, sawfly, Willow leaf beetle, Japanese beetle, Alder spittlebug, lacebug, psyllids, giant Willow aphids, Azalea bark oyster and cottony cushion scales

DISEASE PROBLEMS: *Fusarium* root rot, crown gall, Willow scab, *Physaluspora miyabeana, Hypoxylon, Nectria,* nematodes, smooth patch, *Glomeralla, Venturia,* black canker, leaf spot, powdery mildew, rust and tar spot

ENVIRONMENTAL FACTORS: Needs plenty of room to grow; do not locate near sewer lines or septic tank drain fields because the aggressive roots can cause damage; leaf and twig litter messy and roots can clog small drainage pipes

PRUNING: Prune and train when young to develop a strong structure; maintain a central leader trunk with wide branch crotches

ADDITIONAL NOTES

USES: Screening, specimen, near ponds or lakes, graceful accent plant

URBAN USES: Tolerates temporary flooding; short lived tree; messy, drooping limbs

SUBSTITUTIONS: *Salix alba* 'Tristis', weeping *Prunus*, weeping *Carpinus*, weeping *Malus* or *Ilex vomitoria* 'Pendula'

COMMENTS: The graceful form of Weeping Willow is a nice accent to place around streams, lakes, or pond edges. It needs plenty of room to grow. Do not locate in areas where the soil will be cultivated.

OTHER CULTIVARS: 'Aurea' - bright yellow stems; 'Tristis' - more cold hardy, similar form, very tough, graceful, adaptable Weeping Willow, gold-yellow bark color until stems are three years old

Styrax japonica
Japanese Snowbell
USDA Hardiness Zones: 5-9

DESCRIPTION

NATIVE HABITAT: Japan and Korea
PLANT TYPE: Deciduous, broadleaf, medium size, flowering tree
MATURE SIZE: 20-30' tall by 15-20' wide
FORM/SHAPE: Symmetrical, rounded to vase-shaped crown
BARK: Smooth; attractive bark with orange-brown interlaying fissures
FLOWER: White, bell-shaped to star-shaped flower; blooms May to June; attracts insects
FRUIT: Ovate, small, fleshy green fruit; turns brown in Fall; does not attract wildlife
FOLIAGE: Alternate, simple, elliptic-oblong leaves, crenate to serrulate margin; green leaves turn yellow in Fall

LANDSCAPE CHARACTERISTICS

GROWTH RATE: Slow to Moderate   **DROUGHT TOLERANCE:** Moderate   **SALT TOLERANCE:** Low to Moderate
SOIL REQUIREMENTS: Well-drained and slightly alkaline to acidic clay, loam or sandy soil; prefers humus rich, acidic soil that is moist
LIGHT REQUIREMENTS: Part shade to full sun
PEST PROBLEMS: Stressed trees can attract ambrosia beetles and lacebug
DISEASE PROBLEMS: Root rot in wet soil sites and canker
ENVIRONMENTAL FACTORS: The numerous beautiful flowers of the Japanese Snowbell are followed by numerous seeds about 1/2" long and 3/8" wide, which can cover pedestrian walkways and become hazardous; the seeds sprout and grow prolifically and must be controlled; the flowers attract insects
PRUNING: Little pruning needed and can be trained into multi-trunk or standard single-stem tree form

ADDITIONAL NOTES

USES: Small patio tree, container or above ground container plant, lawn tree and buffer strip plantings
URBAN USES: No proven urban tolerance; good as small street tree or in medians
SUBSTITUTIONS: *Styrax obassia, Styrax grandiflora, Lagerstroemia* cultivars, Chinese Dogwood (*Cornus kousa*) or *Chionanthus retusus*
COMMENTS: *Styrax japonica* and its cultivars are very adaptable to soil and light conditions where *Cornus, Prunus* or *Malus* cultivars may not perform as well due to soil requirements and the affects of disease and insects to those genus.
OTHER CULTIVARS: 'Crystal' - upright to fastigiated habit, black-green foliage, crisp, white flowers with purple pedicels, USDA Hardiness Zone 5; 'Carillon' - grows 1 ft per year, weeping habit, USDA Hardiness Zone 6; 'Pink Chimes' - pink flowers, USDA Hardiness Zone 6; Snow Cone® - tight, upright, broad, cone-shaped crown, very uniform grower

Taxodium distichum
Bald Cypress
USDA Hardiness Zones: 5-10

DESCRIPTION

NATIVE HABITAT: Eastern and Southern United States through Northern Mexico

PLANT TYPE: Deciduous, coniferous, short needle-like leaves, large tree

MATURE SIZE: 60-80' tall by 25-30' wide

FORM/SHAPE: Upright, pyramidal, symmetrical when young; flat topped when very old

BARK: Smooth; reddish brown fibers when young; matures to reddish brown to gray-brown with shallow fissures; ridges are narrow strips, ribbons and bands vertically overlapping

FLOWER: Brownish tan panicle of small male cones; greenish purple female cones composed of fleshy scales form a globus 1-1 1/2" ball; forms in late Winter

FRUIT: Oval, hard, greenish purple to brown cone; attracts birds, squirrels, and other mammals

FOLIAGE: Alternate, simple, lanceolate, needle-like leaves; pale green needles turn coppery red in Fall; leaves are like a soft evergreen needle, but tree is deciduous

LANDSCAPE CHARACTERISTICS

GROWTH RATE: Moderate to Fast   **DROUGHT TOLERANCE:** High   **SALT TOLERANCE:** Moderate

SOIL REQUIREMENTS: Well-drained, slightly alkaline to acidic, clay, loam or sandy soil; will tolerate extended flooding

LIGHT REQUIREMENTS: Full sun to part shade

PEST PROBLEMS: Bagworm, Cypress looper mites, Beech blight aphid, Southern Cypress beetle, Japanese beetle, Cypress gall mites, Cypress twig gall midges

DISEASE PROBLEMS: *Cercospora*, leaf blight, sapwood rot and root knot nematodes

ENVIRONMENTAL FACTORS: Urban plantings may show brownish yellow leaves due to mites, high pH or air pollution

PRUNING: Requires little pruning; prune only to remove dead wood and remove co-dominant leaders

ADDITIONAL NOTES

USES: Large parking lot islands, parking lot buffer strips, reclamation plantings, screening and as a shade tree; can be clipped into a nice soft hedge

URBAN USES: Good for urban areas; great to use in parking lots or medians; Cypress knees do not appear when planted in drier locations, but when growing in saturated soil conditions, knees may be produced

SUBSTITUTIONS: *Metasequoia glyptostroboides* or *Taxodium asendens*

COMMENTS: The Bald Cypress is an outstanding ornamental tree with Winter interest because of its showy trunk and bark. It can even grow where constant flooding may kill other plants. Some cultivars have unusual plant form.

OTHER CULTIVARS: Autumn Gold™ - broad crown, nice golden yellow Fall color; 'Pendens' - central main stem with pendulous limb tips; 'Cascade Falls' PP 12,296 - weeping to prostrate form, if not staked plant will creep on the ground

Taxodium distichum 'Mickelson'
Shawnee Brave® Bald Cypress
USDA Hardiness Zones: 5-9

MATURE SIZE: 55-75' tall by 18-20' wide
FORM/SHAPE: Narrow, pyramidal form
FOLIAGE: Green foliage turns russet-brown to orange-brown in Fall
LIGHT REQUIREMENTS: Full sun to part shade
COMMENTS: Shawneee Brave® has a strong, narrow, pyramidal form that has proven to be widely adaptable to urban environments. This plant is tolerant of water-logged soil but will produce large root structures called "knees" that stick up above the ground in water-logged soil. It also has good cold hardiness in the northern limits of its indigenous range.

Taxodium distichum 'Sofine' PP 13,431
Autumn Gold™ Bald Cypress
USDA Hardiness Zones: 5-10

MATURE SIZE: 50-70' tall by 20-30' wide
FORM/SHAPE: Broad, pyramidal form
FOLIAGE: Medium green foliage turns golden yellow in Fall
LIGHT REQUIREMENTS: Full sun to part shade
COMMENTS: Autumn Gold™ has a broad, pyramidal form with uniform growth. This plant is produced on its own roots and it has yellow Fall color and medium green Summer foliage with a fine texture. It is tolerant of water-logged soil but will produce large root structures called "knees" that stick up above the ground in water-logged soil.

Tilia cordata
Greenspire® Littleleaf Linden
USDA Hardiness Zones: 3-7a

DESCRIPTION

NATIVE HABITAT: British Isles and Europe; cultivar of nursery origin
PLANT TYPE: Deciduous, broadleaf, large tree
MATURE SIZE: 40-60' tall by 35-50' wide
FORM/SHAPE: Dense, pyramidal
BARK: Smooth; gray to black bark, becomes ridged and furrowed when mature
FLOWER: Yellow; small and fragrant; blooms late June to July
FRUIT: Small, round, hard and persistent fruit; not a litter problem
FOLIAGE: Alternate, simple, serrate leaf margins; green leaves turn yellow in Fall

LANDSCAPE CHARACTERISTICS

GROWTH RATE: Moderate   **DROUGHT TOLERANCE:** Moderate   **SALT TOLERANCE:** Low
SOIL REQUIREMENTS: Well-drained, slightly acidic to slightly alkaline, clay, loam or sandy soil; tolerant of occasionally wet soil
LIGHT REQUIREMENTS: Part shade to full sun
PEST PROBLEMS: Japanese beetle, mites, ambrosia beetles, aphids, sawfly, twig girdler, root borer, mealybugs, gypsy moth, forest tent caterpillar and Linden borer
DISEASE PROBLEMS: *Verticillium* wilt, *Ganoderma* trunk rot, *Nectria* stem canker, *Pseudomonas* wilt, canker, *Glomerella, Hypoxylon* and powdery mildew
ENVIRONMENTAL FACTORS: Bark sunburn on trunk, prone to frost injury, moderate air pollution tolerance
PRUNING: Requires little pruning when maintained with a central leader; remove root suckers on grafted trees

ADDITIONAL NOTES

USES: Hedge, large parking lot islands, specimen and as a shade tree
URBAN USES: Good for urban areas, especially when used in buffer strips around parking lots and sidewalk cutouts
SUBSTITUTIONS: *Pyrus calleryana* cultivars or *Lagerstroemia* cultivars
COMMENTS: Greenspire is a strong grower in USDA Hardiness Zones 6 and colder. In colder hardiness zones, it is a good plant for urban areas.
OTHER CULTIVARS: 'Glenleven' - fast growth, straight trunk; 'Morden' - compact, pyramidal crown

Ulmus americana 'Princeton'
Princeton Elm
USDA Hardiness Zones: 2-9

DESCRIPTION

NATIVE HABITAT: Eastern half of North America; cultivar of nursery origin

PLANT TYPE: Deciduous, broadleaf, large tree

MATURE SIZE: 60-80' tall by 60-100' wide

FORM/SHAPE: Broad, upright, vase-shaped

BARK: Grayish brown with ridges and fissures; flakes and scales develop from ridges

FLOWER: Green; inconspicuous; appears in early Spring

FRUIT: Thin, wafer-like seed; appears soon after flowering

FOLIAGE: Alternate, simple, double serrated; dark green leaves in Summer turn yellow in Fall

LANDSCAPE CHARACTERISTICS

GROWTH RATE: Fast   **DROUGHT TOLERANCE:** High   **SALT TOLERANCE:** Moderate to High

SOIL REQUIREMENTS: Well-drained, acidic to alkaline, clay, loam or sandy soil; tolerates extended flooding

LIGHT REQUIREMENTS: Full sun to part shade; grows best in full sun

PEST PROBLEMS: May be affected by one or more pests such as bark beetle, Elm borer, aphids, gypsy moths, mites, scales, Elm leafminer and Fall webworm

DISEASE PROBLEMS: Oak root rot, leaf scorch, canker, butt rot, *Discula*, *Endothia*, *Ganoderma*, leaf spot, *Hypoxylon*, *Nectria*, root rot; reported to have resistance to Dutch Elm disease

ENVIRONMENTAL FACTORS: Roots can lift sidewalks; dropped seeds create a mess; wood is weak and can break in ice or wind storms

PRUNING: Required to develop strong structure; remove limbs with acute limb to trunk unions; remove co-dominant leaders

ADDITIONAL NOTES

USES: Use in reclamation plantings, as a specimen, in urban areas, parks and shade trees

URBAN USES: Use in urban areas as a street tree or in median plantings where less than favorable conditions exist

SUBSTITUTIONS: Hybrid Elm cultivars introduced from the USDA Nursery Crops Laboratory

COMMENTS: American Elms were once a very popular shade and street tree. Use of this tree has declined due to dieback from Dutch Elm disease. 'Princeton' is said to have resistance to Dutch Elm disease and is a fast growing tree.

OTHER CULTIVARS: 'Jefferson', 'Valley Forge' and 'Homestead' are Elm cultivars developed by the USDA Nursery Crops Laboratory which show good resistance to Dutch Elm disease and phloem necrosis

Ulmus parvifolia
Chinese Lacebark Elm
USDA Hardiness Zones: 5b-10a

DESCRIPTION

NATIVE HABITAT: Japan, Korea, Taiwan, Northern and Central China
PLANT TYPE: Deciduous, broadleaf, large tree
MATURE SIZE: 40-50' tall by 35-50' wide
FORM/SHAPE: Irregular outline, rounded, vase-shaped
BARK: Smooth; gray when young; matures to gray, green, orange and brown; showy trunk; bark exfoliates to reveal random mottled patterns
FLOWER: Green; inconspicuous; blooms in late Summer to Fall
FRUIT: Green or brown, flat, membranous samara seed in middle; distal end clefted or notched, 1/2" long by 1/4" wide; in axillary clusters
FOLIAGE: Alternate, simple, elliptical to elliptic-lanceolate and leathery with simple to (crenate) rounded, serrated leafmargin; medium to dark green leaves turn yellow to yellow-brown and shed during Fall

LANDSCAPE CHARACTERISTICS

GROWTH RATE: Moderate   **DROUGHT TOLERANCE:** Moderate   **SALT TOLERANCE:** Moderate
SOIL REQUIREMENTS: Well-drained, moist, fertile, humus rich, slightly alkaline to slightly acidic soil; very adaptable to clay, loam or sandy soil
LIGHT REQUIREMENTS: Full sun to part shade
PEST PROBLEMS: Ambrosia beetles, spindle galls, Elm leaf beetle, bagworm, bark beetle, Japanese beetle, black vine weevil, Locust leafminer, Willow leaf weevil, leafroller, webworm, mites, Oak spider mite, sawfly, twig pruner, Ash borer, Peach bark borer, Alder lacebug, Elm leafhopper, wooly Apple aphid, scales, white Peach scale and oyster scale
DISEASE PROBLEMS: Oak root rot, bark rot, canker, dieback, *Fusarium, Ganoderma, Hypoxylon*, leaf spot, *Nectria*, nematodes, *Oxyporus*, powdery mildew, *Taphrina, Verticillium* wilt, wetwood, *Alternaria* and witches broom
ENVIRONMENTAL FACTORS: Not tolerant of water-logged planting sites; low temperatures can kill shoot tips and split bark in Winter
PRUNING: Prune to develop a strong structure and remove low hanging limbs; trees have a somewhat pendulous limb tip and weeping inner limbs

ADDITIONAL NOTES

USES: Bonsai, parking lots, buffer strips, medians, shade tree and residential street tree
URBAN USES: Grown successfully in urban areas with poor conditions; good for street and median settings
SUBSTITUTIONS: *Lagerstroemia* cultivars, *Zelkova* cultivars, *Quercus* species and cultivars, *Ulmus* hybrids
COMMENTS: This is an excellent tree for multiple landscape uses. Trees vary in growth and plant habit. Use cultivars for better uniform growth. Disease resistance and pest tolerance are better known with *Ulmus* cultivars.
OTHER CULTIVARS: 'Frosty' - old cultivar from England with compact growth, upright crown and creamy, white variegated leaf serrations, turns dark green when leaves mature; 'Dynasty' - small, compact, dome-shaped crown, 30' tall by 20' wide, very useful under powerlines and in urban areas, attractive burgundy-red Fall foliage, samara are reddish pink; 'Catlin', 'Golden Ray', 'Pathfinder' and 'True Green' are other cultivars

Ulmus parvifolia 'BSNUPF' PPAF
Everclear® Elm
USDA Hardiness Zones: 5-9

DESCRIPTION

NATIVE HABITAT: Japan, Korea, Taiwan, Northern and Central China; cultivar of nursery origin
PLANT TYPE: Deciduous, broadleaf, large tree
MATURE SIZE: 30-50' tall by 18-25' wide
FORM/SHAPE: Upright, very narrow, tight form when young
BARK: Smooth; olive to brownish gray when young; mature tree exfoliates puzzle-like bark exposing orange, tan, gray and brown patches
FLOWER: Small, light green to reddish green flowers in axillary clusters; inconspicuous; blooms late Summer to early Fall
FRUIT: Green or brown, flat, membranous samara seed in middle; distal end clefted or notched; 1/2" long by 1/4" wide; in axillary clusters
FOLIAGE: Alternate, simple, elliptical to ovate and leathery, with simple to (crenate) rounded, serrated, leaf margin; medium to dark green leaves turn yellow to brown in Fall

LANDSCAPE CHARACTERISTICS

GROWTH RATE: Moderate to Fast   **DROUGHT TOLERANCE:** High   **SALT TOLERANCE:** Moderate
SOIL REQUIREMENTS: Well-drained, moist, fertile, humus rich, slightly alkaline to slightly acidic soil; very adaptable to clay, loam or sandy soil
LIGHT REQUIREMENTS: Full sun to part shade
PEST PROBLEMS: Ambrosia beetles, spindle galls, Elm leaf beetle, bagworm, bark beetle, Japanese beetle, black vine weevil, Locust leafminer, Willow leaf weevil, leafroller, webworm, mites, Oak spider mite, sawfly, twig pruner, Ash borer, Peach bark borer, Alder lacebug, Elm leafhopper, wooly Apple aphid, scale, white Peach scale and oyster scale
DISEASE PROBLEMS: Oak root rot, bark rot, canker, dieback, *Fusarium, Ganoderma, Hypoxylon*, leaf spot, *Nectria,* nematodes, *Oxyporus*, powdery mildew, *Taphrina, Verticillium* wilt, wetwood, *Alternaria* and witches broom
ENVIRONMENTAL FACTORS: Not tolerant of water-logged planting sites
PRUNING: Minimal pruning needed; remove low hanging limbs and limbs broken due to ice, snow or wind; remove co-dominant leaders and limbs with acute limb crotch angles; prune to distribute the main scaffold limbs into a spiral around the tree's central leader or axis

ADDITIONAL NOTES

USES: Street tree, parking lots, medians, lawn tree, shade tree, planters, specimen, standard or multi-trunk tree and narrow landscape spaces where above ground crown space is limited by width
URBAN USES: Very adaptable to different soil types; good, strong growth in poor planting environments
SUBSTITUTIONS: *Zelkova* cultivars, *Lagerstroemia* cultivars, *Carpinus* cultivars, *Styrax japonica* and cultivars, *Chionanthus retusus, Acer buergerianum* and cultivars
COMMENTS: The Everclear® Elm is a tough, easily managed tree with a more upright limb habit.
OTHER CULTIVARS: 'Frosty' - old cultivar from England with compact growth, upright crown and creamy, white variegated leaf serrations, turns dark green when leaves mature; 'Dynasty' - small, compact, dome-shaped crown, 30' tall by 20' wide, very useful under powerlines and in urban areas, attractive burgundy-red Fall foliage, samara are reddish pink

Ulmus parvifolia 'Drake'
Drake Chinese Elm
USDA Hardiness Zones: 7b-10

DESCRIPTION

NATIVE HABITAT: Japan, Korea, Taiwan and Northern and Central China; cultivar of nursery origin

PLANT TYPE: Semi-evergreen to deciduous, broadleaf, large tree

MATURE SIZE: 35-45'tall by 35-50' wide

FORM/SHAPE: Symmetrical, round, spreading to weeping mature canopy; weeping, vase-shape when young

BARK: Smooth; olive to brownish gray when young; exfoliating bark reveals a mottled pattern of gray, olive-green and tan

FLOWER: Light green; inconspicuous; blooms late Summer to early Fall

FRUIT: Green or brown, flat, membranous samara seed in middle; distal end clefted or notched, 1/2" long by 1/4" wide; in axillary clusters

FOLIAGE: Alternate, simple, elliptical to elliptic-lanceolate and leathery with simple to (crenate) rounded, serrated leaf margin; medium to dark green; nearly evergreen in mild, warm climates; early or previous season's leaves turn yellow to yellow-brown and shed during Winter

LANDSCAPE CHARACTERISTICS

GROWTH RATE: Moderate to Fast   **DROUGHT TOLERANCE:** High   **SALT TOLERANCE:** Moderate

SOIL REQUIREMENTS: Well-drained, moist, fertile, humus rich, slightly alkaline to slightly acidic soil; very adaptable to clay, loam or sandy soil

LIGHT REQUIREMENTS: Full sun to part shade

PEST PROBLEMS: Ambrosia beetles, spindle galls, Elm leaf beetle, bagworm, bark beetle, Japanese beetle, black vine weevil, Locust leafminer, Willow leaf weevil, leafroller, webworm, mites, Oak spider mite, sawfly, twig pruner, Ash borer, Peach bark borer, Alder lacebug, Elm leafhopper, wooly Apple aphid, scales, white Peach scale and oyster scale

DISEASE PROBLEMS: Oak root rot, bark rot, canker, dieback, *Fusarium, Ganoderma, Hypoxylon*, leaf spot, *Nectria,* nematodes, *Oxyporus*, powdery mildew, *Taphrina, Verticillium* wilt, wetwood, *Alternaria* and witches broom

ENVIRONMENTAL FACTORS: Not tolerant of water-logged planting sites; low temperatures can kill shoot tips and split bark in Winter; cold can damage foliage retained throughout Winter

PRUNING: Prune to develop a strong structure and remove low hanging limbs; trees have a somewhat pendulous to weeping limb tip and weeping inner limbs

ADDITIONAL NOTES

USES: Street tree, parking lots, medians, lawn tree, shade tree, planters, specimen, standard or multi-trunk tree

URBAN USES: Very adaptable to different soil types; not prone to produce large surface roots; pendulous, wide spreading may limit use as street tree; give crown enough room to develop

SUBSTITUTIONS: *Zelkova* cultivars, *Lagerstroemia* cultivars, *Carpinus* cultivars, *Styrax japonica* and cultivars, *Chionanthus retusus, Acer buergerianum* and cultivars

COMMENTS: A tough and easily managed tree with a wide, vase-shaped and pendulous limb habit as a young tree. 'Drake' matures to a round, spreading to pendulous limb habit. Trees are more evergreen in warmer climates. Winter cold damage to stem tip may show up in the Spring, and bark splitting and cracks may cause tree loss.

OTHER CULTIVARS: 'Frosty' - old cultivar from England with compact growth, upright, crown and creamy, white, variegated leaf serrations, turns dark green when leaves mature; 'Dynasty' - small, compact, dome-shaped crown, 30' tall by 20" wide, very useful under powerlines and in urban areas, attractive burgundy-red Fall foliage, samara are reddish pink

Ulmus parvifolia 'Emer I' PP 7,551
Athena® Elm

USDA Hardiness Zones: 5b-10a

DESCRIPTION

NATIVE HABITAT: Japan, Korea, Taiwan, Northern and Central China; cultivar of nursery origin

PLANT TYPE: Deciduous, broadleaf, large tree

MATURE SIZE: 30-40' tall by 50-55' wide

FORM/SHAPE: Uniform crown with ascending branches; broad, spreading, dome-shaped crown

BARK: Smooth; olive to brownish gray when young; maturing tree exfoliates puzzle-like patches exposing tan, gray and brown bark

FLOWER: Small, light green to reddish green flowers in axillary clusters; inconspicuous; blooms late Summer to early Fall

FRUIT: Green or brown, flat, membranous samara seed in middle; distal end clefted or notched; 1/2" long by 1/4" wide; in axillary clusters

FOLIAGE: Alternate, simple, elliptical to ovate and leathery with simple to (crenate) rounded, serrated, leaf margin; dark green Summer leaves turn bronzed brown in Fall

LANDSCAPE CHARACTERISTICS

GROWTH RATE: Moderate   **DROUGHT TOLERANCE:** High   **SALT TOLERANCE:** Moderate

SOIL REQUIREMENTS: Well-drained, moist, fertile, humus rich, slightly alkaline to slightly acidic soil; very adaptable to clay, loam or sandy soil

LIGHT REQUIREMENTS: Full sun to part shade

PEST PROBLEMS: Ambrosia beetles, spindle galls, Elm leaf beetle, bagworm, bark beetle, Japanese beetle, black vine weevil, Locust leafminer, Willow leaf weevil, leafroller, webworm, mites, Oak spider mites, sawfly, twig pruner, Ash borer, Peach bark borer, Alder lacebug, Elm leafhopper, wooly Apple aphid, scales, white Peach scale and oyster scale

DISEASE PROBLEMS: Oak root rot, bark rot, canker, dieback, *Fusarium, Ganoderma, Hypoxylon*, leaf spot, *Nectria,* nematodes, *Oxyporus*, powdery mildew, *Taphrina, Verticillium* wilt, wetwood, *Alternaria* and witches broom

ENVIRONMENTAL FACTORS: Not tolerant of water-logged planting sites

PRUNING: Minimal pruning needed; remove low hanging limbs and limbs broken due to ice, snow or wind; remove co-dominant leaders and limbs with acute limb crotch angles; prune to distribute the main scaffold limbs into a spiral around the tree's central leader or axis

ADDITIONAL NOTES

USES: Street tree, parking lots, medians, lawn tree, shade tree, planters, specimen and standard or multi-trunk tree

URBAN USES: Very adaptable to different soil types; strong growth in poor planting environments

SUBSTITUTIONS: *Zelkova* cultivars, *Lagerstroemia* cultivars, *Carpinus* cultivars, *Styrax japonica* and cultivars, *Chionanthus retusus*, *Acer buergerianum* and cultivars, *Ulmus parvifolia* 'Dynasty'

COMMENTS: The Athena® Elm is not affected by leaf scorch during dry summers. It transplants easily and is tolerant of a wide range of soil and conditions. It has been reported to withstand temperatures as low as minus 10 degrees Farenheit and growth hardens off two weeks earlier than the species.

OTHER CULTIVARS: Athena® Classic - uniform, broad, dome-shaped crown, dark green, leathery leaves, trunk and crown are more uniform and easily maintained as tree develops into mature specimen; 'Frosty' - old cultivar from England with compact growth, upright crown and variegated creamy, white serrations turning dark green when the leaves mature; 'Dynasty' - small, compact, dome-shaped crown, 30' tall by 20' wide, very useful under power lines and in urban sites, attractive Fall foliage, burgundy-red and seed samara are reddish pink

Ulmus parvifolia 'Emer II' PP 7,552
Allee® Elm
USDA Hardiness Zones: 5-9

DESCRIPTION

NATIVE HABITAT: Japan, Korea, Taiwan, Northern and Central China; cultivar of nursery origin
PLANT TYPE: Deciduous, broadleaf, large tree
MATURE SIZE: 50-60' tall by 35-40' wide
FORM/SHAPE: Vase to upright, dome-shaped
BARK: Smooth; olive to brownish gray when young; mature tree exfoliates puzzle-like bark exposing orange, tan, gray and brown patches
FLOWER: Small, light green to reddish green flowers in axillary clusters; inconspicuous; blooms late Summer to early Fall
FRUIT: Green or brown, flat, membranous samara seed in middle; distal end clefted or notched; 1/2" long by 1/4" wide; in axillary clusters
FOLIAGE: Alternate, simple, elliptical to ovate and leathery with simple to (crenate) round, serration, leaf margin; bright green leaves turn yellow to bronzed yellow in Fall

LANDSCAPE CHARACTERISTICS

GROWTH RATE: Fast **DROUGHT TOLERANCE:** High **SALT TOLERANCE:** Moderate
SOIL REQUIREMENTS: Well-drained, moist, fertile, humus rich, slightly alkaline to slightly acidic soil; very adaptable to clay, loam or sandy soil
LIGHT REQUIREMENTS: Full sun to part shade
PEST PROBLEMS: Ambrosia beetles, spindle galls, Elm leaf beetle, bagworm, bark beetle, Japanese beetle, black vine weevil, Locust leafminer, Willow leaf weevil, leafroller, webworm, mites, Oak spider mite, sawfly, twig pruner, Ash borer, Peach bark borer, Alder lacebug, Elm leaf hopper, wooly Apple aphids, scale, white Peach scale and oyster scale
DISEASE PROBLEMS: Oak root rot, bark rot, canker, dieback, *Fusarium, Ganoderma, Hypoxylon*, leaf spot, *Nectria,* nematodes, *Oxyporus*, powdery mildew, *Taphrina, Verticillium* wilt, wetwood, *Alternaria* and witches broom
ENVIRONMENTAL FACTORS: Not tolerant of water-logged planting sites
PRUNING: Minimal pruning needed; remove low hanging limbs and limbs broken due to ice, snow or wind; remove co-dominant leaders and limbs with acute limb crotch angles; prune to distribute the main scaffold limbs into a spiral around the tree's central leader or axis

ADDITIONAL NOTES

USES: Street tree, parking lots, medians, lawn tree, shade tree, planters, specimen, standard or multi-trunk tree
URBAN USES: Very adaptable to different soil types; strong growth in poor planting environments
SUBSTITUTIONS: *Acer rubrum* cultivars, *Zelkova* cultivars, *Carpinus* cultivars, *Lagerstroemia* cultivars, *Quercus* cultivars, *Taxodium* cultivars, *Ulmus americana* cultivars and hybrids
COMMENTS: The Allee® Elm is a tall, fast growing, upright branching tree. Limb breakage from weak limb crotch angles should be corrected when tree is young so limb pruning scars will heal in a few years.
OTHER CULTIVARS: 'Frontier' - 40' tall by 30' wide, broad, oval, upright form, glossy green foliage turns burgundy in Fall, U.S. National Arboretum introduction; 'Homestead' - 55' tall by 35' wide, upright branching and narrow, oval form, dark green foliage turns yellow in Fall, U.S. National Arboretum introduction

Ulmus parvifolia 'UPMTF' PP 11,295
Bosque® Elm
USDA Hardiness Zones: 5-9

DESCRIPTION

NATIVE HABITAT: Japan, Korea, Taiwan, Northern and Central China; cultivar of nursery origin
PLANT TYPE: Deciduous, broadleaf, large tree
MATURE SIZE: 60-65' tall by 30-35' wide
FORM/SHAPE: Broad, oval
BARK: Smooth; olive to brownish gray when young; mature tree exfoliates puzzle-like bark exposing orange, tan, gray and brown patches
FLOWER: Small, light green to reddish green flowers in axillary clusters; inconspicuous; blooms late Summer to early Fall
FRUIT: Green or brown, flat, membranous samara seed in middle; distal end clefted or notched; 1/2" long by 1/4" wide; in axillary clusters
FOLIAGE: Alternate, simple, elliptical to ovate and leathery with a simple to (crenate) rounded, serrated, leaf margin; medium to dark green leaves turn yellow-orange to yellow-brown in Fall

REQUIREMENTS & CHARACTERISTICS

GROWTH RATE: Moderate to Fast   **DROUGHT TOLERANCE:** High   **SALT TOLERANCE:** Moderate
SOIL REQUIREMENTS: Well-drained, moist, fertile, humus rich, slightly alkaline to slightly acidic soil; very adaptable to clay, loam or sandy soil
LIGHT REQUIREMENTS: Full sun to part shade
PEST PROBLEMS: Ambrosia beetles, spindle galls, Elm leaf beetle, bagworm, bark beetle, Japanese beetle, black vine weevil, Locust leafminer, Willow leaf weevil, leafroller, webworm, mites Oak spider mite, sawfly, twig pruner, Ash borer, Peach bark borer, Alder lacebug, Elm leafhopper, wooly Apple aphids, scale, white Peach scale and oyster scale
DISEASE PROBLEMS: Oak root rot, bark rot, canker, dieback, *Fusarium, Ganoderma, Hypoxylon*, leaf spot, *Nectria,* nematodes, *Oxyporus*, powdery mildew, *Taphrina, Verticillium* wilt, wetwood, *Alternaria* and witches broom
ENVIRONMENTAL FACTORS: Not tolerant of water-logged planting sites
PRUNING: Minimal pruning needed; remove low hanging limbs and limbs broken due to ice, snow or wind; remove co-dominant leaders and limbs with acute limb crotch angles; prune to distribute the main scaffold limbs into a spiral around the tree's central leader or axis

ADDITIONAL NOTES

USES: Street tree, parking lots, medians, lawn tree, shade tree, planters, specimen, standard or multi-trunk tree
URBAN USES: Very adaptable to different soil types; strong growth in poor planting environments
SUBSTITUTIONS: *Zelkova* cultivars, *Lagerstroemia* cultivars, *Carpinus* cultivars, *Styrax japonica* and cultivars, *Chionanthus retusus, Acer buergerianum* and cultivars
COMMENTS: This tough and easily managed tree has an upright limb habit and is easily transplanted as a ball and burlap tree with high transplant success.
OTHER CULTIVARS: 'Frosty' - old cultivar from England with compact growth, upright crown and creamy, white, variegated leaf serrations, turn dark green when leaves mature; 'Dynasty' - small, compact, dome-shaped crown, 30' tall by 20" wide, very useful under power lines and in urban areas, attractive burgundy-red Fall foliage, samara are reddish pink

Vitex agnus-castus 'Shoal Creek'
Shoal Creek Chastetree
USDA Hardiness Zones: 7b-11

DESCRIPTION

NATIVE HABITAT: Mediterranean region to Central and Western Asia; cultivar of nursery origin

PLANT TYPE: Deciduous, broadleaf, large shrub or small tree

MATURE SIZE: 10-15' tall by 15-20' wide

FORM/SHAPE: Irregular outline, rounded vase-shaped

BARK: Smooth; gray to tan when young; rough, dark gray when very old

FLOWER: Lavender-blue; showy and fragrant; blooms in Spring and Summer; attracts bees

FRUIT: Black; 1/8-3/16" round drupe-like fruit produced after flowers shed from slender racemes

FOLIAGE: Opposite, palmately compound leaves; blue-green to green leaves with no noticeable color change before leaves drop in Fall

LANDSCAPE CHARACTERISTICS

GROWTH RATE: Fast   **DROUGHT TOLERANCE:** High   **SALT TOLERANCE:** Moderate

SOIL REQUIREMENTS: Well-drained, moist, fertile, acidic or alkaline, clay, loam or sandy soil

LIGHT REQUIREMENTS: Full sun to part shade

PEST PROBLEMS: Oleander scale and *Pittosporum* scale

DISEASE PROBLEMS: Leaf spot and root rot

ENVIRONMENTAL FACTORS: May reseed in landscaped areas

PRUNING: Prune to develop strong structure and keep clearance under the canopy when used as a small tree form

ADDITIONAL NOTES

USES: Container or above ground planter, buffer or median strip planting, trainable as a standard specimen and beautiful as a multi-trunk tree

URBAN USES: No proven urban tolerance; good street tree if located away from street edge so that low branches will not impede circulation

SUBSTITUTIONS: *Lagerstroemia* cultivars, *Malus* cultivars, *Prunus* cultivar, *Hibiscus syracus*

COMMENTS: Vitex is used in mixed shrub borders or as a specimen. It is a good choice for a multi-trunk tree or in medians because the tree will not grow too large. In colder climates, severe Winters can cause cold damage dieback.

OTHER CULTIVARS: 'Alba' - white flowers, similar growth habit as species; 'Blushing Spires' - soft pink flowers, compact growth habit; 'Salina's Pink' - medium pink flowers

Zelkova serrata
Green Vase® Zelkova
USDA Hardiness Zones: 5b-8

DESCRIPTION

NATIVE HABITAT: China, Japan, Korea and Taiwan; culitvar of nursery origin

PLANT TYPE: Deciduous, broadleaf, large tree

MATURE SIZE: 50' tall by 40' wide

FORM/SHAPE: Vase-shaped, moderately dense

BARK: Smooth; gray; corky lenticels; with age may develop shallow furrows and exfoliated patches at trunk base

FLOWER: Yellowish green clusters of male flowers separate from female flowers; inconspicuous; blooms in Spring

FRUIT: Small, round, green fruit; inconspicuous; ripens in Fall

FOLIAGE: Alternate, simple, ovate to oblanceolate leaves with serrated margins; green to dark green leaves turn burnt umber to reddish bronze in Fall; very showy Fall color

LANDSCAPE CHARACTERISTICS

GROWTH RATE: Fast   **DROUGHT TOLERANCE:** Moderate to High   **SALT TOLERANCE:** Low

SOIL REQUIREMENTS: Well-drained, moist, fertile, humus rich, slightly acidic to slightly alkaline clay, loam or sandy soil; adaptable to many soil types

LIGHT REQUIREMENTS: Full sun to part shade

PEST PROBLEMS: Scales, Elm leaf beetle, ambrosia beetles, Japanese beetle and Horse Chestnut scale

DISEASE PROBLEMS: Bacterial canker, dieback, leaf spot, *Nectria* and black spot

ENVIRONMENTAL FACTORS: Not tolerant of water-logged, compacted soil; avoid deep planting of root flare; exhibits ozone tolerance; limbs tend to split during wind, ice and snow storms due to acute limb angles and included bark at the trunk and limb junction

PRUNING: Prune to maintain a central leader and spiral limb distribution

ADDITIONAL NOTES

USES: Park plantings, gardens, street tree, parking areas, shade tree and as a specimen tree

URBAN USES: Adaptable to most soil types, but soil must be well-drained

SUBSTITUTIONS: *Zelkova serrata* 'Musashino', *Zelkova serrata* Myrimar®, *Styrax japonica* Snow Cone®, *Quercus robur* 'Fastigiata', *Pyrus calleryana* 'Capital', or *Prunus sargentii* 'Columnaris'

COMMENTS: Good branching structure is crucial to strong development in the Green Vase® Zelkova. Look for trees with branches that are spaced out. Crowns will grow together if planted on 30' centers to form a shaded planting.

OTHER CULTIVARS: 'Village Green' - dark green leaves, spreading crown, fast growing, good cold hardiness; 'Spring Grove' - dark green leaves, upright, vase-shaped, very large, growing 40-80' tall by 40-60' wide, red Fall color; 'Goshiki' - dark green leaves, variegated, with splashes of cream colored markings

Zelkova serrata 'C Creek I'
Gold Falls® Zelkova
USDA Hardiness Zones: 5-8

DESCRIPTION

NATIVE HABITAT: China, Japan, Korea and Taiwan; cultivar of nursery origin
PLANT TYPE: Deciduous, broadleaf, large tree
MATURE SIZE: 30-35' tall by 15-20' wide
FORM/SHAPE: Upright, vase-shaped, weeping inner branches
BARK: Smooth; gray; corky lenticels; with age may develop shallow furrows and exfoliated patches at trunk base
FLOWER: Yellowish green clusters of male flowers separate from female flowers; inconspicuous; blooms in Spring
FRUIT: Small, round, green; inconspicuous; ripens in Fall
FOLIAGE: Alternate, simple, ovate to oblanceolate leaves with serrate margins; green to dark green leaves turn bright yellow in Fall; very showy Fall color

LANDSCAPE CHARACTERISTICS

GROWTH RATE: Moderate   **DROUGHT TOLERANCE:** Moderate to High   **SALT TOLERANCE:** Low
SOIL REQUIREMENTS: Well-drained, moist, fertile, humus rich, slightly acidic to slightly alkaline, clay, loam or sandy soil; adaptable to many soil types
LIGHT REQUIREMENTS: Full sun to part shade
PEST PROBLEMS: Scales, Elm leaf beetle, ambrosia beetles, Japanese beetle and Horse Chestnut scale
DISEASE PROBLEMS: Bacterial canker, dieback, leaf spot, *Nectria* and black spot
ENVIRONMENTAL FACTORS: Not tolerant of water-logged, compacted soil; avoid deep planting of root flare; exhibits ozone tolerance
PRUNING: Can be pruned to maintain a central leader or to create a multi-leader tree; remove low hanging limbs

ADDITIONAL NOTES

USES: Park plantings, gardens, street tree, parking areas and as a specimen tree
URBAN USES: Adaptable to most soil types, but soil must be well-drained
SUBSTITUTIONS: *Zelkova serrata* 'Musashino', *Styrax japonica* Snow Cone®, *Quercus robur* 'Fastigiata', *Pyrus calleryana* 'Capital' or *Prunus sargentii* 'Columnaris'
COMMENTS: Gold Falls® has a unique form with upright main limbs and pendulous, small twigs and branches. Fall foliage is a golden yellow. The narrow, upright form is useful in narrow landscape spaces.
OTHER CULTIVARS: 'Village Green' - dark green leaves, spreading crown, fast growing, good cold hardiness; 'Spring Grove' - dark green leaves, upright, vase-shaped, very large, growing 40-80' tall by 40-60' wide, red Fall color; 'Goshiki' - dark green leaves, variegated, with splashes of cream colored markings

Zelkova serrata 'Musashino'
Musashino Zelkova
USDA Hardiness Zones: 5-9

DESCRIPTION

NATIVE HABITAT: China, Japan, Korea and Taiwan; cultivar of nursery origin
PLANT TYPE: Deciduous, broadleaf, large tree
MATURE SIZE: 45' tall by 15' wide
FORM/SHAPE: Upright, columnar, narrow crowned, vase-shaped
BARK: Smooth; gray; corky lenticels; with age may develop shallow furrows and exfoliated patches at trunk base
FLOWER: Yellowish green clusters of male flowers separate from female flowers; inconspicuous; blooms in Spring
FRUIT: Small, round, green; inconspicuous; ripens in Fall
FOLIAGE: Alternate, simple, ovate to oblanceolate leaves with serrated margins; green to dark green leaves turn bright yellow in Fall; very showy Fall color

LANDSCAPE CHARACTERISTICS

GROWTH RATE: Fast   **DROUGHT TOLERANCE:** Moderate to High   **SALT TOLERANCE:** Low
SOIL REQUIREMENTS: Well-drained, moist, fertile, humus rich, slightly acidic to slightly alkaline, clay, loam or sandy soil; adaptable to many soil types
LIGHT REQUIREMENTS: Full sun to part shade
PEST PROBLEMS: Scales, Elm leaf beetle, ambrosia beetles, Japanese beetle and Horse Chestnut scale
DISEASE PROBLEMS: Bacterial canker, dieback, leaf spot, *Nectria* and black spot
ENVIRONMENTAL FACTORS: Not tolerant of water-logged, compacted soil; avoid deep planting of root flare; exhibits ozone tolerance; limbs tend to split during wind, ice, and snow storms due to acute limb angles and included bark at the trunk and limb junction
PRUNING: Prune to maintain a central leader and to remove low hanging limbs

ADDITIONAL NOTES

USES: Streetscapes, accent and specimen
URBAN USES: Adaptable to most soil types, but soil must be well-drained; where tree crown has limited space; adaptable to narrow planting sites; shape and form allow for good visibility
SUBSTITUTIONS: *Zelkova serrata* 'Musashino', *Styrax japonica* Snow Cone®, *Quercus robur* 'Fastigiata', *Pyrus calleryana* 'Capital' or *Prunus sargentii* 'Columnaris'
COMMENTS: The 'Musashino' Zelkova has a uniquely narrow crown and is useful where space is limited in width but there is a need for vertical height. Proper tree development of the limb and trunk structure is needed to reduce the tendency of crown splitting.
OTHER CULTIVARS: 'Village Green' - dark green leaves, spreading crown, fast growing, good cold hardiness; 'Spring Grove' - dark green leaves, upright, vase-shaped, very large, growing 40-80' tall by 40-60' wide, red Fall color; 'Goshiki' - dark green leaves, variegated, with splashes of cream colored markings

Zelkova serrata 'Village Green'
Village Green Zelkova
USDA Hardiness Zones: 5-8

DESCRIPTION

NATIVE HABITAT: China, Japan, Korea and Taiwan; cultivar of nursery origin
PLANT TYPE: Deciduous, broadleaf, large tree
MATURE SIZE: 50-60' tall by 45-50' wide
FORM/SHAPE: Upright, vase-shaped, spreading
BARK: Smooth; gray; corky lenticels; with age may develop shallow furrows and exfoliated patches at trunk base
FLOWER: Yellowish green clusters of male flowers separate from female flowers; inconspicuous; blooms in Spring
FRUIT: Small, round, green; inconspicuous; ripens in Fall
FOLIAGE: Alternate, simple, ovate to oblanceolate leaves with serrated margins; green to dark green leaves turn bronze-red in Fall; very showy Fall color

LANDSCAPE CHARACTERISTICS

GROWTH RATE: Moderate to Fast   **DROUGHT TOLERANCE:** Moderate to High   **SALT TOLERANCE:** Low
SOIL REQUIREMENTS: Well-drained, moist, fertile, humus rich, slightly acidic to slightly alkaline clay, loam or sandy soil; adaptable to many soil types
LIGHT REQUIREMENTS: Full sun to part shade
PEST PROBLEMS: Scales, Elm leaf beetle, ambrosia beetles, Japanese beetle and Horse Chestnut scale
DISEASE PROBLEMS: Bacterial canker, dieback, leaf spot, *Nectria* and black spot
ENVIRONMENTAL FACTORS: Not tolerant of water-logged, compacted soil; avoid deep planting of root flare; exhibits ozone tolerance; limbs tend to split during wind, ice, and snow storms due to acute limb angles and included bark at the trunk and limb junction
PRUNING: Prune to maintain a central leader and spiral limb distribution; remove low hanging limbs

ADDITIONAL NOTES

USES: Parking lot islands, lawns, streetscapes, shade tree and residential areas
URBAN USES: Successfully grown in urban areas with poor conditions; a good choice for a street or parking lot tree; adaptable to most soil types, but soil must be well-drained
SUBSTITUTIONS: *Zelkova serrata* 'ZSFKF', *Zelkova serrata* 'Spring Grove', *Quercus* species and culitvars, *Lagerstroemia* cultivars, *Acer rubrum* culitvars or *Ulmus* cultivars
COMMENTS: 'Village Green' is a rapidly growing, large tree with dark green leaves and good cold hardiness. It has many years of dependable use in landscape plantings. 'Village Green' Zelkova is a good replacement for American Elm. Good branch structure is crucial to strong development. It is one of the few *Zelkova* cultivars that can be produced on its own roots, instead of grafted .
OTHER CULTIVARS: 'Spring Grove' - dark green leaves, upright, vase-shaped, very large, growing 40-80' tall by 40-60' wide, red Fall color; 'Goshiki' - dark green leaves, variegated, with splashes of cream colored markings

Zelkova serrata 'ZSFKF'
Myrimar® Zelkova
USDA Hardiness Zones: 5-8

DESCRIPTION

NATIVE HABITAT: China, Japan, Korea and Taiwan; cultivar of nursery origin
PLANT TYPE: Deciduous, broadleaf, large tree
MATURE SIZE: 50-60' tall by 40-45' wide
FORM/SHAPE: Broad, vase-shaped
BARK: Smooth; gray; corky lenticels; with age may develop shallow furrows and exfoliated patches at trunk base
FLOWER: Yellowish green clusters of male flowers separate from female flowers; inconspicuous; blooms in Spring
FRUIT: Small, round, green; inconspicuous; ripens in Fall
FOLIAGE: Alternate, simple, ovate to oblanceolate leaves with serrated margins; green to dark green leaves turn bronze- yellow in Fall

LANDSCAPE CHARACTERISTICS

GROWTH RATE: Moderate   **DROUGHT TOLERANCE:** Moderate to High   **SALT TOLERANCE:** Low
SOIL REQUIREMENTS: Well-drained, moist, fertile, humus rich, slightly acidic to slightly alkaline, clay, loam or sandy soil; adaptable to many soil types
LIGHT REQUIREMENTS: Full sun to part shade
PEST PROBLEMS: Scales, Elm leaf beetle, ambrosia beetles, Japanese beetle and Horse Chestnut scale
DISEASE PROBLEMS: Bacterial canker, dieback, leaf spot, *Nectria* and black spot
ENVIRONMENTAL FACTORS: Not tolerant of water-logged, compacted soil; avoid deep planting of root flare; exhibits ozone tolerance
PRUNING: Prune to maintain a central leader and spiral limb distribution; remove low hanging limbs

ADDITIONAL NOTES

USES: Specimen, street tree and parking lots
URBAN USES: Adaptable to most soil types, but soil must be well-drained
SUBSTITUTIONS: *Zelkova serrata* 'Village Green', *Zelkova serrata* 'Spring Grove', *Quercus* species and culitvars, *Lagerstroemia* cultivars, *Acer rubrum* culitvars or *Ulmus* cultivars
COMMENTS: A fibrous root system anchors and nourishes the Myrimar® Zelkova and makes it one of few Zelkovas that grows on its own root stock. This tree has good heat and drought tolerance.
OTHER CULTIVARS: 'Village Green' - dark green leaves, spreading crown, fast growing, good cold hardiness; 'Spring Grove' - dark green leaves, upright, vase-shaped, very large, growing 40-80' tall by 40-60' wide, red Fall color; 'Goshiki' - dark green leaves, variegated, with splashes of cream colored markings

Evergreen Trees

Cedrus deodara
Deodar Cedar
USDA Hardiness Zones: 7-9

DESCRIPTION

NATIVE HABITAT: Afghanistan, Kashmir, Northern India and Western Himalayas
PLANT TYPE: Evergreen, coniferous, short needle-like leaves, large tree
MATURE SIZE: 40-60' tall by 20-30' wide
FORM/SHAPE: Broad, conical when young; irregular, broad, pyramidal as it matures
BARK: Smooth; greenish brown matures to grayish brown; develops fissures and plates with age
FLOWER: Green to brown male cones produce yellow pollen in Fall; greenish female cones with resin; turns brown after two years and sheds in Fall throughout Winter
FRUIT: Green resin coated female cones mature to brown, 3-4" long by 2-3" wide
FOLIAGE: Needle-like leaves 1" long in clusters; needles have three to four flat sides, in cross-section; color ranges from green, blue-green, silver blue-green, powdery blue-green or yellow-green; old inner needles turn yellow to brown and shed in Fall and again in Spring as new growth emerges

LANDSCAPE CHARACTERISTICS

GROWTH RATE: Moderate   **DROUGHT TOLERANCE:** High   **SALT TOLERANCE:** Low to Moderate
SOIL REQUIREMENTS: Well-drained, clay, loam or sandy, well-limed soil; good soil drainage critical for plant survival
LIGHT REQUIREMENTS: Full sun
PEST PROBLEMS: Pine needle scale, pale weevil, bagworm, bowlegged Fir aphid, Deodar weevil, redheaded Pine sawfly, mealybugs and black scale
DISEASE PROBLEMS: *Cylindrocladium* root rot, *Pestalotiopsis*, root rot, Pine wood nematodes and butt rot
ENVIRONMENTAL FACTORS: Not tolerant of water-logged or compacted soil; damaged by late Spring freezes; not tolerant of severe air pollution; requires large area for crown and root growth
PRUNING: Pruning minimal, but maintain a single leader; best when kept limbed to the ground, but can be limbed up if necessary

ADDITIONAL NOTES

USES: Specimen, lawn tree, large screening evergreen, street and median planting only where soil is well-drained
URBAN USES: Not tolerant of severe air pollution, water-logged or compacted soil; very drought tolerant
SUBSTITUTIONS: *Cedrus atlantica* in colder regions, Juniper cultivars, *Calodedrus* species, *Cupressus* cultivars, *Sequoia* cultivars, *Picea* cultivars, *Pinus* cultivars
COMMENTS: Seedling trees of *Cedrus deodara* vary dramatically, but cultivars offer consistent growth and foliage color. Regional selections of cultivars for the Southeastern United States have expanded the use of Deodar Cedar in the landscape. Many cultivars exist including dwarf, weeping, blue foliage, yellow foliage, large growing columnar forms. Own root production allow the tree to be used in all types of landscape settings. Where adaptable, Deodar Cedar is the most graceful conifer for southern landscapes. It does not tolerate smog, and water drainage is critical for plant survival.
OTHER CULTIVARS: 'Aurea' - yellow needles, moderate growth, large tree; 'Bill's Blue' - blue-green foliage, moderate growth, foliage color retained year round; 'Blue Ice' - powder blue foliage color, moderate growth, dense branching, foliage color maintained year round; 'Crystal Falls' - gray-green needles and upright with weeping limb growth; 'Karl Fuchs' - blue-gray foliage, very cold hardy; Patty Faye™ - powder blue, broad, pyramidal, dense form

Cedrus deodara 'BBC'
Bracken's Best Deodar Cedar
USDA Hardiness Zones: 7-9

MATURE SIZE: 40-60' tall by 20-30' wide
FORM/SHAPE: Narrow, pyramidal
FOLIAGE: Gray-green needles; shorter than species; foliage color maintained throughout the year
COMMENTS: Young 'BBC' trees are open, but the plant is a vigorous grower and quickly becomes dense with age. The mature tree is more narrow than other Deodar Cedar cultivars. 'BBC' has a better tolerance of normal *Cedrus* problems.

Cedrus deodara 'Bill's Blue'
Bill's Blue Deodar Cedar
USDA Hardiness Zones: 7-9

MATURE SIZE: 40-60' tall by 20-30' wide
FORM/SHAPE: Pyramidal; maintains broad pyramidal form with age
FOLIAGE: Medium to long, blue-green needles
COMMENTS: 'Bill's Blue' grows vigorously and dense with blue-green foliage maintained throughout the year. Minimal pruning is required to create a dense limb structure. Ascending limb tips helps lessen breakage when tying for digging and transplanting.

Cedrus deodara 'Sander's Blue'
Blue Velvet™ Deodar Cedar
USDA Hardiness Zones: 7-9

MATURE SIZE: 30-40' tall by 20-25' wide
FORM/SHAPE: Broad, open pyramid with drooping limbs; irregular and open in youth; becomes a rounded pyramid with age
FOLIAGE: The most powdery blue foliage of all *C. deodaras*, short needles held in spiral clusters
COMMENTS: The blue foliage of 'Sander's Blue' rivals many blue foliage forms of Blue Spruce. Blue Velvet™ Deodar Cedar is slow growing with open, pendulous limbs. This tree will have a slower growth habit in its southern cold hardiness range.

Cryptomeria japonica 'Yoshino'
Japanese Cedar or Cryptomeria
USDA Hardiness Zones: 6-8

DESCRIPTION

NATIVE HABITAT: China and Japan; cultivar of nursery origin

PLANT TYPE: Evergreen, coniferous, large tree

MATURE SIZE: 40-60' tall by 20-25' wide

FORM/SHAPE: Upright, symmetrical, dense, pyramidal

BARK: Green when young; reddish gray-brown when mature; old bark hangs in ribbons, fibers or strips

FLOWER: Not especially showy; male cones yellowish brown; female cones green turning brown in late Winter to Spring

FRUIT: Spherical female cone, green turning brown; appear in late Winter and remain on plant for several years

FOLIAGE: Spirally arranged on the stem, awl to needle-like; dark green when well fertilized and watered during Summer, light green if water and nutrition are lacking; develops a yellow, copper, bronze color with cold temperatures and Winter sun; old leaves turn brown and remain on the stem

LANDSCAPE CHARACTERISTICS

GROWTH RATE: Moderate to Fast   **DROUGHT TOLERANCE:** Low to Moderate   **SALT TOLERANCE:** Moderate to High

SOIL REQUIREMENTS: Moist, well-drained, sandy, clay or loam soil; adapts to many soil types and fertility levels; soil should have adequate lime; mulch to maintain soil moisture

LIGHT REQUIREMENTS: Full sun to part shade; best in full sun for dense branching and form

PEST PROBLEMS: Mites and bagworm

DISEASE PROBLEMS: No serious problems on older maturing trees, but young plants in nurseries and landscapes with overhead irrigation or poor air circulation show severe needle blight, die back, *Phomopsis*, and root rot; young or old trees may be affected by canker, southern stem blight, root rot, and needle blight

ENVIRONMENTAL FACTORS: Plants with overhead irrigation and poor air circulation may favor diseases; severe windy sites can result in top kill and limb death in Winter; plants over-fertilized, over-watered, and stressed by drought can suffer from bark burst, rot, and decline; heavily shaded conditions favor needle blight

PRUNING: Pruning not normally needed, but heavy pruning should occur in early Spring before new growth emerges; avoid pruning during Summer

ADDITIONAL NOTES

USES: Specimen tree, large, tall screen or hedge and background for other landscape and structural features

URBAN USES: Good adaptability to urban conditions; allow enough space for mature size; provide good soil preparation and irrigation

SUBSTITUTIONS: 'Green Giant' Arborvitae, Leyland Cypress, *Picea abies*, *Tsuga canadensis*, *Ilex* species and cultivars

COMMENTS: 'Yoshino' is a popular evergreen conifer tree for replacing Leyland Cypress. Cryptomeria tolerates part shade to full sun and exhibits good disease resistance and insect tolerance. A much better tree than Leyland Cypress. Winter bronzing will be less noticed when 'Yoshino' is well-fertilized and grown in part shade.

OTHER CULTIVARS: 'Ben Franklin' - shows better cold hardiness and reported to have good salt tolerance; 'Kitayama' - is more cold hardy than most; 'Sekkan Sugi' - golden tipped foliage needing full sun for best color, tips will winter burn; 'Winter Mint' - more compact

Cryptomeria japonica var. sinensis 'Radicans'
Radicans Cryptomeria
USDA Hardiness Zones: 6-9

DESCRIPTION

NATIVE HABITAT: China and Japan; cultivar of nursery origin

PLANT TYPE: Evergreen, coniferous, large tree

MATURE SIZE: 30-40' tall by 10-15' wide

FORM/SHAPE: Narrow, pyramidal, dense crown

BARK: Green when young; reddish gray-brown when mature; old bark hangs in ribbons, fibers or strips

FLOWER: Not especially showy; male cones yellowish brown; female cones green turning brown in late Winter to Spring

FRUIT: Spherical, green female cone turns brown; appears in late Winter and remain on the plant for several years

FOLIAGE: Spirally arranged on the stem; awl to needle-like; dark bluish green when well-fertilized and watered during Summer, light green if water and nutrition are lacking; foliage color does not bronze with cold temperatures and Winter sun; old leaves turn brown and remain on the stem

LANDSCAPE CHARACTERISTICS

GROWTH RATE: Moderate   **DROUGHT TOLERANCE:** Low to Moderate   **SALT TOLERANCE:** Moderate to High

SOIL REQUIREMENTS: Moist, well-drained, sandy, clay or loam soil; adapts to many soil types and fertility levels; soil should have adequate lime; mulch to maintain soil moisture

LIGHT REQUIREMENTS: Full sun to part shade; best in full sun for dense branching and form

PEST PROBLEMS: Mites and bagworm

DISEASE PROBLEMS: No serious problems on older maturing trees, but young plants in nurseries and landscapes with overhead irrigation or poor air circulation show some needle blight, dieback, *Phomopsis*, and root rot; young or old trees may be affected by canker, southern stem blight, root rot and needle blight

ENVIRONMENTAL FACTORS: Plants with overhead irrigation and poor air circulation may favor diseases; severe windy sites can result in top kill and limb death in Winter; not tolerant of prolonged drought stress

PRUNING: Pruning not normally needed, but heavy pruning should occur in early Spring before new growth emerges; avoid pruning during the Summer

ADDITIONAL NOTES

USES: Specimen tree, large tall screen or hedge and background for other landscape and structural features

URBAN USES: Good adaptability to urban conditions; allow enough space for mature size, provide good soil preparation and irrigation

SUBSTITUTIONS: 'Green Giant' Arborvitae, Leyland Cypress, *Picea abies, Tsuga canadensis, Ilex* species and cultivars, *Thuja plicata* 'Clemson Select', *Juniper* cultivars

COMMENTS: 'Radicans' Cryptomeria is of the Chinese (*sinensis syn. fortunei*) forms exhibiting a more coarse, loose plant habit, slender shape and is considered more cold hardy. 'Radicans' show less Winter bronzing with a small maturing height and less disease problems.

OTHER CULTIVARS: 'Tarheel Blue' - very blue-green foliage, very loose, open plant habit, Winter color rusty-plum; 'Yakusugi' - loose, open habit, silvery blue-green foliage, needles are more spiny; 'Kitayama' - dark, bright green foliage, narrow, pyramidal form, more cold hardy; 'Purple Sentinel' - dark green foliage, open pyramidal growth, Winter color is plum-purple with cold temperatures and full sun

Cupressus arizonica var. glabra 'Carolina Sapphire'
Carolina Sapphire Arizona Cypress
USDA Hardiness Zones: 7-9

DESCRIPTION

NATIVE HABITAT: Regions of Arizona, New Mexico and Northern Mexico; cultivar of nursery origin
PLANT TYPE: Evergreen, coniferous, large tree
MATURE SIZE: 25-30' tall by 15-20' wide
FORM/SHAPE: Broad, pyramidal
BARK: Smooth, peeling bark; gray-green to reddish brown; blistering and exfoliating in thin plates
FLOWER: Produces male and female cones; male cones yellowish brown; female cones bluish gray-green; matures in two years; appears Winter through Spring
FRUIT: Small, fleshy, female cone; dry, woody, scale-like, male cone
FOLIAGE: Opposite, scale-like needles; bluish gray-green; foliage covers the twigs and branches for two growing seasons before shedding; older inner foliage turns yellow to brown and gradually sheds as the bark develops

LANDSCAPE CHARACTERISTICS

GROWTH RATE: Fast   **DROUGHT TOLERANCE:** High   **SALT TOLERANCE:** Moderate
SOIL REQUIREMENTS: Well-drained, sandy-clay, loam to clay soil; should be well-limed
LIGHT REQUIREMENTS: Full sun; not tolerant of shade
PEST PROBLEMS: Cypress sawfly, bagworm, mites, leaf miner, Cypress tipminer, Juniper scale, cottony Cypress scale, Cypress bark scale, mealybugs and cottony cushion scale
DISEASE PROBLEMS: Root rot, dieback, canker, *Phomopsis*, *Seiridium* canker, *Pestalotiopsis* and *Cercospora*
ENVIRONMENTAL FACTORS: Multi-leader or co-dominant leaders in trees are prone to splitting from wind, ice or snow; not tolerant of shade or poorly drained soil
PRUNING: Prune to maintain good structure; should be grown with a strong central leader; trees with co-dominant leaders are prone to splitting of the tree crown

ADDITIONAL NOTES

USES: Large screens, specimen plant, group plantings with other plants, large containers in USDA Hardiness Zones 7b-9 and as a sheared Christmas tree
URBAN USES: Good adaptability to dry climates; needs plenty of space for wide limb spread
SUBSTITUTIONS: *Cupressus arizonica var. glabra* 'Silver Smoke', 'Blue Ice', 'Blue Pyramid' and 'Clemson Green Spire', *Juniperus silicicola* 'Brodie', *Juniperus virginiana* 'Burkii' and *Thuja occidentalis* 'Degroot's Spire', 'Emerald', 'Zmatlic'
COMMENTS: *Cupressus arizonica var. glabra* is synonymous with *Cupressus glabra*. Cultivars of *Cupressus arizonica* are a better choice than seedling trees because of the high variability in plant form, foliage color, cold tolerance and tolerance to insects and diseases. 'Carolina Sapphire' is a strongly rooted tree that resists blowing over in windy conditions.
OTHER CULTIVARS: 'Blue Pyramid' - broad, upright tree, powder blue foliage, reddish brown bark, USDA Hardiness Zone 6; 'Golden Pyramid' - narrow, pyramidal form, horizontal branch arrangement, golden yellow foliage, 20' tall by 6-8' wide, USDA Hardiness Zone 7; 'Silver Smoke' - narrow, pyramidal form, silver to blue-green foliage, reddish brown bark, 20' tall by 6-8' wide, USDA Hardiness Zone 6

Cupressus sempervirens
Italian Cypress or Mediterranean Cypress
USDA Hardiness Zones: 7-9

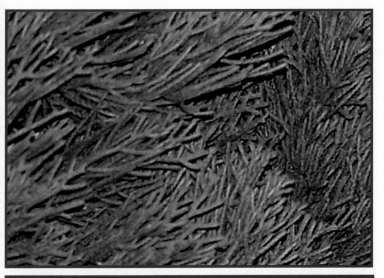

DESCRIPTION

NATIVE HABITAT: Mediterranean region and Western Asia
PLANT TYPE: Evergreen, coniferous, large tree
MATURE SIZE: 40-60' tall by 3-6' wide
FORM/SHAPE: Upright, very narrow, columnar
BARK: Brownish gray forming fibrous strips of peeling bark; matures to thin plates with fissures and ridges
FLOWER: Green to yellow-green; inconspicuous; blooms in Spring
FRUIT: Oval cones; 1/2"-1" long; whitish green in Summer; brown in Fall
FOLIAGE: Simple, scale-like, whorled around stem, grows on the branchlets like tiles; bright green to dark green in Summer; dark green in Winter; old leaves turn brown on interior of plant in Winter

LANDSCAPE CHARACTERISTICS

GROWTH RATE: Moderate   **DROUGHT TOLERANCE:** High   **SALT TOLERANCE:** Moderate to High
SOIL REQUIREMENTS: Well-drained, sandy, clay or loam soil; should be well-limed
LIGHT REQUIREMENTS: Full sun; not tolerant of shade
PEST PROBLEMS: Cypress sawfly, bagworm, mites, leaf miner, Cypress tipminer, Juniper scale, cottony Cypress scale, Cypress bark scale, mealybugs and cottony cushion scale
DISEASE PROBLEMS: Root rot, dieback, canker, *Phomopsis*, *Seiridium* canker, *Pestalotiopsis* and *Cercospora*
ENVIRONMENTAL FACTORS: Not tolerant of shade or poorly drained soil; multi-leader or co-dominant leaders of trees are prone to split from wind, ice or snow
PRUNING: Prune to keep good structure; should be grown with a strong central leader; trees with co-dominant leaders are prone to splitting of the tree crown

ADDITIONAL NOTES

USES: Framing for large buildings, screens, accent around tall buildings, avenues, specimen plant, large containers in the warmer USDA Hardiness Zones 8-9
URBAN USES: Good adaptability to dry climate regions and where limited spaces require a tall, narrow tree
SUBSTITUTIONS: *Juniperus silicicola* 'Brodie', *Juniperus virginiana* 'Idyllwild', *Thuja occidentalis* 'Degroot's Spire', *Thuja occidentalis* 'Emerald', *Thuja occidentalis* 'Zmatlic', *Ilex crenata* 'Sky Pencil', *Juniperus scopulorum* 'Skyrocket'
COMMENTS: Several cultivars may be known by the same name such as 'Green Spire', 'Fastigiata' or 'Stricta' and some may be seedling with variable plant habit. Young plants can be injured by cold while other plants, or those in protected planting sites, show no damage. In humid climate regions, diseases and scales are more problematic.
OTHER CULTIVARS: 'Gracillis' - narrow, compact, columnar form; 'Green Pencil' syn. 'Green Spire' - slender, columnar form, bright green foliage and reported to be more cold hardy

Eriobotrya japonica
Loquat
USDA Hardiness Zones: 8-10

DESCRIPTION

NATIVE HABITAT: China and Japan

PLANT TYPE: Evergreen, broadleaf, small tree or large shrub

MATURE SIZE: 15-20' tall by 12-15' wide

FORM/SHAPE: Upright, rounded and spreading

BARK: Young stems are green and downy; older stems brownish gray with exfoliating flakes and plates

FLOWER: White; small, 5" long panicles; very showy; appear from November to December; attracts insects

FRUIT: Yellow; obovate to oblong shaped, edible fruit; 1-2"; develop by Spring; attracts insects and wildlife

FOLIAGE: Alternate, simple, 6-10" long, oval-oblong shape; coarsely serrate to dentate leaf margins; dark green, downy leaves; old leaves turn yellow-green in Fall and shed as new growth begins in Spring

LANDSCAPE CHARACTERISTICS

GROWTH RATE: Fast   **DROUGHT TOLERANCE:** Moderate   **SALT TOLERANCE:** Moderate

SOIL REQUIREMENTS: Moist, well-drained, loam soil; adaptable to coastal and beach soil with high pH

LIGHT REQUIREMENTS: Sun to light shade

PEST PROBLEMS: Ambrosia beetles, cottony cushion scale, latania scale, leaf-footed bug, carpenter worm, Dogwood borer and greedy scale

DISEASE PROBLEMS: Anthracnose, fireblight, Oak root rot, canker, dieback, leaf spot, root rot, southern stem blight and fruit scab

ENVIRONMENTAL FACTORS: Not tolerant of exposure to severe wind and water-logged or flooded soil

PRUNING: Prune to establish good structure and preferred shape; can be trained to be tree-form or espaliered

ADDITIONAL NOTES

USES: Specimen with tropical look, espalier, container planting with Winter protection and fruiting plant in warmer regions

URBAN USES: Used in warm climate regions and in micro-climate planting areas in and around urban buildings

SUBSTITUTIONS: In tropical regions many large leaf plants may be substituted for Loquat; in colder regions substitute *Magnolia grandiflora* cultivars, *Viburnum* cultivars, *Daphniphyllum*, *Rhododendron*

COMMENTS: Plant Loquat in micro-climates and protected areas in and around buildings for best survival in colder regions. Insects are problematic in microclimate planting areas due to warm, dry conditions. The fruit and flower are killed by freezing temperatures in colder regions.

OTHER CULTIVARS: Most plants in commerce are seed grown; some cultivars selected for fruit quality or foliage variegation

Ilex cornuta 'Burfordii'
Burford Holly
USDA Hardiness Zones: 6b-9

DESCRIPTION

NATIVE HABITAT: Species of China and Korea; cultivar of nursery origin
PLANT TYPE: Evergreen, broadleaf, large shrub to small tree; female
MATURE SIZE: 15-25' tall by 15-25' wide
FORM/SHAPE: Rounded, dense, thick crown; can be trained as a vase-shaped, multi-stemmed small tree
BARK: Smooth; gray; showy when plant is limbed up; trunk should be protected because of thin bark
FLOWER: White; somewhat showy; fragrant; blooms in Spring; attracts bees and other insects
FRUIT: Large, bright, red, berries; long lasting and persistent through Fall and Winter; good fruiter; attracts birds and can become a litter problem; can set fruit without a male pollenator
FOLIAGE: Alternate, simple, oblong, single spined, 2-4" long; leaves remain glossy, dark green in Fall; old inner foliage turns yellow and sheds through Winter and into Spring when new growth emerges

LANDSCAPE CHARACTERISTICS

GROWTH RATE: Moderate to Fast   **DROUGHT TOLERANCE:** Moderate to High   **SALT TOLERANCE:** Moderate to High
SOIL REQUIREMENTS: Well-drained, moist, fertile, humus rich, slightly acidic soil; very adaptable to many soil types and fertility levels
LIGHT REQUIREMENTS: Full sun; tolerates part shade, but it may limit flower and berry production
PEST PROBLEMS: Ambrosia beetles, Holly pit scale, leaf miner, aphids, native Holly leafminer, tea scale, Japanese weevil, gypsy moth, spider mites, Holly bud moth, cambium miner, mealybugs, Oleander scale, wax scale, Florida wax scale, cottony cushion scale, *Euonymus* scale, Cranberry rootworm, whitefly; mice and rabbits feed on bark
DISEASE PROBLEMS: *Alternaria*, blight, canker, butt rot, black root rot, dieback, nematodes, leaf spot, *Nectria*, tar spot, sap wood rot, *Hypoxylon*, powdery mildew and algal leaf spot
ENVIRONMENTAL FACTORS: Not tolerant of water-logged soil, excessively dry soil or alkaline soil conditions; heavy bloom production attracts bees and other insects; heavy berry production attracts flocks of birds and other animals; avoid pedestrian areas
PRUNING: Prune to develop shape, density and to control size; tolerant of severe pruning; best to prune heavily in late Winter to early Spring before new growth emerges; avoid pruning in Fall; can be grown in multi-stem form; best kept when limbed to the ground

ADDITIONAL NOTES

USES: Container or planter, espalier, hedge or screen, parking lots, wildlife habitat, lawn tree, buffer strips, residential plantings and urban areas
URBAN USES: Very adaptable to urban environments; tolerant of air pollutants, compacted soil and common drought stresses; diseases and insects may be problematic in urban micro-climates
SUBSTITUTIONS: *Ilex cornuta* 'Burfordii Nana', *Ilex cornuta* 'Fine Line', *Osmanthus* cultivars, *Viburnum* cultivars
COMMENTS: Typically pruned into formal hedge plantings, Burford Holly is also ideal for unpruned natural plantings because of its graceful drooping branches. The plant is popular as a multi-stemmed small tree and should be used more in this form. Burford Holly is a great plant choice for low maintenance landscapes as long as plenty of space is allotted for the plant to reach its mature size.
OTHER CULTIVARS: 'Needle Point' - narrow, wavy leaf, compact, upright form, heavy berry production

Ilex cornuta 'Needle Point'
Needle Point Holly
USDA Hardiness Zones: 6b-9

DESCRIPTION

NATIVE HABITAT: Seedling selection of *Ilex cornuta*
PLANT TYPE: Evergreen, broadleaf, large shrub to small tree; female
MATURE SIZE: 15' tall by 10-15' wide
FORM/SHAPE: Conical in youth; broader when mature
BARK: Smooth; gray; showy when plant is limbed up
FLOWER: Dull white; small; blooms late March to April; attracts bees and insects
FRUIT: Vivid, bright red berries; persistent through Winter; good fruiter; attracts insects, birds and animals
FOLIAGE: Alternate, simple, oblong to rectangular, single spined; dark green leaves with a yellow-green underside; old inner foliage turns yellow and begins to shed in Fall and again in Spring when new growth emerges

LANDSCAPE CHARACTERISTICS

GROWTH RATE: Moderate   **DROUGHT TOLERANCE:** Moderate   **SALT TOLERANCE:** Moderate to High
SOIL REQUIREMENTS: Well-drained, moist, fertile, humus rich, slightly acidic soil; very adaptable to many soil types and fertility levels
LIGHT REQUIREMENTS: Full sun; tolerates part shade, but it may limit flower and berry production
PEST PROBLEMS: Ambrosia beetles, Holly pit scale, leaf miner, aphids, native Holly leafminer, tea scale, Japanese weevil, gypsy moth, spider mites, Holly bud moth, cambium miner, mealybugs, Oleander scale, wax scale, Florida wax scale, cottony cushion scale, *Euonymus* scale, Cranberry rootworm, whitefly; mice and rabbits feed on bark
DISEASE PROBLEMS: *Alternaria*, blight, canker, butt rot, black root rot, dieback, nematodes, leaf spot, *Nectria*, tar spot, sap wood rot, *Hypoxylon*, powdery mildew and algal leaf spot
ENVIRONMENTAL FACTORS: Not tolerant of water-logged soil, excessively dry soil, or alkaline soil conditions; heavy bloom production attracts bees and other insects; heavy berry production attracts flocks of birds and other animals; avoid pedestrian areas
PRUNING: Prune to develop shape, density and to control size; tolerant of severe pruning; best to heavily prune in late Winter to early Spring before new growth emerges; avoid pruning in Fall; can be grown in multi-stem form; best kept when limbed to the ground

ADDITIONAL NOTES

USES: Screen, mass or group planting, hedges, wildlife habitat, single trunk or multi-trunk form and specimen plant
URBAN USES: Very adaptable to urban environments; moderately tolerant of air pollutants; diseases and insects may be problematic in urban micro-climates
SUBSTITUTIONS: *Ilex cornuta* 'Burfordii Nana', *Ilex cornuta* 'Fine Line', *Osmanthus* cultivars, *Viburnum* cultivars
COMMENTS: The plant is also known as *Ilex cornuta syn.* 'Anicet Delcambre' and *Ilex cornuta syn.* 'Willow Leaf'. 'Needlepoint' is great for low maintenance landscapes, screening and mass plantings. This plant is a heavy berry producer.
OTHER CULTIVARS: 'Burfordii Nana' - compact, dome-shaped, red fruit; 'Fine Line' - compact, upright shape, red fruit; 'D'Or' - slow growing 'Burfordii' type with yellow berries; 'Sunrise' - slow growing 'Burfordii' type, overlayed bright yellow, olive-green leaves, bright, light red berries

Ilex opaca 'Croonenburg'
Croonenburg American Holly
USDA Hardiness Zones: 5-9

DESCRIPTION

NATIVE HABITAT: Eastern United States; culitvar of garden origin
PLANT TYPE: Evergreen, broadleaf, large tree; female
MATURE SIZE: 15-30' tall by 10-20' wide
FORM/SHAPE: Compact, pyramidal to columnar
BARK: Smooth; tannish gray; matures to smooth, dark gray
FLOWER: Greenish white; inconspicuous; fragrant; attracts insects
FRUIT: Bright, vividly, red berries; 1/4-3/8" in diameter; very showy in Fall through Winter; attracts wildlife
FOLIAGE: Alternate, simple, wavy leaves; less spiny than species; deep, glossy green ovate foliage; old inner foliage turns yellow to yellow-green and sheds in Spring when new growth emerges

LANDSCAPE CHARACTERISTICS

GROWTH RATE: Moderate   **DROUGHT TOLERANCE:** Moderate to High   **SALT TOLERANCE:** Moderate
SOIL REQUIREMENTS: Well-drained, moist, fertile, humus rich, slightly acidic soil; very adaptable to many soil types and fertility levels; tolerant of short duration flooding during dormant season
LIGHT REQUIREMENTS: Full sun to part shade; best plant form, flower and fruit set in full sun
PEST PROBLEMS: Ambrosia beetles, Holly pit scale, leafminer, aphids, native Holly leaf miner, tea scale, Japanese weevil, gypsy moth, spider mites, Holly bud moth, cambium miner, mealybugs, Oleander scale, wax scale, Florida wax scale, cottony cushion scale, *Euonymus* scale, Cranberry rootworm, whitefly; mice and rabbits feed on bark
DISEASE PROBLEMS: *Alternaria*, blight, canker, butt rot, black root rot, cankers, dieback, root rot, nematodes, leaf spot, *Nectria*, tar spot, sap wood rot, *Hypoxylon*, powdery mildew and algal leaf spot
ENVIRONMENTAL FACTORS: Not tolerant of water-logged soil, excessively dry soil or alkaline pH conditions; heavy bloom production attracts bees and other insects; heavy berry production will attract flocks of birds and other animals; avoid using in pedestrian areas
PRUNING: Prune to develop shape, density and control size; tolerant of severe pruning; heavy pruning is best done in late Winter to early Spring before new growth emerges; avoid pruning in Fall; can be grown in a multi-stem or standard form; best kept when limbed to the ground

ADDITIONAL NOTES

USES: Hedges, parking lot islands, lawn tree, buffer strip plantings, screening, reclamation plantings, residential street tree, naturalizing and planted for wildlife habitat
URBAN USES: Tolerant of air pollutants, poorly drained, compacted soil and moderate drought stresses
SUBSTITUTIONS: *Ilex opaca* 'Carolina No. 2', *Ilex opaca* 'Christmas Tree' or *Ilex opaca* 'Dan Fenton'
COMMENTS: 'Croonenburg' is a heavy fruiting cultivar of American Holly with faster and more compact growth than the species. It is reported to produce some male flowers along with many female flowers, ensuring annual fruit sets.
OTHER CULTIVARS: 'Carolina No. 2' - red fruit, dark green leaves are ovate with two to six spines on upper half of leaf, broad pyramidal to dome-shaped plant form; 'Dan Fenton' - red fruit, dark, glossy green leaves are ovate to elliptical with wavy margins, twelve to sixteen spines, a strong grower that keeps a dominant central leader

Ilex vomitoria
Yaupon Holly
USDA Hardiness Zones: 7-9

DESCRIPTION

NATIVE HABITAT: Eastern North America through Southern United States
PLANT TYPE: Evergreen, broadleaf, small tree or large shrub
MATURE SIZE: 15-25' tall by 15-20' wide
FORM/SHAPE: Upright, spreading, rounded, vase-shaped crown
BARK: Smooth; gray when mature; twigs green to purple
FLOWER: White; inconspicuous; blooms in Spring; attracts bees
FRUIT: Female plants produce red berries; showy Fall through Winter;
1/4-3/8" in diameter; pollinated by *Ilex vomitoria* male forms or cultivars; attracts wildlife
FOLIAGE: Alternate, simple, crenate, ovate, less than 2" long; dark, green to gray-green, leathery leaves

LANDSCAPE CHARACTERISTICS

GROWTH RATE: Moderate   **DROUGHT TOLERANCE:** High   **SALT TOLERANCE:** High
SOIL REQUIREMENTS: Well-drained, moist, fertile, humus rich, acidic to slightly alkaline soil
LIGHT REQUIREMENTS: Full sun; tolerates part shade, but it may limit flower and berry production
PEST PROBLEMS: Ambrosia beetles, Holly pit scale, leaf miner, aphids, native Holly leafminer, tea scale, Japanese weevil, gypsy moth, spider mites, Holly bud moth, cambium miner, mealybugs, Oleander scale, wax scale, Florida wax scale, cottony cushion scale, *Euonymus* scale, Cranberry rootworm, whitefly; mice and rabbits feed on bark
DISEASE PROBLEMS: *Alternaria*, blight, canker, butt rot, black root rot, dieback, nematodes, leaf spot, *Nectria*, tar spot, sap wood rot, *Hypoxylon*, powdery mildew and algal leaf spot
ENVIRONMENTAL FACTORS: Not tolerant of water-logged soil, excessively dry soil or very alkaline soil conditions; heavy bloom production attracts bees and other insects; heavy berry production attracts flocks of birds and other animals; avoid pedestrian areas; plants sprout easily from roots and produces shoots at the base of the plant
PRUNING: Requires little pruning for a strong structure; prune to develop shape, density and to control size; tolerant of severe pruning; best to heavily prune in late Winter to early Spring before new growth emerges, avoid pruning in Fall; can be grown in multi-stem form; best kept when limbed to the ground; remove root sucker growth to maintain neat appearance

ADDITIONAL NOTES

USES: Container or planter, topiary, espaliered, hedge, lawn tree, parking lots, buffer strips, accent near deck or patios, residential foundation plantings, streetscapes, reclamation and wildlife habitat
URBAN USES: Successfully grown in urban areas; tolerates compacted soil, air pollutants, poor drainage and drought stresses
SUBSTITUTIONS: *Ilex vomitoria* cultivars, *Loropetalum* cultivars, *Osmanthus* cultivars
COMMENTS: This is a tough native plant of the Southern United States that grows in various conditions and locations. The crowns grow thin in shade. It is tolerant of drought and coastal conditions and will seed itself in the landscape. Cultivars are a better choice for low maintenance areas.
OTHER CULTIVARS: 'Dodd's Suspensa' - red fruit, upright, weeping form, dark olive-green leaves; 'Hoskin Shadow' - red fruit, compact spreading form, large, dark green, round-ovate leaves, cold hardy; 'Kathy Ann' - red fruit, multi-stemmed, upright spreading form, large, dark green round-elliptical leaves

Ilex vomitoria 'Pendula'
Weeping Yaupon Holly
USDA Hardiness Zones: 7-9

DESCRIPTION

NATIVE HABITAT: Eastern North America through Southern United States; cultivar of nursery origin
PLANT TYPE: Evergreen, broadleaf, weeping, narrow to spreading, large shrub to small tree
MATURE SIZE: 15-30' tall by 8-20' wide
FORM/SHAPE: Upright, weeping, open, irregularly outlined crown
BARK: Smooth; gray bark; branches droop as tree grows
FLOWER: White; inconspicuous; blooms in Spring
FRUIT: Female cultivars have round, fleshy, red berries if pollinated by *Ilex vomitoria* forms on male cultivars; showy Fall through Winter; attracts wildlife
FOLIAGE: Alternate, simple, crenate, ovate, less than 2" long; dark green or gray-green leathery leaves

LANDSCAPE CHARACTERISTICS

GROWTH RATE: Slow to Moderate   **DROUGHT TOLERANCE:** Moderate to High   **SALT TOLERANCE:** High
SOIL REQUIREMENTS: Well-drained, moist, fertile, humus rich, acidic to slightly alkaline soil
LIGHT REQUIREMENTS: Full sun; tolerates part shade, but it may limit flower and berry production
PEST PROBLEMS: Ambrosia beetles, Holly pit scale, leaf miner, aphids, native Holly leafminer, tea scale, Japanese weevil, gypsy moth, spider mites, Holly bud moth, cambium miner, mealybugs, Oleander scale, wax scale, Florida wax scale, cottony cushion scale, *Euonymus* scale, Cranberry rootworm, whitefly; mice and rabbits feed on bark
DISEASE PROBLEMS: *Alternaria*, blight, canker, butt rot, black root rot, dieback, nematodes, leaf spot, *Nectria*, tar spot, sap wood rot, *Hypoxylon*, powdery mildew and algal leaf spot
ENVIRONMENTAL FACTORS: Not tolerant of water-logged soil, excessively dry soil or very alkaline soil conditions; heavy bloom production attracts bees and other insects; heavy berry production attracts flocks of birds and other animals; avoid pedestrian areas; plant sprouts easily from roots and produces shoots at the base of the plant
PRUNING: Requires little pruning for a strong structure; prune to develop shape, density and to control size; tolerant of severe pruning; best to heavily prune in late Winter to early Spring before new growth emerges, avoid pruning in Fall; can be grown in multi-stem form; best kept when limbed to the ground; remove root sucker growth to maintain neat appearance; prune to allow for vehicular or pedestrian circulation

ADDITIONAL NOTES

USES: Container or planter, specimen, median strips and lawn tree
URBAN USES: Good choice for urban areas; tolerates air pollutants, compacted soil and common drought stresses
SUBSTITUTIONS: *Ilex vomitoria* cultivars, *Loropetalum* cultivars, weeping forms of *Picea*, *Tsuga* and *Pinus*
COMMENTS: Seedlings of *Ilex vomitoria* 'Pendula' will be a male or female plants. Weeping Yaupon Holly is often used as an accent or specimen due to its unusual form. It can be used as a screen in full sun if planted 8-10' on center. Weeping Yaupon Holly performs well when used in urban areas due to its tolerance of harsh, urban conditions.
OTHER CULTIVARS: 'Dodd's Suspensa' - red fruit, upright, weeping form, dark olive-green leaves; 'Folsom's Weeping' - red fruit, upright, weeping habit, cultivar name may apply to female and male cultivars

Ilex x 'Emily Bruner'
Emily Bruner Holly
USDA Hardiness Zones: 7-9

DESCRIPTION

NATIVE HABITAT: Hybrid of two Asian species
(*Ilex cornuta* and *Ilex latifolia*); cultivar of garden origin
PLANT TYPE: Evergreen, broadleaf, large shrub to small tree; female
MATURE SIZE: 20' tall by 15' wide
FORM/SHAPE: Broad, dense, pyramidal form that rounds out with age
BARK: Smooth; light gray; showy feature when limbed up into a small multi-trunk tree
FLOWER: White; blooms in Spring; attracts bees and other insects
FRUIT: Clusters of red berries that fade to a dull red; berries encircle the stems; showy Fall through Winter; attracts insects, birds and animals
FOLIAGE: Alternate, simple, glossy, spiny; oblong to ovate, slightly wavy and twisted; dark green color; old inner foliage turns yellow and begins to shed in Fall and again once new growth emerges in the Spring

LANDSCAPE CHARACTERISTICS

GROWTH RATE: Moderate   **DROUGHT TOLERANCE:** Moderate   **SALT TOLERANCE:** Moderate
SOIL REQUIREMENTS: Well-drained, moist, fertile, humus rich, slightly acidic soil; very adaptable to many soil types and fertility levels
LIGHT REQUIREMENTS: Full sun; tolerates part shade, but it may limit flower and berry production
PEST PROBLEMS: Ambrosia beetles, Holly pit scale, leaf miner, aphids, native Holly leafminer, tea scale, Japanese weevil, gypsy moth, spider mites, Holly bud moth, cambium miner, mealybugs, Oleander scale, wax scale, Florida wax scale, cottony cushion scale, *Euonymus* scale, Cranberry rootworm, whitefly; mice and rabbits feed on bark
DISEASE PROBLEMS: *Alternaria*, blight, canker, butt rot, black root rot, dieback, nematodes, leaf spot, *Nectria*, tar spot, sap wood rot, *Hypoxylon*, powdery mildew and algal leaf spot
ENVIRONMENTAL FACTORS: Not tolerant of water-logged soil, excessively dry soil or alkaline soil conditions; heavy bloom production attracts bees and other insects; heavy berry production attracts flocks of birds and other animals; avoid pedestrian areas
PRUNING: Prune to develop shape, density and to control size; tolerant of severe pruning; best to heavily prune in late Winter to early Spring before new growth emerges; avoid pruning in Fall; can be grown in multi-stem form; best kept when limbed to the ground

ADDITIONAL NOTES

USES: Screening, buffer strips, specimen plant, hedges, wildlife habitat, single trunk or multi-trunk form
URBAN USES: Very adaptable to urban environments, moderately tolerant of air pollutants; diseases and insects may be problematic in urban micro-climates
SUBSTITUTIONS: *Ilex* cultivars, *Magnolia grandiflora* cultivars, *Osmanthus* cultivars, *Viburnum* cultivars
COMMENTS: Emily Bruner Holly is a great choice for screen and border plantings. The plant has a beautiful and showy berry display.
OTHER CULTIVARS: 'Ginny Bruner' - smaller leaf, good fruit set with red berries on young plants; 'James Swan' - smaller leaf, male cultivar; 'Bob Bruner' - smaller leaf, male cultivar

Ilex x 'HL10-90' PP 14,477
Christmas Jewel® Holly
USDA Hardiness Zones: 6-9

DESCRIPTION

NATIVE HABITAT: Seedling selection of *Ilex pernyi;* cultivar of nursery origin
PLANT TYPE: Evergreen, broadleaf, large shrub
MATURE SIZE: 8-10' tall by 4-6' wide
FORM/SHAPE: Upright, columnar to compact, pyramidal
BARK: Smooth; green bark on twigs, matures to tannish gray
FLOWER: Abundant greenish white; inconspicuous; blooms late March to April; attracts bees and other insects
FRUIT: Deep, vivid red berries; showy Fall through Winter; attracts insects, birds and animals
FOLIAGE: Alternate, simple, small, narrow leaves with five to seven blunt spines; lustrous dark green; old inner foliage turns yellow-green and begins to shed in Fall and once again as new growth emerges in Spring

LANDSCAPE CHARACTERISTICS

GROWTH RATE: Slow to Moderate   **DROUGHT TOLERANCE:** Moderate to High   **SALT TOLERANCE:** Moderate to High
SOIL REQUIREMENTS: Well-drained, moist, fertile, humus rich, slightly acidic soil; very adaptable to many soil types and fertility levels
LIGHT REQUIREMENTS: Full sun; tolerates part shade and keeps dense foliage, but it may limit flower and berry production
PEST PROBLEMS: Common Holly pests are not serious, but can be affected by ambrosia beetles, Holly pit scale, leaf miner, aphids, native Holly leafminer, tea scale, Japanese weevil, gypsy moth, spider mites, Holly bud moth, cambium miner, mealybugs, Oleander scale, wax scale, Florida wax scale, cottony cushion scale, *Euonymus* scale, Cranberry rootworm, whitefly; mice and rabbits feed on bark
DISEASE PROBLEMS: *Alternaria*, blight, canker, butt rot, black root rot, dieback, nematodes, leaf spot, *Nectria*, tar spot, sap wood rot, *Hypoxylon*, powdery mildew and algal leaf spot
ENVIRONMENTAL FACTORS: Not tolerant of water-logged soil, excessively dry soil or very alkaline soil conditions; heavy bloom production attracts bees and other insects; heavy berry production attracts flocks of birds and other animals; avoid pedestrian areas
PRUNING: Prune to develop shape, density and to control size; tolerant of severe pruning; best to heavily prune in late Winter to early Spring before new growth emerges; avoid pruning in Fall; can be grown in multi-stem form; best kept when limbed to the ground

ADDITIONAL NOTES

USES: Specimen, screening, group plantings, narrow hedges, single trunk or multi-trunk form, wildlife habitats
URBAN USES: Very adaptable to urban environment; moderately tolerant of air pollutants; diseases and insects may be problematic in urban micro-climates
SUBSTITUTIONS: *Ilex x* 'Carolina Sentinel', *Ilex x* 'Patricia Varner'
COMMENTS: Christmas Jewel® produces abundant, large, red berries without the need of a pollinator. It produces a dense, narrow specimen plant or hedge with light pruning and maintains dark green foliage even with a heavy fruit load.
OTHER CULTIVARS: 'Carolina Sentinel' - red fruit, small, dark green leaves with five to seven spines, open, upright, broad, pyramidal form; Meschick Dragon Lady® - red fruit, small, dark green leaves with three to five sharp spines, upright, pyramidal form; 'Doctor Kassab' - red fruit, dark, glossy, green leaves with three to five spines, compact, pyramidal form

Ilex x 'Mary Nell'
Mary Nell Holly
USDA Hardiness Zones: 7-9

DESCRIPTION

NATIVE HABITAT: Hybrid of three Asian species
(*I. cornuta x I. pernyi x I. latifolia*); cultivar of nursery origin
PLANT TYPE: Evergreen, broadleaf, small tree or large shrub; female
MATURE SIZE: 15' tall by 10' wide
FORM/SHAPE: Upright, pyramidal
BARK: Smooth; tannish gray
FLOWER: White; blooms in Spring; attracts insects
FRUIT: Red berries; showy in Fall through Winter; needs pollinator
for fruit set; attracts wildlife
FOLIAGE: Alternate, ovate to lanceolate leaves with ten to twenty
small, uniform spines; glossy, bright green new leaves turn glossy, dark olive-green; old inner foliage turns yellow-green
in Fall and sheds in Spring as new growth emerges

LANDSCAPE CHARACTERISTICS

GROWTH RATE: Slow to Moderate **DROUGHT TOLERANCE:** Moderate to High **SALT TOLERANCE:** Moderate to High
SOIL REQUIREMENTS: Well-drained, moist, fertile, humus rich, slightly acidic soil; very adaptable to many soil types
and fertility levels; will tolerate slightly alkaline soil
LIGHT REQUIREMENTS: Full sun; tolerates part shade, but it may limit flower and berry production
PEST PROBLEMS: Ambrosia beetles, Holly pit scale, leaf miner, aphids, native Holly leafminer, tea scale, Japanese
weevil, gypsy moth, spider mites, Holly bud moth, cambium miner, mealybugs, Oleander scale, wax scale, Florida wax
scale, cottony cushion scale, *Euonymus* scale, Cranberry rootworm, whitefly; mice and rabbits feed on bark
DISEASE PROBLEMS: *Alternaria*, blight, canker, butt rot, black root rot, dieback, nematodes, leaf spot, *Nectria*, tar spot,
sap wood rot, *Hypoxylon*, powdery mildew and algal leaf spot
ENVIRONMENTAL FACTORS: Not tolerant of water-logged soil, excessively dry soil or very alkaline soil conditions;
heavy bloom production attracts bees and other insects; heavy berry production attracts flocks of birds and other
animals; avoid pedestrian areas
PRUNING: Prune to develop shape, density and to control size; tolerant of severe pruning; best to heavily prune in late
Winter to early Spring before new growth emerges; avoid pruning in Fall; can be grown in multi-stem form; best kept
when limbed to the ground

ADDITIONAL NOTES

USES: Hedges, screening, parking lot islands, median strip plantings, specimen, residential plantings, streetscapes,
naturalizing and wildlife habitat
URBAN USES: Moderately tolerant of air pollutants, poor drainage, compacted soils, and drought stresses
SUBSTITUTIONS: *Ilex x* 'Emily Bruner', *Ilex x* 'James Swan', *Ilex x* 'Conot' PP 12,010 Patriot™
COMMENTS: Distinctive foliage, compact, pyramidal shape, and red berries make Mary Nell Holly a beautiful specimen
or accent plant. It needs heavy pruning when young to develop density. A pollinator is required for fruit set.
OTHER CULTIVARS: 'Emily Bruner' - red fruit, large, olive-green leaves, rapid growth, broad, dome-shaped;
'James Swan' - male pollinator, medium, dark olive-green leaves, medium growth, broad, dome-shaped

Ilex x 'Nellie R. Stevens'
Nellie R. Stevens Holly
USDA Hardiness Zones: 6-9

DESCRIPTION

NATIVE HABITAT: Hybrid of two species (*Ilex aquifolium x Ilex cornuta*); cultivar of nursery origin
PLANT TYPE: Evergreen, broadleaf, large shrub or tree; female
MATURE SIZE: 20-30' tall by 10-15' wide
FORM/SHAPE: Oval, pyramidal, symmetrical canopy
BARK: Smooth; green bark on young shoots, matures to tannish gray; showy when plant is limbed up
FLOWER: White; inconspicuous; blooms in Spring; attracts bees and other insects
FRUIT: Red berries; showy Fall through Winter; 3/8-1/2" diameter; produced without pollinator; attracts insects, birds and animals
FOLIAGE: Alternate, simple, oblong to ovate, spiny leaf with one to seven blunt spines; glossy, dark green leaves; old inner foliage turns yellow to yellow-green and sheds in Fall and again once new growth emerges in Spring

LANDSCAPE CHARACTERISTICS

GROWTH RATE: Moderate   **DROUGHT TOLERANCE:** Moderate to High   **SALT TOLERANCE:** Moderate
SOIL REQUIREMENTS: Well-drained, moist, fertile, humus rich, slightly acidic soil; very adaptable to many soil types and fertility levels
LIGHT REQUIREMENTS: Full sun; tolerates part shade, but it may limit flower and berry production
PEST PROBLEMS: Ambrosia beetles, Holly pit scale, leaf miner, aphids, native Holly leafminer, tea scale, Japanese weevil, gypsy moth, spider mites, Holly bud moth, cambium miner, mealybugs, Oleander scale, wax scale, Florida wax scale, cottony cushion scale, *Euonymus* scale, Cranberry rootworm, whitefly; mice and rabbits feed on bark
DISEASE PROBLEMS: *Alternaria*, blight, canker, butt rot, black root rot, dieback, nematodes, leaf spot, *Nectria*, tar spot, sap wood rot, *Hypoxylon*, powdery mildew and algal leaf spot
ENVIRONMENTAL FACTORS: Not tolerant of water-logged soil, excessively dry soil or alkaline soil conditions; heavy bloom production attracts bees and other insects; heavy berry production attracts flocks of birds and other animals; avoid pedestrian areas
PRUNING: Requires little pruning to develop a strong structure; prune to develop shape, density and to control size; tolerant of severe pruning; best to heavily prune in late Winter to early Spring before new growth emerges; avoid pruning in Fall; can be grown in multi-stem form; best kept when limbed to the ground

ADDITIONAL NOTES

USES: Container or planter, hedge, screening, parking lot islands, lawn tree, buffer strips and residential plantings
URBAN USES: Very adaptable to urban environments; moderately tolerant of air pollutants; diseases and insects may be problematic in urban micro-climates
SUBSTITUTIONS: *Ilex x* 'Edward J. Stevens', *Ilex x* 'Maplehurst', *Ilex x* 'Wyeriv' PP 8793 River Queen™
COMMENTS: This is one of the best Holly varieties for warmer regions. 'Nellie R. Stevens' is a great choice as a screen or border planting, but make sure to leave enough space for the plant to spread at the base. The plant does not need a pollinator for fruit set.
OTHER CULTIVARS: 'Edward J. Stevens' - male flowered, dark green foliage similar to 'Nellie R. Stevens', narrow, pyramidal form, heavy flower production; 'Maplehurst' - male flower, narrow, dark green foliage, broad, pyramidal form

Ilex x attenuata 'East Palatka'
East Palatka Holly
USDA Hardiness Zones: 7b-9

DESCRIPTION

NATIVE HABITAT: Hybrid of three North American species
(*Ilex opaca x, Ilex myrtifolia x, Ilex cassine*); cultivar of nursery origin
PLANT TYPE: Evergreen, broadleaf, large shrub to small tree; female
MATURE SIZE: 30-45' tall by 10-15' wide
FORM/SHAPE: Tight, pyramidal, uniform growth
BARK: Smooth; tannish gray; single or multi-stemmed
FLOWER: White; inconspicuous; blooms in Spring; attracts insects
FRUIT: Female plants produce red berries when pollinated; showy Fall through Winter; 1/4-3/8" in diameter; attracts insects and animals
FOLIAGE: Alternate, simple, rounded leaves, one spine at leaf tip; entire margin; bright olive-green

LANDSCAPE CHARACTERISTICS

GROWTH RATE: Moderate   **DROUGHT TOLERANCE:** Moderate to High   **SALT TOLERANCE:** Moderate to High
SOIL REQUIREMENTS: Well-drained, moist, fertile, humus rich, slightly acidic soil; in high pH soils plant will have light green foliage and slower growth
LIGHT REQUIREMENTS: Full sun; tolerates part shade, but it may limit flower and berry production
PEST PROBLEMS: Ambrosia beetles, Holly pit scale, leaf miner, aphids, native Holly leafminer, tea scale, Japanese weevil, gypsy moth, spider mites, Holly bud moth, cambium miner, mealybug, Oleander scale, wax scale, Florida wax scale, cottony cushion scale, *Euonymus* scale, Cranberry rootworm, whitefly; mice and rabbits feed on bark
DISEASE PROBLEMS: *Alternaria*, blight, canker, butt rot, black root rot, dieback, nematodes, leaf spot, *Nectria*, tar spot, sap wood rot, *Hypoxylon*, powdery mildew and algal leaf spot
ENVIRONMENTAL FACTORS: Not tolerant of water-logged soil, excessively dry soil or alkaline soil conditions; heavy bloom production attracts bees and other insects; heavy berry production attracts flocks of birds and other animals; avoid pedestrian areas
PRUNING: Prune to develop a strong central leader, shape, density and to control size; tolerant of severe pruning; best to heavily prune in late Winter to early Spring before new growth emerges; avoid pruning in Fall; can be grown in a multi-stem form; best kept when limbed to the ground

ADDITIONAL NOTES

USES: Container or planter, hedge, screening, parking lot islands, lawn tree, buffer strips, specimen, residential lots and streetscapes and naturalizing
URBAN USES: Very adaptable to urban environments; moderately tolerant of air pollutants; diseases and insects may be problematic in urban micro-climates
SUBSTITUTIONS: Savannah Holly, *Ilex x attenuata* 'Hume No. 2'
COMMENTS: 'East Palatka' is a durable street tree that is very drought tolerant once established. The plant is often sheared in the nursery trade and landscape plantings. The natural form is rarely seen, but is a graceful pyramid with drooping branches. Great choice for Winter interest with an abundant red berry display (on female plants) and a showy bark. 'East Palatka' shows Winter cold injury in USDA Hardiness Zone 7a, so it is best used in Hardiness Zone 8 or warmer.
OTHER CULTIVARS: 'Foster No. 2' - dark green foliage, narrow, pyramidal plant form, red berries; 'Savannah' - light green foliage, broad leaf with few spines, pyramidal plant form, abundant red berries

Ilex x attenuata 'Foster No. 2'
Foster No. 2 Holly
USDA Hardiness Zones: 6b-9

DESCRIPTION

NATIVE HABITAT: Hybrid of 3 North American species
(*Ilex opaca x, Ilex myritifolia x, Ilex cassine*); cultivar of nursery origin
PLANT TYPE: Evergreen, broadleaf, large shrub to small tree; female
MATURE SIZE: 15-25' tall by 8-12' wide
FORM/SHAPE: Columnar, pyramidal, dense with symmetrical canopy
BARK: Smooth; twigs purplish green, tannish gray when mature
FLOWER: White; inconspicuous; blooms in Spring; attracts insects
FRUIT: Round, red berries; showy Fall through Winter; 3/8-1/2" in diameter; not a litter problem; attracts wildlife
FOLIAGE: Alternate, simple, entire, spiny; very dark green obovate to oblanceolate leaves

LANDSCAPE CHARACTERISTICS

GROWTH RATE: Slow to Moderate   **DROUGHT TOLERANCE:** Moderate to High   **SALT TOLERANCE:** Low to Moderate
SOIL REQUIREMENTS: Well-drained, moist, fertile, humus rich, slightly acidic soil; very adaptable to many soil types and fertility levels
LIGHT REQUIREMENTS: Full sun; tolerates part shade, but it may limit flower and berry production
PEST PROBLEMS: Ambrosia beetles, Holly pit scale, leaf miner, aphids, native Holly leafminer, tea scale, Japanese weevil, gypsy moth, spider mites, Holly bud moth, cambium miner, mealybugs, Oleander scale, wax scale, Florida wax scale, cottony cushion scale, *Euonymus* scale, Cranberry rootworm, whitefly; mice and rabbits feed on bark
DISEASE PROBLEMS: *Alternaria*, blight, canker, butt rot, black root rot, dieback, nematodes, leaf spot, *Nectria*, tar spot, sap wood rot, *Hypoxylon*, powdery mildew and algal leaf spot
ENVIRONMENTAL FACTORS: Not tolerant of water-logged soil, excessively dry soil or alkaline soil conditions; heavy bloom production attracts bees and other insects; heavy berry production attracts flocks of birds and other animals; avoid pedestrian areas
PRUNING: Prune to develop shape, density and to control size; tolerant of severe pruning; best to heavily prune in late Winter to early Spring before new growth emerges; avoid pruning in Fall; can be grown in multi-stem form; best kept when limbed to the ground; maintain a central leader by removing co-dominant leaders

ADDITIONAL NOTES

USES: Container or planter, hedge, screening, large parking lot islands, lawn tree, buffer strips, residential plantings and streetscapes
URBAN USES: Very adaptable to urban environments; moderately tolerant of air pollutants; diseases and insects may be problematic in urban micro-climates; should be used more in urban applications
SUBSTITUTIONS: *Ilex x attenuata* cultivars, *Ilex x* 'HL10-90' PP 14,477 Christmas Jewel®
COMMENTS: This is a good tree to use in tall, narrow spaces. 'Foster No. 2' Holly has a showy berry display and creates attractive Winter interest. It is a great plant choice for urban and residential areas in the South because of its high drought tolerance.
OTHER CULTIVARS: 'Mountain' - male flower, olive-green foliage, hardy in USDA Hardiness Zone 5; 'Nasa' - red fruit, dark green foliage, upright, pyramidal form; 'Oriole' - red fruit, dark green foliage, pyramidal form

Ilex x attenuata 'Greenleaf'
Greenleaf Holly
USDA Hardiness Zones: 6b-9

DESCRIPTION

NATIVE HABITAT: Hybrid of three North American species
(*Ilex opaca x, Ilex myrtifolia x, Ilex cassine*); cultivar of nursery origin
PLANT TYPE: Evergreen, broadleaf, large tree
MATURE SIZE: 20-30' tall by 15-20' wide
FORM/SHAPE: Broad, dense, pyramidal; softer form than *Opaca* species
BARK: Smooth; greenish gray when young, matures to a light gray
FLOWER: Greenish white; inconspicuous; fragrant; attracts insects
FRUIT: Bright red berries, 1/4-3/8" in diameter; persistent and abundant
berry production; very showy Fall through Winter; attracts wildlife
FOLIAGE: Alternate, simple, entire, spiny, oval; glossy, medium green leaves turn a darker green in Fall and throughout
Winter

LANDSCAPE CHARACTERISTICS

GROWTH RATE: Slow to Moderate **DROUGHT TOLERANCE:** Moderate to High **SALT TOLERANCE:** Moderate to High
SOIL REQUIREMENTS: Well-drained, moist, fertile, humus rich, slightly acidic soil; very adaptable to many soil types
and fertility levels
LIGHT REQUIREMENTS: Full sun; tolerates part shade, but it may limit flower and berry production
PEST PROBLEMS: Ambrosia beetles, Holly pit scale, leaf miner, aphids, native Holly leafminer, tea scale, Japanese
weevil, gypsy moth, spider mites, Holly bud moth, cambium miner, mealybugs, Oleander scale, wax scale, Florida wax
scale, cottony cushion scale, *Euonymus* scale, Cranberry rootworm, whitefly; mice and rabbits feed on bark
DISEASE PROBLEMS: *Alternaria*, blight, canker, butt rot, black root rot, dieback, nematodes, leaf spot, *Nectria*, tar spot,
sap wood rot, *Hypoxylon*, powdery mildew and algal leaf spot
ENVIRONMENTAL FACTORS: Not tolerant of water-logged soil, excessively dry soil or alkaline soil conditions; heavy
bloom production attracts bees and other insects; heavy berry production attracts flocks of birds and other animals; avoid
pedestrian areas
PRUNING: Prune to develop shape, density and to control size; tolerant of severe pruning; best to heavily prune in late
Winter to early Spring before new growth emerges; avoid pruning in Fall; can be grown in multi-stem form; best kept
when limbed to the ground

ADDITIONAL NOTES

USES: Hedges, screening, parking lot islands, median strip plantings, specimen, residential plantings, streetscapes,
naturalizing and wildlife habitat
URBAN USES: Tolerant of air pollutants, moderately poor drainage, compacted soils and moderate drought stresses
SUBSTITUTIONS: *Ilex x attenuata* 'Foster No. 2', *Ilex x attenuata* 'East Palatka', *Ilex x attenuata* 'Hume #2', *Ilex opaca*
'Carolina No. 2', *Ilex opaca* 'Christmas Tree', *Ilex opaca* 'Croonenberg', *Ilex opaca* 'Dan Fenton'
COMMENTS: 'Greenleaf' is a good plant to use in natural areas. It will attract wildlife and is an excellent food source.
Beautiful showy berries are persistent through Winter months. This is a good hybrid of American Hollies for the
Southeastern United States because of its tolerance to hot Summers. It can get Winter leaf burn in colder regions or
during extreme Winters. Confused in the trade and once considered a straight *Ilex opaca*, most authorities now consider
'Greenleaf' to be an *Ilex x attenuata*.
OTHER CULTIVARS: 'Foster No. 2' - dark green foliage, narrow, pyramidal plant form, red berries; 'Savannah' - light
green foliage, broad leaf with few spines, pyramidal plant form, abundant berry production

Ilex x attenuata 'Savannah'
Savannah Holly
USDA Hardiness Zones: 6-9

DESCRIPTION

NATIVE HABITAT: Hybrid of three North American species (*Ilex cassine, Ilex opaca x, Ilex myrtifolia*); cultivar of nursery origin
PLANT TYPE: Evergreen, broadleaf, large tree
MATURE SIZE: 30-45' tall by 10-15' wide
FORM/SHAPE: Columnar to loose, pyramidal, smooth outline
BARK: Smooth; tannish gray to chalky gray
FLOWER: White; inconspicuous; blooms in Spring; attracts insects
FRUIT: Round, red berries in heavy clusters; very showy; lasts from Fall through Winter; attracts wildlife
FOLIAGE: Alternate, simple, three to six pairs of blunt spines and terminal spines; dull, medium green, ovate leaves

LANDSCAPE CHARACTERISTICS

GROWTH RATE: Moderate to Fast   **DROUGHT TOLERANCE:** Moderate to High   **SALT TOLERANCE:** Moderate
SOIL REQUIREMENTS: Well-drained, moist, fertile, humus rich, slightly acidic soil; very adaptable to many soil types and fertility levels
LIGHT REQUIREMENTS: Full sun; tolerates part shade, but it may limit flower and berry production
PEST PROBLEMS: Ambrosia beetles, Holly pit scale, leaf miner, aphids, native Holly leafminer, tea scale, Japanese weevil, gypsy moth, spider mites, Holly bud moth, cambium miner, mealybugs, Oleander scale, wax scale, Florida wax scale, cottony cushion scale, *Euonymus* scale, Cranberry rootworm, whitefly; mice and rabbits feed on bark
DISEASE PROBLEMS: *Alternaria*, blight, canker, butt rot, black root rot, dieback, nematodes, leaf spot, *Nectria*, tar spot, sap wood rot, *Hypoxylon*, powdery mildew and algal leaf spot
ENVIRONMENTAL FACTORS: Not tolerant of water-logged soil, excessively dry soil or alkaline soil conditions; heavy bloom production attracts bees and other insects; heavy berry production attracts flocks of birds and other animals; avoid pedestrian areas
PRUNING: Requires little pruning to develop structure; tolerant of severe pruning; best to heavily prune in late Winter to early Spring before new growth emerges; avoid pruning in Fall; can be grown in multi-stem form; best kept when limbed to the ground

ADDITIONAL NOTES

USES: Hedges, parking lots, lawn tree, buffer strips, screening, wildlife habitat, specimen, residential plantings, streetscapes; ideal for naturalizing
URBAN USES: Very adaptable to urban environments; moderately tolerant of air pollutants; diseases and insects may be problematic in urban micro-climates
SUBSTITUTIONS: 'Nellie R. Stevens' Holly, Foster Holly
COMMENTS: This is a plant to use in natural areas and to create screen or buffer plantings. Savannah Holly has a more loose, open canopy than some of the other Hollies. The berries attract wildlife and birds. The foliage is light green to yellow-green and requires heavy fertilization to maintain a medium to dark green color.
OTHER CULTIVARS: 'Greenleaf' - red fruit, medium to dark green foliage, broad, pyramidal plant; 'Hume No. 2' - red fruit, dark green, broad foliage, broad, open, pyramidal form

Juniperus chinensis 'Kaizuka'
Hollywood Juniper
USDA Hardiness Zones: 5-9

DESCRIPTION

NATIVE HABITAT: Cultivar of Japanese garden origin
PLANT TYPE: Evergreen, coniferous, small tree or shrub
MATURE SIZE: 8-12' tall by 5-7' wide
FORM/SHAPE: Upright, irregular, more open at top
BARK: Rough; reddish brown; develops fiber strips and ribbons; mature bark is dark brown, exfoliates thin plates
FLOWER: Pale yellow; inconspicuous; blooms late Winter to Spring
FRUIT: Berry-like; 1/4 - 1/2"; light green; matures to dark blue-violet; matures in Fall
FOLIAGE: Opposite pairs, scale-like, deep, bright green year-round; old foliage turns yellow to brown and sheds throughout Winter

LANDSCAPE CHARACTERISTICS

GROWTH RATE: Moderate   **DROUGHT TOLERANCE:** Moderate to High   **SALT TOLERANCE:** Moderate
SOIL REQUIREMENTS: Well-drained, moist, fertile, humus rich soil; tolerant of high pH soil
LIGHT REQUIREMENTS: Full sun
PEST PROBLEMS: Bagworm, spider mites, Juniper scale, Juniper midge, Juniper webworm, black scale, Cypress leafminer and Juniper spittlebug
DISEASE PROBLEMS: *Phomopsis*, twig blight, rust, *Seiridium*, *Cercospora*, *Kabatina* blight
ENVIRONMENTAL FACTORS: Not tolerant of shade or water-logged soil; moderately tolerant of air pollutants
PRUNING: Looks best when unpruned, taking on an oriental form; very adaptable to pruning for shape and size control; responds well when pruned into topiary forms

ADDITIONAL NOTES

USES: Bold accent plant; rock, stone or Japanese gardens
URBAN USES: Adaptable to small spaces and many soil types, but soil must be well-drained
SUBSTITUTIONS: *Chamaecyparis filicoides*, *Chamaecyparis gracilis*, *Cryptomeria japonica* 'Taisho Tamasugi'
COMMENTS: Hollywood Juniper is a tough, adaptable plant and each one is unique in its form. Use the plant as an accent or specimen, however it has been overused in some landscape designs and regions.
OTHER CULTIVARS: 'Columnaris' - upright, coarse, green foliage; 'Kaizuka Variegata' - compact, bushy, conical, scale-like foliage with flecks of creamy yellow to white; 'Monarch' - upright, conical bush with open habit and ascending, spreading, arm-like branches; 'Robusta Green' - upright, columnar form, gray-green foliage

Juniperus silicicola 'Brodie'
Brodie Juniper
USDA Hardiness Zones: 6-9

DESCRIPTION

NATIVE HABITAT: Southeastern United States; cultivar of nursery origin
PLANT TYPE: Evergreen, coniferous, large tree
MATURE SIZE: 20-30' tall by 6-10' wide
FORM/SHAPE: Pyramidal, dense, strongly upright
BARK: Rough; grayish to reddish brown; exfoliates; scales and thin fiber
FLOWER: Inconspicuous; blooms in late Winter
FRUIT: Blue-green, drupe-like (Juniper berry); inconspicuous
FOLIAGE: Opposite, whorled, simple, scale-like, pressed to stem and overlapping; deep bright green foliage color is maintained throughout Fall and Winter

LANDSCAPE CHARACTERISTICS

GROWTH RATE: Moderate   **DROUGHT TOLERANCE:** Moderate to High   **SALT TOLERANCE:** High
SOIL REQUIREMENTS: Well-drained, moist, fertile, humus rich soil; needs well-limed soil for optimal growth; tolerates sandy soil of coastal regions and barrier islands
LIGHT REQUIREMENTS: Full sun
PEST PROBLEMS: Eriophyid mite, Juniper scale, Juniper midge, Eastern Juniper bark beetle, bagworm, Cypress tip miner, gypsy moth, Cypress sawfly, Spruce spider mite, aphids, pales weevil and spittlebug
DISEASE PROBLEMS: *Alternaria*, stem canker, Cedar Apple rust, nematodes, root rot, rust, sooty mold, *Phomopsis*, wood rot and Quince rust
ENVIRONMENTAL FACTORS: Not tolerant of shade or water-logged soil
PRUNING: Minimal pruning required; remove co-dominant leader and maintain tree with central leader, allowing limbs to spread weight of snow and ice evenly around the tree axis; can be pruned into a narrow, columnar form or topiary

ADDITIONAL NOTES

USES: Specimen, wind break, screening, mass planting and naturalizing
URBAN USES: Good plant for urban areas, tolerates fluorides, sulfur dioxide, ozone air pollutants, heat and humidity
SUBSTITUTIONS: *Juniperus virginiana* species, *Juniperus silicicola* species, *Juniperus chinensis* 'Spartan', *Juniperus chinensis* 'Columnaris'
COMMENTS: Brodie Juniper needs root pruning when young to develop a strong root system that will hold the plant steady in strong winds. It maintains a deep bright green color throughout Winter and when pruned to a narrow form is a great replacement for Italian Cypress. 'Brodie' maintains good resistance to foliar diseases common to *Juniperus virginiana* species and cultivars.
OTHER CULTIVARS: 'Hoven's Blue' - broad, pyramidal form with gray-green foliage

Juniperus virginiana
Eastern Red Cedar
USDA Hardiness Zones: 3-9

DESCRIPTION

NATIVE HABITAT: Eastern United States
PLANT TYPE: Evergreen, coniferous, large tree
MATURE SIZE: 30-50' tall by 10-25' wide
FORM/SHAPE: Upright and columnar in youth; becomes an open, irregular oval with age, plant form is highly variable
BARK: Rough; tan-gray to reddish brown; older bark exfoliates in fibers and ribbons
FLOWER: Male cones yellowish brown; female cones yellowish green; inconspicuous; appears early to late Winter
FRUIT: Fleshy, oval, drupe-like (Juniper berry); 1/4" blue-purple; glaucous
FOLIAGE: Opposite, whorled, simple, scale-like to awl-like; medium to dark green foliage; older inner foliage turns yellow and sheds throughout Winter; cold temperatures and sun exposure give foliage a bronze to purple cast

LANDSCAPE CHARACTERISTICS

GROWTH RATE: Moderate to Fast   **DROUGHT TOLERANCE:** Moderate to High   **SALT TOLERANCE:** Moderate to High
SOIL REQUIREMENTS: Well-drained, moist, fertile, humus rich soil; needs well-limed soil for optimal growth; tolerates sandy soil of coastal regions and barrier islands; lime should be added to acidic soils
LIGHT REQUIREMENTS: Full sun
PEST PROBLEMS: Spider mites, bagworm, Juniper scale, Juniper midges, Juniper webworm, black scale, Cypress leafminer and Juniper spittlebug
DISEASE PROBLEMS: Juniper blight, Cedar Apple rust, Hawthorn rust, Quince rust, *Phomopsis* twig blight, *Seiridium*, *Cercospora* and *Kabatina* blight
ENVIRONMENTAL FACTORS: Not tolerant of shade or water-logged soil; moderately tolerant of air pollutants; multi-leader plants may split from ice and snow
PRUNING: Pruning can increase density; too much pruning results in poor air circulation, tender growth at pruning sites can have disease problems

ADDITIONAL NOTES

USES: Specimen, naturalizing, windbreak, screen, hedge and group plantings with other plants
URBAN USES: Moderately tolerant of air pollutants and dry planting sites
SUBSTITUTIONS: 'Green Giant' Arborvitae, *Picea abies*, *Thuja plicata* cultivars, *Thuja occidentalis* cultivars, Leyland Cypress cultivars
COMMENTS: *Juniperus virginiana* is commonly grown from seed. It exhibits many variable plant forms and color variations, as well as disease and pest resistance. Cold hardiness and tolerance to heat and humidity are unknown in seedlings. When making plant selections, choose cultivars with positive characteristics and good resistance to diseases, pests and environmental stresses. Large trees with dead inner foliage are a fire hazard. The foliage gets very dry inside the tree canopy and produces volatile oils which can burn quickly. Needles are pointed and will prick skin causing an itchy skin irritation.
OTHER CULTIVARS: 'Burkii' - broad, columnar, compact form with steel blue foliage; 'Hillspire' syn. 'Cupressifolia' - dense, columnar forms, fastigiate branching habit with green scale-like foliage

Juniperus virginiana 'Burkii'
Burkii Red Cedar
USDA Hardiness Zones: 3-9

DESCRIPTION

NATIVE HABITAT: Eastern United States; cultivar of nursery origin

PLANT TYPE: Evergreen, coniferous, large tree

MATURE SIZE: 20-25' tall by 8-15' wide

FORM/SHAPE: Pyramidal, dense

BARK: Rough; tan-gray to reddish brown bark; older bark exfoliates in fibers and ribbons

FLOWER: Inconspicuous; yellowish green; blooms early to late Winter

FRUIT: Fleshy, oval, drupe-like (Juniper berry); 1/4" blue-purple; glaucous

FOLIAGE: Opposite, whorled, simple, awl-like to scale-like; steel blue or blue-green foliage turns a reddish purple in cold temperatures and with exposure to Winter sun

LANDSCAPE CHARACTERISTICS

GROWTH RATE: Moderate to Fast   **DROUGHT TOLERANCE:** Moderate to High   **SALT TOLERANCE:** Moderate to High

SOIL REQUIREMENTS: Well-drained, moist, fertile, humus rich soil; needs well-limed soil for optimal growth; tolerates sandy soil of coastal regions and barrier islands; lime should be added to acidic soil

LIGHT REQUIREMENTS: Full sun

PEST PROBLEMS: Spider mites, bagworm, Juniper scale, Juniper midges, Juniper webworm, black scale, Cypress leafminer and Juniper spittlebug

DISEASE PROBLEMS: Juniper blight, Cedar Apple rust, Hawthorn rust, Quince rust, *Phomopsis* twig blight, *Seiridium*, *Cercospora* and *Kabatina* blight

ENVIRONMENTAL FACTORS: Not tolerant of shade or water-logged soil; moderately tolerant of air pollutants; multi-leader plants may split from ice and snow

PRUNING: Pruning can increase density; too much pruning results in poor air circulation, tender growth at pruning sites can have disease problems

ADDITIONAL NOTES

USES: Screen, windbreaks, specimen tree, border plantings, naturalizing and group plantings with other plants

URBAN USES: Moderately tolerant of air pollutants and dry planting sites

SUBSTITUTIONS: *Juniperus silicicola* 'Brodie', *Thuja plicata* cultivars, *Thuja occidentalis* cultivars, *Picea pungens* cultivars

COMMENTS: 'Burkii' has good tolerance to most disease problems when grown in full sun with a well-drained, lime rich soil. Large 'Burkii' trees with dead inner foliage are a fire hazard. The volatile oils produced in the dry inner tree canopy foliage can easily catch fire and burn quickly. Needles are pointed and will prick skin causing an itchy skin irritation.

OTHER CULTIVARS: 'Manhattan Blue' - conical, compact form with bluish green foliage; 'Glauca' - narrow, columnar form, medium height, with blue-green to silver-green foliage

Ligustrum japonicum 'Recurvifolium'
Wavy Leaf Ligustrum
USDA Hardiness Zones: 6b-10

DESCRIPTION

NATIVE HABITAT: Japan, Korea, Taiwan and Northern China; cultivar of nursery origin
PLANT TYPE: Evergreen, broadleaf, small tree or shrub
MATURE SIZE: 8-12' tall by 6-8' wide
FORM/SHAPE: Upright, broad dome
BARK: Smooth; whitish gray with heavy lenticel development
FLOWER: White flowers in clusters; strong, unpleasant fragrance; blooms late Spring to early Summer; attracts insects
FRUIT: Blue drupe; 3/8-1/2" long by 1/4" wide in large clusters; fruit ripens in late Summer through Fall; somewhat attractive to animals
FOLIAGE: Opposite, simple, ovate, entire margin, narrower leaf than species; shiny, dark green color and wavy leaf margins; medium green quickly turns dark green; in Fall, the older previous season's leaves turn yellow and shed throughout the dormant season until the start of new growth

LANDSCAPE CHARACTERISTICS

GROWTH RATE: Moderate   **DROUGHT TOLERANCE:** Moderate   **SALT TOLERANCE:** Low to Moderate
SOIL REQUIREMENTS: Well-drained, moist, fertile, humus rich, clay, loam or sandy soil; very adaptable to different pH levels, but performs best in soil that is adequately limed
LIGHT REQUIREMENTS: Light shade to full sun
PEST PROBLEMS: Japanese weevil, black vine weevil, caterpillars, snails, Lilac leafminer, Privet rust mite, mites, sawfly, Lilac borer, leafhopper, leaf-footed bugs, scales, white Peach scale, *Euonymus* scale and *Camellia* mining scale; mice and rabbits feed on bark
DISEASE PROBLEMS: Nematodes, *Alternaria*, anthracnose, canker, dieback, edema gall, *Glomerella,* leaf spot, *Nectria, Phomopsis*, powdery mildew, root rot, *Verticillium* wilt, *Pseudomonas* and crown gall
ENVIRONMENTAL FACTORS: Not tolerant of water-logged or flooded soil; has a high tolerance to air pollution; foliage may be damaged by Winter sunscald or hard, late freezes
PRUNING: Normally pruned as a shrub with limbs maintained to the ground; can be limbed up to develop a multi-trunk tree; can be pruned as a topiary; constant pruning in unfavorable weather conditions can result in disease such as dieback

ADDITIONAL NOTES

USES: Buffer and screen plantings, small specimen tree, median plantings, parking lot islands, topiaries and large foundation plantings
URBAN USES: Very adaptable in urban landscapes; tolerant of most pests and diseases
SUBSTITUTIONS: *Ilex cornuta* cultivars, *Ilex x* 'HL 10-90' PP 14,477 Christmas Jewel®, *Magnolia grandiflora* 'Little Gem', *Loropetalum* cultivars, *Elaeagnus* cultivars, *Osmanthus* cultivars, *Kalmia* cultivars, *Illicium* species and cultivars
COMMENTS: 'Recurvifolium' is more compact with a more upright growth habit than the species. The leaves are glossy with wavy margins and are more attractive than the species. It is considered to be more cold hardy than the species in USDA Hardiness Zones 6b-7a. Old cultivar literature lists 'Suwanee River' which may be the same cultivar as 'Recurvifolium'.
OTHER CULTIVARS: *Ligustrum japonicum* - evergreen, broadleaf shrub with opposite, ovate, thick, dark green, broad, wavy leaves, very adaptable to varying soil types and light conditions, 15' tall by 20' wide, tolerant of frequent severe pruning, hardy in USDA Hardiness Zones 7-9; 'Howard' - typical of species, foliage is bright gold to yellow-green with maximum sunlight; 'Jack Frost' - small, compact grower, gray-green foliage with white and silver variegation; 'Rotundifolium' - dark green leaves, rounded, leaves tight fitting around the stem, compact and upright growth

Loropetalum chinense rubrum 'Zhuzhou Fuchsia'
Zhuzhou Red Leaf Loropetalum
USDA Hardiness Zones: 6b-9

DESCRIPTION

NATIVE HABITAT: China and Japan; cultivar of nursery origin
PLANT TYPE: Evergreen, broadleaf, flowering shrub or small tree
MATURE SIZE: 10-15' tall by 10' wide
FORM/SHAPE: Irregularly rounded shrub, arching branches, upright
BARK: Smooth; rich brown; old stems exfoliate in large, thin strips on plates
FLOWER: Deep fuchsia-pink flowers; fascile of strap-like petals; 3/4" long; fragrant; blooms March to April
FRUIT: Woody; rounded to oval; dehiscent, nut-like capsule
FOLIAGE: Alternate, small ovate to lanceolate, 1 1/2 - 2 1/4" long by 1" wide; purple-maroon leaves in Summer; may change to shades of bronze, purple and green if not grown vigorously; old inner foliage turns yellow, orange and red; sheds in Fall and again in Spring as new growth emerges

LANDSCAPE CHARACTERISTICS

GROWTH RATE: Fast   **DROUGHT TOLERANCE:** Moderate   **SALT TOLERANCE:** Low
SOIL REQUIREMENTS: Well-drained, slightly acidic soil with high organic matter; does not perform well in soil with a high pH, extremely dry or water-logged soil; copper deficiency results in small deformed leaves and dieback of stem tip
LIGHT REQUIREMENTS: Sun to light shade; will maintain purple-maroon leaf in light shade
PEST PROBLEMS: Ambrosia beetles, spider mites, caterpillars and aphids
DISEASE PROBLEMS: Leaf spot, dieback, frost injury due to late Spring hard freezes, *Phyllostica* and root rot
ENVIRONMENTAL FACTORS: Late Spring freezes cause stem dieback; tolerant of light frost when in bloom; avoid severe pruning during hot dry Summer conditions as it causes sunscald to foliage and bark
PRUNING: Vigorous grower; will need size control in foundation plantings; tree-formed plants need lower limb suckers removed and will need removing several mores times during the growing season

ADDITIONAL NOTES

USES: Large foundation shrub, accent, purple foliage shrub or small multi-trunk tree, buffer planting, medians and streetscapes
URBAN USES: Very adaptable to urban conditions
SUBSTITUTIONS: Other *Loropetalum* cultivars such as 'Blush', 'Fire Dance' and 'Burgundy', *Ilex* cultivars, *Ligustrum* cultivars, *Osmanthus* cultivars, *Acer palmatum* red leaf cultivars
COMMENTS: *Loropetalum chinense* make large, trouble-free shrubs or small trees. 'Zhuzhou' is a good variety to use in urban settings where space is limited. This plant makes a good screen for tight locations and is very pest and disease resistant.
OTHER CULTIVARS: 'Blush' - 8-12' tall by 8-10' wide, large, medium, green leaves, stocky, compact, broad, upright form, fuchsia-pink flowers; 'Burgundy' - 8-12' tall by 8-10' wide, purple-'maroon, medium, narrow, ovate to lanceolate leaves

Magnolia grandiflora 'Bracken's Brown Beauty'
Bracken's Brown Beauty Magnolia
USDA Hardiness Zones: 5b-9

DESCRIPTION

NATIVE HABITAT: Eastern and Southeastern United States to Eastern Texas; cultivar of nursery origin
PLANT TYPE: Evergreen, broadleaf, large flowering tree
MATURE SIZE: 40' tall by 20' wide
FORM/SHAPE: Pyramidal, dense, oval
BARK: Smooth; brownish gray when young; matures to grayish black
FLOWER: Fragrant, white flowers 6-8" wide; blooms May to September; attracts insects
FRUIT: Red berries in a large, dry, hard, woody cone; sometimes considered messy
FOLIAGE: Alternate, simple, ovate to elliptical, medium to large-sized leaves; medium to dark green with a heavily felted dark brown back in Summer; old leaves turn yellow to brown and shed in Fall and again in Spring as new growth begins

LANDSCAPE CHARACTERISTICS

GROWTH RATE: Moderate to Fast   **DROUGHT TOLERANCE:** Moderate to High **SALT TOLERANCE:** Moderate to High
SOIL REQUIREMENTS: Well-drained, moist, fertile, humus rich soil that is well-limed; tolerant of slightly acidic soil
LIGHT REQUIREMENTS: Full sun to part shade; best growth and flower production in full sun
PEST PROBLEMS: *Magnolia* scale, black twig borer, leaf miner, Oleander scale, false Oleander scale, spider mites and Tulip Tree scale
DISEASE PROBLEMS: Leaf spot, stem canker, root rot, *Verticillium* wilt and wetwood
ENVIRONMENTAL FACTORS: Needs adequate soil moisture and fertility for optimal growth and aesthetics; adaptable to less desirable environmental conditions; spreading root system can make trees difficult to preserve on construction sites
PRUNING: Can be heavily pruned in Spring before new growth begins to maintain size without reducing flowers; pruning strengthens limb structure; can be limbed up to create a tree-form plant, but best kept when limbed to the ground

ADDITIONAL NOTES

USES: Large specimen plant, mass planted as a large hedge or screen, naturalizing and lawn tree
URBAN USES: Shows no significant problems in urban planting sites
SUBSTITUTIONS: *Magnolia grandiflora* Teddy Bear®, *Magnolia grandiflora* 'Hasse', *Ilex latifolia* and cultivars, 'Green Giant' Arborvitae, *Cryptomeria japonica*
COMMENTS: 'Bracken's Brown Beauty' is adaptable to heat, humidity and drought stresses. 'Bracken's Brown Beauty' has proven very cold hardy in USDA Hardiness Zone 5b and was selected by the Pennsylvania Horticulture Society as a Gold Medal Plant Award Winner in 2003.
OTHER CULTIVARS: 'CoCo' - similar in plant form with a larger flower; 'D. D. Blanchard' - dark green leaves with felted backs; 'Edith Bogue'- has large leaves and is the most cold tolerant *Magnolia*

Magnolia grandiflora 'Claudia Wannamaker'
Claudia Wannamaker Magnolia
USDA Hardiness Zones: 7-10

DESCRIPTION

NATIVE HABITAT: Eastern and Southeastern United States to Eastern Texas; cultivar of nursery origin
PLANT TYPE: Evergreen, broadleaf, large flowering tree
MATURE SIZE: 50-60' tall by 30-40' wide
FORM/SHAPE: Broad, uniform, pyramidal
BARK: Smooth; grayish brown to blackish gray
FLOWER: Fragrant, white flowers are 6-8" wide; blooms May to June; attracts insects
FRUIT: Red berries in a large, hard, woody cone; sometimes considered messy
FOLIAGE: Alternate, simple, ovate to elliptical, 5-10" long; medium green leaves with tannish brown underside; older, inner leaves turn yellow to brown and shed in Fall and again in Spring as new growth begins; leaf litter can be messy

LANDSCAPE CHARACTERISTICS

GROWTH RATE: Moderate to Fast   **DROUGHT TOLERANCE:** Moderate to High   **SALT TOLERANCE:** Low to Moderate
SOIL REQUIREMENTS: Well-drained, moist, fertile, humus rich soil that is well-limed; tolerant of slightly acidic soil
LIGHT REQUIREMENTS: Full sun produces best growth and flower; tolerates part shade
PEST PROBLEMS: Oleander scale, false Oleander scale, spider mites, Tulip Tree scale, black twig borer, leaf miner, and *Magnolia* scale
DISEASE PROBLEMS: Leaf spot, blight, canker, stem canker, root rot, *Verticillium* wilt and wetwood
ENVIRONMENTAL FACTORS: Needs adequate soil moisture and fertility for optimal growth and aesthetics; adaptable to less desirable environmental conditions; spreading root system makes trees difficult to preserve on construction sites
PRUNING: Can be heavily pruned in Spring before new growth begins to maintain size, but will somewhat reduce flowering; pruning strengthens limb structure; can be limbed up to create a tree-form plant, but best when kept limbed to the ground

ADDITIONAL NOTES

USES: Lawn tree, specimen plant, naturalizing, screening, buffer strips in parking lots and median plantings
URBAN USES: Shows no significant problem in urban planting sites
SUBSTITUTIONS: *Magnolia grandiflora* Teddy Bear®, *Magnolia grandiflora* 'Hasse', *Ilex latifolia* and cultivars, 'Green Giant' Arborvitae, *Cryptomeria japonica*, *Magnolia grandiflora* 'Bracken's Brown Beauty'
COMMENTS: 'Claudia Wannamaker' is a good specimen to use for a traditional southern planting. It will bloom at a young age and is a dense, uniform grower.
OTHER CULTIVARS: 'Coco' - broad, pyramidal, large tree; large, green, lanceolate, wavy-marginated leaves with tannish brown felted leaf backs and large flowers borne on young plants; fast growth and dense branching; 'Edith Bogue' - broad, dome-shaped large tree; large, green, long, oblong to elliptical shaped leaves, large flowers infrequently produced, old plants have an open limb structure, very cold hardy

Magnolia grandiflora 'D. D. Blanchard'
D. D. Blanchard Magnolia
USDA Hardiness Zones: 6-10

DESCRIPTION

NATIVE HABITAT: Eastern and Southeastern United States to Eastern Texas; cultivar of nursery origin
PLANT TYPE: Evergreen, broadleaf, large flowering tree
MATURE SIZE: 50-70' tall by 30-50' wide
FORM/SHAPE: Broad, pyramidal, open, loose growing
BARK: Smooth; grayish brown to blackish gray
FLOWER: Fragrant, white flowers are 6-8" wide; blooms May to June; slow to begin flowering; attracts insects
FRUIT: Red berries in a large, hard, woody cone; sometimes considered messy
FOLIAGE: Alternate, simple, elliptical to oblong, 5-10" long; dark green leaves with rich reddish brown undersides; older, inner leaves turn yellow to brown and shed in Fall and again in Spring as new growth begins; leaf litter can be messy

LANDSCAPE CHARACTERISTICS

GROWTH RATE: Slow to Moderate **DROUGHT TOLERANCE:** Moderate to High **SALT TOLERANCE:** Low to Moderate
SOIL REQUIREMENTS: Well-drained, moist, fertile, humus rich soil that is well-limed; tolerant of slightly acidic soil
LIGHT REQUIREMENTS: Full sun produces best growth and flower; tolerates part shade
PEST PROBLEMS: Oleander scale, false Oleander scale, spider mites, Tulip Tree scale, black twig borer, leaf miner and *Magnolia* scale
DISEASE PROBLEMS: Leaf spot, blight, canker, stem canker, root rot, *Verticillium* wilt and wetwood
ENVIRONMENTAL FACTORS: Needs adequate soil moisture and fertility for optimal growth and aesthetics; adaptable to less desirable environmental conditions; spreading root system makes trees difficult to preserve on construction sites
PRUNING: Can be heavily pruned in Spring before new growth begins to maintain size, but will reduce flowering; pruning strengthens limb structure; can be limbed up to create a tree form plant, but best when kept limbed to the ground

ADDITIONAL NOTES

USES: Lawn tree, specimen plant, naturalizing, screening, buffer strips in parking lots and median plantings
URBAN USES: Shows no significant problem in urban planting sites
SUBSTITUTIONS: *Magnolia grandiflora* Teddy Bear®, *Magnolia grandiflora* 'Hasse', *Ilex latifolia* and cultivars, 'Green Giant' Arborvitae, *Cryptomeria japonica*, *Magnolia grandiflora* 'Bracken's Brown Beauty'
COMMENTS: This plant is desired for its large, dark green leaves with vibrant reddish brown undersides. Shows above average cold hardiness. It can be many years before flowering occurs and only a limited number of flowers are produced.
OTHER CULTIVARS: 'Bracken's Brown Beauty' - pyramidal, large tree, dark green foliage with wavy margins and heavy felted, dark brown back, flowers from young age and one of the most cold hardy cultivars; 'Southern Charm' PP 13,049 Teddy Bear® - compact plant form, dark green leaves and season long blooming

Magnolia grandiflora 'Little Gem'
Little Gem Magnolia
USDA Hardiness Zones: 7-9

DESCRIPTION

NATIVE HABITAT: Eastern and Southeastern United States to Eastern Texas; cultivar of nursery origin

PLANT TYPE: Evergreen, broadleaf, medium size flowering tree

MATURE SIZE: 25' tall by 15' wide

FORM/SHAPE: Dense, dome

BARK: Smooth; brownish gray bark when young and matures to grayish black

FLOWER: Fragrant, white flowers 6-8" wide; blooms May to December and begins when young plant is one to two years old; attracts insects

FRUIT: Rose-red berries in a small, hard, woody cone

FOLIAGE: Alternate, simple, ovate to elliptical, small to medium-sized leaves, dark green with a heavily felted brown back in Summer; older leaves turn yellow to brown and shed in Fall and again in Spring as new growth begins; leaf litter can be messy

LANDSCAPE CHARACTERISTICS

GROWTH RATE: Slow to Moderate   **DROUGHT TOLERANCE:** Moderate to High   **SALT TOLERANCE:** Low to Moderate

SOIL REQUIREMENTS: Well-drained, moist, fertile, humus rich soil that is well-limed; tolerant of slightly acidic soil

LIGHT REQUIREMENTS: Full sun produces best growth and flower; tolerates part shade

PEST PROBLEMS: Oleander scale, false Oleander scale, spider mites, Tulip Tree scale, black twig borer, leaf miner and *Magnolia* scale

DISEASE PROBLEMS: Leaf spot, blight, canker, stem canker, root rot, *Verticillium* wilt and wetwood

ENVIRONMENTAL FACTORS: Needs adequate soil moisture and fertility for optimal growth and aesthetics; adaptable to less desirable environmental conditions; spreading root system makes trees difficult to preserve on construction sites

PRUNING: Can be heavily pruned in Spring before new growth to maintain size without reducing flowering; pruning strengthens limb structure

ADDITIONAL NOTES

USES: Medium size specimen plant, mass plantings, large hedge or screen; can be espaliered to walls or trellises

URBAN USES: Shows no significant problem in urban planting sites

SUBSTITUTIONS: *Magnolia* cultivars, *Ilex latifolia* and cultivars, other large leaf cultivars of *Ilex* and *Daphniphyllum* species, *Osmanthus* species or cultivars, *Viburnum japonicum*, large *Rhododendron* species or cultivars

COMMENTS: 'Little Gem' is adaptable to heat, humidity and drought stresses. It exhibits a long season of heavy blooming on young trees. Annual fertilization will maintain abundant, dark green foliage and continuous season-long blooming.

OTHER CULTIVARS: 'Southern Charm' PP 13,049 Teddy Bear® - compact plant form, dark green leaves and season-long blooming

Magnolia grandiflora 'Mgtig' PP 9,243
Greenback™ Magnolia or Migtig Magnolia
USDA Hardiness Zones: 7-10

DESCRIPTION

NATIVE HABITAT: Eastern and Southeastern United States to Eastern Texas; cultivar of nursery origin
PLANT TYPE: Evergreen, broadleaf, medium size flowering tree
MATURE SIZE: 30' tall by 12' wide
FORM/SHAPE: Dense, broad, pyramidal, tightly-branched
BARK: Smooth; grayish brown to blackish gray
FLOWER: Fragrant, white flowers; blooms May to June; attracts insects
FRUIT: Red berries in an eliptical to large, hard, woody cone; sometimes considered messy
FOLIAGE: Alternate, simple, oblong; waxy, green leaves with a greenish gray pubescent underside; older leaves turn yellow to brown and shed in Fall and again in Spring as new growth begins; litter can be messy

LANDSCAPE CHARACTERISTICS

GROWTH RATE: Slow to Moderate   **DROUGHT TOLERANCE:** Moderate to High   **SALT TOLERANCE:** Low to Moderate
SOIL REQUIREMENTS: Well-drained, moist, fertile, humus rich soil that is well-limed; tolerant of slightly acidic soil
LIGHT REQUIREMENTS: Full sun produces best growth and flower; tolerates part shade
PEST PROBLEMS: Oleander scale, false Oleander scale, spider mites, Tulip Tree scale, black twig borer, leaf miner and *Magnolia* scale
DISEASE PROBLEMS: Leaf spot, blight, canker, stem canker, root rot, *Verticillium* wilt and wetwood
ENVIRONMENTAL FACTORS: Needs adequate soil moisture and fertility for optimal growth and aesthetics; adaptable to less desirable environmental conditions; spreading root system makes trees difficult to preserve on construction sites
PRUNING: Can be heavily pruned in Spring before new growth begins to maintain size, but will reduce flowering; pruning strengthens limb structure; can be limbed up to create a tree-form plant, but best kept limbed to the ground

ADDITIONAL NOTES

USES: Lawn tree, specimen plant , buffer or screen, parking lot median planting and naturalizing
URBAN USES: Shows no significant problem in urban planting sites
SUBSTITUTIONS: *Magnolia* cultivars, *Ilex latifolia* and cultivars, other large leaf cultivars of *Ilex* and *Daphniphyllum* species, *Osmanthus* species or cultivars, *Viburnum japonicum*, large *Rhododendron* species or cultivars
COMMENTS: This plant does not exhibit a brown back to the leaf, hence the name Greenback™. Plant exhibits a narrow plant form allowing it to be used where crown space is limited. Plant is slow to flower with no repeat bloom.
OTHER CULTIVARS: 'Southern Charm' PP 13,049 Teddy Bear® - compact plant form, dark green leaves and season-long blooming; 'Hasse' - narrow, pyramidal, large tree form, foliage very dark green with light, reddish brown felted back, slow to flower, no repeat bloom

Magnolia grandiflora 'Southern Charm' PP 13,049
Teddy Bear® Magnolia
USDA Hardiness Zones: 7-9

DESCRIPTION

NATIVE HABITAT: Southeastern United States to Eastern Texas; cultivar of nursery origin

PLANT TYPE: Evergreen, broadleaf, medium size flowering tree

MATURE SIZE: 20' tall by 12' wide

FORM/SHAPE: Dense, pyramidal

BARK: Smooth; brownish gray when young; matures to smooth grayish black

FLOWER: Fragrant, white flowers 6-8" wide; blooms May to November; attracts insects

FRUIT: Red berries in a small, dry, hard, woody cone

FOLIAGE: Alternate, simple, broad-ovate; small to medium-sized leaves; lustrous dark green with a heavily felted reddish-brown back in Summer; old leaves turn yellow to brown and shed in Fall and again in Spring as new growth begins; less leaf litter, but can be messy

LANDSCAPE CHARACTERISTICS

GROWTH RATE: Slow to Moderate **DROUGHT TOLERANCE:** Moderate to High **SALT TOLERANCE:** Low to Moderate

SOIL REQUIREMENTS: Well-drained, moist, fertile, humus rich soil that is well-limed; tolerant of slightly acidic soil

LIGHT REQUIREMENTS: Full sun produces best growth and flower; tolerates light shade

PEST PROBLEMS: Oleander scale, false Oleander scale, spider mites, Tulip Tree scale, black twig borer and leaf miner

DISEASE PROBLEMS: Leaf spot, blight, canker, stem canker, root rot, *Verticillium* wilt and wetwood

ENVIRONMENTAL FACTORS: No serious problems; needs adequate soil moisture and fertility for optimal growth and aesthetics; adaptable to less desirable environmental conditions; spreading root system makes trees difficult to preserve on construction sites

PRUNING: Little pruning needed, but can be pruned every few years to maintain a dense, small plant size; can be heavily pruned in Spring before new growth to maintain size without reducing flowering; pruning will strengthen limb structure

ADDITIONAL NOTES

USES: Medium size specimen plant, mass plantings as a large hedge or screen and accent plant

URBAN USES: Shows no significant problem in urban planting sites

SUBSTITUTIONS: *Magnolia* cultivars, *Ilex latifolia* and cultivars, other large leaf cultivars of *Ilex*, *Daphnipyllum* species, *Osmanthus* species or cultivars, *Viburnum japonica*, large *Rhododendron* species or cultivars

COMMENTS: Teddy Bear® is adaptable to heat, high humidity and drought stresses. Because of its self-branching growth habit and long, continuous flowering season, Teddy Bear® is a more compact *Magnolia*. Pruning every few years will also help maintain a dense, small plant size.

OTHER CULTIVARS: 'Little Gem' - small, dark green leaves on a medium-sized, narrow, dome-shaped tree, heavy flowering

Magnolia grandiflora 'TMGH' PP 11,612
Alta® Magnolia
USDA Hardiness Zones: 7-9

DESCRIPTION

NATIVE HABITAT: Eastern and Southern United States to Eastern Texas; cultivar of nursery origin

PLANT TYPE: Evergreen, broadleaf, medium size flowering tree

MATURE SIZE: 20-25' tall by 8-10' wide

FORM/SHAPE: Upright, dense, columnar

BARK: Smooth; grayish brown to blackish gray

FLOWER: Fragrant, white flowers are 6-8" wide; blooms May to June; attracts insects

FRUIT: Small, hard, woody cone with rose-red berries; sometimes considered messy

FOLIAGE: Alternate, simple, ovate to elliptical, medium to small-sized leaves; glossy, dark green leaves with light brown underside; older leaves turn yellow to brown and shed in Fall and again in Spring as new growth begins; leaf litter can be messy

LANDSCAPE CHARACTERISTICS

GROWTH RATE: Slow to Moderate   **DROUGHT TOLERANCE:** Moderate to High   **SALT TOLERANCE:** Low to Moderate

SOIL REQUIREMENTS: Well-drained, moist, fertile, humus rich soil that is well-limed; tolerant of slightly acidic soil

LIGHT REQUIREMENTS: Full sun produces best growth and flower; tolerates part shade

PEST PROBLEMS: Oleander scale, false Oleander scale, spider mites, Tulip Tree scale, black twig borer, leaf miner and *Magnolia* scale

DISEASE PROBLEMS: Leaf spot, blight, canker, stem canker, root rot, *Verticillium* wilt and wetwood

ENVIRONMENTAL FACTORS: Needs adequate soil moisture and fertility for optimal growth and aesthetics; adaptable to less desirable environmental conditions; spreading root system makes trees difficult to preserve on construction sites

PRUNING: Can be heavily pruned in Spring before new growth begins to maintain size, but will reduce flowering; pruning strengthens limb structure; can be limbed up to create a tree form plant, but best kept limbed to the ground

ADDITIONAL NOTES

USES: Lawn tree, specimen plant, buffer or screen, parking lot median and naturalizing

URBAN USES: Shows no significant problem in urban planting sites

SUBSTITUTIONS: *Magnolia* cultivars, *Ilex latifolia* and cultivars, other large leaved cultivars of *Ilex* and *Daphniphyllum* species, *Osmanthus* species or cultivars, *Viburnum japonicum*, large *Rhododendron* species or cultivars

COMMENTS: Alta® is great to use as a screen since the plant is not as wide as other *Magnolia* varieties. The light brown back of the leaves fade to a silvery gray in late Summer through Winter. The plant is slow to flower with no repeat bloom.

OTHER CULTIVARS: 'Hasse' - narrow, pyramidal, large tree, small to medium-sized foliage with light reddish brown felted back, slow to flower, no repeat bloom; 'Southern Charm' PP 13,049 Teddy Bear® - compact plant form, dark green leaves and season-long blooming

Magnolia virginiana
Sweetbay Magnolia
USDA Hardiness Zones: 5-10a

DESCRIPTION

NATIVE HABITAT: Eastern and Southern United States to Eastern Texas
PLANT TYPE: Evergreen to semi-evergreen, broadleaf, large flowering tree
MATURE SIZE: 40-50' tall by 15-25' wide
FORM/SHAPE: Columnar, upright tree with a symmetrical, rounded canopy
BARK: Smooth; light gray
FLOWER: White blooms 3-5" diameter; showy and fragrant; blooms June through September; attracts insects
FRUIT: Small, dry, hard cone with red berries; attracts wildlife; sometimes considered messy
FOLIAGE: Alternate, simple, elliptical to oblong; small to medium-sized leaves are dark green with silvery white underside; older leaves turn yellow to brown and shed in Fall and again in Spring as new growth begins; leaf litter can be messy

LANDSCAPE CHARACTERISTICS

GROWTH RATE: Moderate to Fast   **DROUGHT TOLERANCE:** Moderate   **SALT TOLERANCE:** Low
SOIL REQUIREMENTS: Well-drained, moist, fertile, humus rich soil that is well-limed; tolerant of slightly acidic soil; tolerant of water-logged soil in native habitats
LIGHT REQUIREMENTS: Full sun to light shade
PEST PROBLEMS: Oleander scale, false Oleander scale, spider mites, Tulip Tree scale, black twig borer, leaf miner and *Magnolia* scale
DISEASE PROBLEMS: Leaf spot, blight, canker, stem canker, root rot, *Verticillium* wilt and wetwood
ENVIRONMENTAL FACTORS: Needs adequate soil moisture and fertility for optimal growth and aesthetics; adaptable to less desirable environmental conditions; spreading root system makes trees difficult to preserve on construction sites
PRUNING: Can be heavily pruned in Spring before new growth begins to maintain size, but will somewhat reduce flowering; pruning strengthens limb structure

ADDITIONAL NOTES

USES: Espalier, lawn tree, buffer strip and medians, accent near patio or deck, residential street tree and naturalizing
URBAN USES: Shows no significant problem in urban planting sites
SUBSTITUTIONS: *Magnolia grandiflora* cultivars, *M. tripetala*, *M. pyramidata*, *M. macrophylla*, *M. acuminata*, Asian species and hybrid cultivars of *Magnolia*, *Ilex latifolia*
COMMENTS: Sweetbay is a beautiful specimen tree that should be used more often. This plant is native to swampy areas of the Southeastern United States and is tolerant of boggy and low lying areas. This plant is a perfect choice for tight and narrow urban areas with limited crown space.
OTHER CULTIVARS: *Magnolia virginiana var. australis* - typical of species, found in more northern regions of its native range; 'Henry Hicks' - typical of species, reported to be more cold hardy; 'Jim Wilson' PP 12,065 Moonglow® - typical of species, reported to be more cold hardy

Myrica cerifera
Wax Myrtle

USDA Hardiness Zones: 7b-11

DESCRIPTION

NATIVE HABITAT: Bermuda, West Indies to Central America; Eastern and Coastal United States through the Gulf to Texas

PLANT TYPE: Evergreen, broadleaf, large shrub or small tree

MATURE SIZE: 15-25' tall by 20-25' wide

FORM/SHAPE: Rounded, vase-shaped, irregular outline; can be multi-trunked

BARK: Smooth; brown-gray to greenish gray

FLOWER: Green; inconspicuous; blooms in Spring

FRUIT: Blue color; round; fleshy and waxy inconspicuous, but plant produces large amounts on the previous season's growth; attracts wildlife

FOLIAGE: Alternate, simple, entire on lower half of the oblanceolate leaf, serrated margin on upper half; glossy green to olive-green leaves, covered by sparse yellow-gold glandular hairs

LANDSCAPE CHARACTERISTICS

GROWTH RATE: Moderate   **DROUGHT TOLERANCE:** Moderate   **SALT TOLERANCE:** Moderate to High

SOIL REQUIREMENTS: Well-drained, acidic to alkaline soil; clay, loam to sandy soil; tolerates extended flooding; adapts to many soil types and conditions

LIGHT REQUIREMENTS: Full sun to part shade; tolerates light shade, but growth will be very open

PEST PROBLEMS: Caterpillars, mites, webworms, aphids, mealybugs, Peony scale, Dogwood borer, *Camellia* mining scale, Cranberry root worm and Mulberry whitefly

DISEASE PROBLEMS: Cankers, *Fusarium*, *Oxyporus*, dieback, rust, algal leaf spot and leaf spot

ENVIRONMENTAL FACTORS: Plant sprouts from the roots; defoliated by severe cold injury; becomes invasive from seed spread by birds and root sprouts

PRUNING: Prune to allow circulation for pedestrians or vehicular traffic; prune up limbs to show trunk aesthetics; prune for density and height control

ADDITIONAL NOTES

USES: Container or planter, hedge, parking lot plantings, buffer strips, accent near a deck or patio, screening, street tree, specimen and naturalizing

URBAN USES: An adaptable plant for coastal areas due to its high salt tolerance

SUBSTITUTIONS: *Ilex cornuta* cultivars, *Ilex vomitoria*, *Illicium floridanum*, *Pyracantha*, *Pittosporum* cultivars

COMMENTS: The Wax Myrtle is very tough and easily grown. It tolerates a wide range of conditions and is a native plant that grows fast. It is best planted in regions where it is locally native. The plant is very invasive from seed spread by birds.   The severe cold will top kill or defoliate plants.

OTHER CULTIVARS: 'Don's Dwarf Wax Myrtle' - leaf and stem size smaller than species, 4-6' tall by 4-6' wide; 'Hiawassee' - typical of species, possibly more cold tolerant

Osmanthus fragrans
Fragrant Tea Olive
USDA Hardiness Zones: 7b-9

DESCRIPTION

NATIVE HABITAT: Japan and Southeastern China
PLANT TYPE: Evergreen, broadleaf, large flowering shrub or small tree
MATURE SIZE: 15-30' tall by 15-20' wide
FORM/SHAPE: Broad, columnar, upright, symmetrical canopy
BARK: Somewhat smooth; brownish gray with large lenticel scars when young; develops shallow fissures on lower trunk with age
FLOWER: White flower; very fragrant; blooms in Fall, Winter and Spring; attracts insects
FRUIT: Black to blue: oblong to round; fleshy; inconspicuous and not commonly produced
FOLIAGE: Opposite, serrulate, oval to elliptical; dark green leaves are attractive through Winter months

LANDSCAPE CHARACTERISTICS

GROWTH RATE: Moderate   **DROUGHT TOLERANCE:** Moderate   **SALT TOLERANCE:** Low
SOIL REQUIREMENTS: Well-drained, moist, fertile, humus rich, slightly acidic soil
LIGHT REQUIREMENTS: Full sun to light shade; best shape in full sun
PEST PROBLEMS: Oleander scale, *Camellia* mining scale, tea scale, American Plum borer, mealybugs, *Euonymus* scale and ambrosia beetles
DISEASE PROBLEMS: Southern stem blight, Oak root rot, *Verticillium* wilt, gall, white root rot, *Pseudomonas*, anthracnose, *Glomerella*, *Phytophthora* root rot and nematodes
ENVIRONMENTAL FACTORS: Very adaptable to various soil, light and moisture conditions; frost injury is a possibility in Fall and Spring
PRUNING: Little pruning required; can be clipped to maintain a more dense canopy; can be limbed up to create a small multi-trunk tree

ADDITIONAL NOTES

USES: Hedge, screen, specimen near a deck or patio, large fragrant shrub and foundation plantings
URBAN USES: Good resistance to pests and diseases; fairly drought tolerant, once established; cold injury is the major problem in USDA Hardiness Zones 7b-8a which can result in stem dieback and other wood invading diseases
SUBSTITUTIONS: *Ilex* cultivars, *Osmanthus x fortunei*, *Osmanthus heterophyllus* cultivars, *Ilex cornuta* cultivars, *Ligustrum* cultivars, *Viburnum* cultivars
COMMENTS: This plant produces very fragrant blossoms that can be enjoyed near entrances, walkways or outdoor sitting areas. These plants should be used more for screening, especially in residential settings.
OTHER CULTIVARS: 'Fudingzhu' - heavy flowering, extremely fragrant, flowers heavily at a young age; *O. f. aurantiacus* - orange flowers, fragrant, early Fall flowering in mid October, large, upright branching shrub 10-15' tall by 6-8' wide, prefers light shade; *O.f. thunbergii* - Chinese Yellow Flowering Tea Olive, soft yellow, fragrant flowers, larger leaves, more cold hardy - USDA Hardiness Zones 7-9

Osmanthus x fortunei
Fortune's Tea Olive
USDA Hardiness Zones: 7-9

DESCRIPTION

NATIVE HABITAT: Hybrid of two Asiatic species, *O. fragrans* and *O. heterophyllus,* introduced in the 1860's by Robert Fortune; of garden origin

PLANT TYPE: Evergreen, broadleaf, large flowering shrub or small tree

MATURE SIZE: 15-20' tall by 8-15' wide

FORM/SHAPE: Upright, oval, symmetrical canopy

BARK: Somewhat smooth; brownish gray with large lenticel scars when young; develops shallow fissures on lower trunk with age

FLOWER: White flower; very fragrant; blooms in Fall; attracts insects

FRUIT: Seldom, if any, fruit produced; similar in appearance to *O. fragrans*

FOLIAGE: Opposite, simple, serrate, ovate 2-4" long, pronounced dull spines on the serrations as juvenile leaves, adult leaves have entire margins with one spine at the leaf apex; dark, lustrous green leaves with conspicuously expressed veins on surface

LANDSCAPE CHARACTERISTICS

GROWTH RATE: Moderate **DROUGHT TOLERANCE:** Moderate **SALT TOLERANCE:** Low

SOIL REQUIREMENTS: Well-drained, moist, fertile, humus rich, slightly acidic soil

LIGHT REQUIREMENTS: Full sun to light shade; best shape in full sun

PEST PROBLEMS: Oleander scale, *Camellia* mining scale, tea scale, American Plum borer, mealybugs, *Euonymus* scale and ambrosia beetles

DISEASE PROBLEMS: Southern stem blight, Oak root rot, nematodes, *Verticillium* wilt, gall, white root rot, *Pseudomonas*, anthracnose, *Glomerella* and *Phytophthora* root rot

ENVIRONMENTAL FACTORS: Very adaptable to various soil, light and moisture conditions; may show Winter sunscald on foliage in sunny exposed sites after severe cold temperatures

PRUNING: Little pruning required; can be clipped to maintain a more dense canopy; can be limbed up to create a small multi-trunk tree; flowers form on old growth and pruning may reduce flower production

ADDITIONAL NOTES

USES: Container or planter, hedge, screen, specimen near a deck or patio, large multi-trunk accent tree, foundation plantings and as a low maintenance plant for commercial landscapes

URBAN USES: Very adaptable; more cold hardy; shows less stem injury and dieback problems from cold temperatures

SUBSTITUTIONS: *Ilex x* 'HL 10-90' PP 14,477 Christmas Jewel®, *Osmanthus heterophyllus* and cultivars, *Ilex cornuta* cultivars, *Ligustrum* cultivars, *Viburnum* cultivars, *Magnolia grandiflora* 'Little Gem' and 'Southern Charm' PP 13,049 Teddy Bear®

COMMENTS: Fortune's Tea Olive is one of the most cold tolerant *Osmanthus* cultivars. It has very fragrant flowers that appear in Fall and is a good choice for adding fragrance to the landscape.

OTHER CULTIVARS: 'San Jose' - similar, interspecific hybrid of U.S. origin, leaves more narrow with more spines, similar flowers

Picea abies
Norway Spruce
USDA Hardiness Zones: 2b-7a

DESCRIPTION

NATIVE HABITAT: Central Europe through Northern Europe
PLANT TYPE: Evergreen, coniferous, short needle-like leaves, large tree
MATURE SIZE: 80-100' tall by 25-40' wide
FORM/SHAPE: Symmetrical, graceful, pyramidal with drooping branchlets
BARK: Thin and scaly; tannish brown when young; develops grayish brown flakes or plates as it matures
FLOWER: Yellow to brown, small male cones; green, long, drooping female cones mature to grayish brown; forms in late Winter to Spring
FRUIT: Grayish brown female cone is long and in drooping clusters
FOLIAGE: Spiraled arrangement on tips, may be flattened arrangement on underside of stems; simple, short needle-like leaves; new growth emerges light green and matures to dark green; older, inner needles turn yellow to brown in Fall and shed before new growth emerges

LANDSCAPE CHARACTERISTICS

GROWTH RATE: Moderate to Fast   **DROUGHT TOLERANCE:** Moderate   **SALT TOLERANCE:** Low to Moderate
SOIL REQUIREMENTS: Well-drained, moist, fertile, slightly alkaline to acidic, clay, loam or sandy soil
LIGHT REQUIREMENTS: Full sun, but can tolerate some part shade
PEST PROBLEMS: Very sensitive to mites in Summer; also affected by galls, adelgids, bagworm, needle miner, redheaded sawfly, Spruce weevil, White Pine weevil and pitch mass borer
DISEASE PROBLEMS: *Cytospora* canker, needle casts (cause needles to turn yellow or brown and fall off), root rot and wood rot
ENVIRONMENTAL FACTORS: Not tolerant of overly wet or dry soil; more adaptable to colder climates
PRUNING: Maintain central leader in large growing trees; most dwarf cultivars need no pruning; trees can be pruned as hedges or Christmas trees

ADDITIONAL NOTES

USES: Screening, specimen, windbreak and live Christmas tree
URBAN USES: Urban tolerance to ozone; sensitive to sulfur dioxide pollution; adaptable tree where climate and soil are suitable; can be used along streetscapes with enough space; good for medians when good soil and moisture are present
SUBSTITUTIONS: *Cryptomeria* cultivars, *Thuja* cultivars, *Pinus* species and cultivars, *Cedrus deodara* cultivars
COMMENTS: Norwary Spruce is best used as a specimen in a lawn area, as a windbreak or as a screen. This tree transplants easily as a balled and burlapped or container grown plant and can be grown as a live Christmas tree.
OTHER CULTIVARS: 'Clanbrassiliana' - small, spreading, mounding dwarf form; 'Cupressina' - slender, columnar, medium height form; 'Pendula Major' - medium height, central leader with pendulous and weeping limbs

Picea omorika
Serbian Spruce
USDA Hardiness Zones: 4-7

DESCRIPTION

NATIVE HABITAT: Region of Eastern Europe

PLANT TYPE: Evergreen, coniferous, short needle-like leaves, large tree

MATURE SIZE: 45-50' tall by 15-20' wide

FORM/SHAPE: Narrow, pyramidal

BARK: Chestnut-brown; scales off in thin plates as tree grows

FLOWER: Inconspicuous; forms in Spring

FRUIT: Yellow male cones; conspicuous, purple, female cones mature to light chestnut-brown; persistent

FOLIAGE: Spiraled arrangement; short needle-like leaves are green to blue-green when young; older inner needles turn yellow to brown and shed in Fall and again in Spring before new growth emerges

LANDSCAPE CHARACTERISTICS

GROWTH RATE: Slow to Moderate   **DROUGHT TOLERANCE:** Moderate   **SALT TOLERANCE:** Low

SOIL REQUIREMENTS: Well-drained, moist, fertile, slightly alkaline to acidic, clay, loam or sandy soil

LIGHT REQUIREMENTS: Part shade to full sun; grows best with some shelter from mid-day heat in warmer climate regions

PEST PROBLEMS: Long term health not usually affected, but can have a few pests: galls, Spruce bagworm larvae, Spruce needle miner, spider mites and sawfly larvae

DISEASE PROBLEMS: Needle cast, butt rot, nematodes, root rot, rust and *Cytospora* canker

ENVIRONMENTAL FACTORS: Avoid wet and extremely dry planting sites

PRUNING: Allow tree to maintain limbs to the ground; maintain a central leader to reduce wind and ice damage

ADDITIONAL NOTES

USES: Lawn tree, parking lot buffer strips, highway medians, screen or windbreak planting and as a specimen

URBAN USES: Adaptable to moderate urban conditions; keep limbed to ground for a better looking tree; allow enough space for growth; soil should be well-drained, moist and fertile

SUBSTITUTIONS: *Picea abies* or *Cedrus deodara* cultivars

COMMENTS: *Picea omorika* is a very adaptable species as well as its many cultivars. The tree should be used more in the southern limits of its hardiness range.

OTHER CULTIVARS: 'Nana' - medium size, dense, conical bush; 'Pendula' - slender tree with slightly drooping branches

Picea pungens
Colorado or Blue Spruce
USDA Hardiness Zones: 4-7

DESCRIPTION

NATIVE HABITAT: High mountain elevations of Western North America

PLANT TYPE: Evergreen, coniferous, short needle-like leaves, large tree

MATURE SIZE: 30-50' tall by 10-20' wide

FORM/SHAPE: Symmetrical, columnar to pyramidal; dense once fully grown

BARK: Orange-brown; scales off in thin plates as plant matures

FLOWER: Orange male cones; green to purple female cones mature to brown; inconspicuous; blooms in Spring

FRUIT: Short, oval, dry, brown cone

FOLIAGE: Spiraled arrangement, simple, short needle-like leaves; blue, blue-green or green foliage; older inner needles turn yellow to brown and shed in Fall and again in Spring before new growth emerges

LANDSCAPE CHARACTERISTICS

GROWTH RATE: Slow   **DROUGHT TOLERANCE:** Moderate   **SALT TOLERANCE:** Moderate to High

SOIL REQUIREMENTS: Well-drained, moist, fertile, humus rich, acidic, clay, loam or sandy soil; should be irrigated in dry weather

LIGHT REQUIREMENTS: Part shade to full sun; grows best with some shelter from mid-day heat in warmer climate regions

PEST PROBLEMS: Galls, Spruce bagworm larvae, needle miner, Pine needle scale, aphids and mites

DISEASE PROBLEMS: Needle cast, butt rot, nematodes, root rot, Pine wood nematodes, rust and *Cytospora* canker

ENVIRONMENTAL FACTORS: Late Spring freezes kill new growth; irrigate during extremely dry weather

PRUNING: Should be grown with a single leader; prune to shape and control size; limbs should be left to ground

ADDITIONAL NOTES

USES: Screen, specimen or as a Christmas tree in mountain regions

URBAN USES: Can grow in urban areas; not the best choice for street or median plantings

SUBSTITUTIONS: *Picea omorika, Abies firma, Picea abies, Cedrus deodara* cultivars

COMMENTS: *Picea pungens* is best grown in high elevations where air and soil temperatures are cool and in soil that provides excellent water drainage. It is adaptable to cold, windy and full sun sites. Many clonal and cultivar forms are grown from dwarf to weeping plant forms and with many different foliage colors.

OTHER CULTIVARS: 'Iseli Foxtail' - glaucous blue foliage, needles long at base of new growth and short at the tip; 'Glauca Pendula' - glaucous foliage, spreading plant form; 'Hoopsii' - powder blue foliage, pyramidal form

Pinus elliottii
Slash Pine
USDA Hardiness Zones: 7-11

DESCRIPTION

NATIVE HABITAT: Coastal and Southern United States
PLANT TYPE: Evergreen, coniferous, long needle-like leaves, large tree
MATURE SIZE: 75-100' tall by 35-50' wide
FORM/SHAPE: Irregular outline; oval, pyramidal, open
BARK: Thin, purple-brown; peels in thin plates; mature bark is dark
reddish brown with rough irregular plates and furrows; plates slough off layers continuously
FLOWER: Purple male cone, 1 1/2-2" long by 1/2-5/8" wide; brown to pinkish purple female cone matures to reddish brown; forms in January to February
FRUIT: Ripe cone reddish brown, 3 1/2-5 1/2" long by 3-3 1/2" wide, matures in Fall; male cones are large and can create litter
FOLIAGE: Spiraled arrangement; two long, needle-like leaves per fascicle; stout, ridged, slightly twisted, 7-10" long; dark, glossy green; older inner needles turn yellow to brown and shed through Winter and abundantly before new growth in Spring

LANDSCAPE CHARACTERISTICS

GROWTH RATE: Moderate to Fast   **DROUGHT TOLERANCE:** High   **SALT TOLERANCE:** Moderate to High
SOIL REQUIREMENTS: Well-drained, slightly acidic to slightly alkaline, clay, loam or sandy soil; tolerant of infrequently wet soil and soil with moderate to low fertility
LIGHT REQUIREMENTS: Full sun
PEST PROBLEMS: Black carpenter beetle, aphids, spider mites, Southern Pine beetle, Pine needle miner, bagworm, redheaded pin sawfly, sawfly, pales weevil, Deodar weevil, Nantucket tipmoth, Pine spittlebug, Pine scale, Pine webworm, Pine tortoise scale and other scale insects
DISEASE PROBLEMS: Canker, blister rust, butt rot, *Fusarium*, *Ganoderma*, needle blight, needle rust, nutrient deficiencies, *Pestalotiopsis*, *Phytophthora*, pitch canker, sooty mold, gall, cone rust and Pine wood nematodes
ENVIRONMENTAL FACTORS: Self-pruning lower limbs can be a hazard to people and property; moderate tolerance to infrequent flooding; moderate tolerance of air pollutants; needles may be shaded out by excessive growth of Spanish moss in warmer, humid zones
PRUNING: Prune to remove low hanging limbs; remove storm, wind and ice damaged limbs; self-pruning and dropping limbs are a hazard; remove inferior, dead or dying limbs

ADDITIONAL NOTES

USES: Parking lot buffer strips, median strip, reclamation plantings and shade tree
URBAN USES: Use when space allows but limbs, cones and needles cause litter
SUBSTITUTIONS: *Pinus glabra*, *Pinus echinata*, *Pinus palustris*, *Pinus serotina*, or *Pinus clausa*
COMMENTS: The Slash Pine's open canopy allows underplantings of shade requiring small trees, shrubs and plants. Slash Pine does not like a high pH soil. Branches can break in ice storms. Slash Pine makes a natural landscape setting plant in coastal regions.
OTHER CULTIVARS: No known commercial cultivars are presently grown

Pinus nigra
Austrian Pine
USDA Hardiness Zones: 5-8a

DESCRIPTION

NATIVE HABITAT: Austria to Central Italy, Greece and Yugoslavia
PLANT TYPE: Evergreen, coniferous, needle-like leaves, large tree
MATURE SIZE: 40-50' tall by 25-35' wide
FORM/SHAPE: Pyramidal, moderately dense
BARK: Dark brown to gray-brown furrowed; forms irregular plates on the ridges
FLOWER: Yellow, inconspicuous; blooms in Spring
FRUIT: Small, brown male cones; yellow-green, female cones turn brown when mature; 2 1/2" long by 1 3/8" wide
FOLIAGE: Spiraled arrangement; two 3-4" long green needle-like leaves per fascile; older inner needles turn yellow to brown and shed in Fall and again in Spring at time of new growth

LANDSCAPE CHARACTERISTICS

GROWTH RATE: Moderate to Fast   **DROUGHT TOLERANCE:** High   **SALT TOLERANCE:** Moderate to High
SOIL REQUIREMENTS: Well-drained, slightly alkaline to slightly acidic, clay, loam or sandy soil
LIGHT REQUIREMENTS: Full sun
PEST PROBLEMS: Black carpenter beetle, aphids, spider mites, Southern Pine beetle, Pine needle miner, bagworm, redheaded pin sawfly, sawfly, pales weevil, Deodar weevil, Nantucket tipmoth, Pine spittlebug, Pine scale, Pine webworm, Pine tortoise scale and other scale insects
DISEASE PROBLEMS: Canker, blister rust, butt rot, *Fusarium*, *Ganoderma*, needle blight, needle rust, nutrient deficiencies, *Pestalotiopsis*, *Phytophthora*, pitch canker, sooty mold, gall, cone rust and Pine wood nematodes
ENVIRONMENTAL FACTORS: Not tolerant of shade or wet soil sites; moderately tolerant of air pollution
PRUNING: Low hanging limbs; prune for topiary or screen

ADDITIONAL NOTES

USES: Bonsai, buffer strips or medians in parking lots, screening, specimen or as a topiary
URBAN USES: Successfully grown in areas where air pollution, compacted soil or drought is common
SUBSTITUTIONS: *Pinus thunbergii*, *Pinus glabra*, *Pinus echinata*, or *Pinus rigida*
COMMENTS: The Austrian Pine is a good tree to use in Texas because it will withstand dryness and sun exposure. The tree is well adapted to urban conditions, but unfortunately is very susceptible to tip blight in the East and should be used sparingly in this region.
OTHER CULTIVARS: 'Columnaris' - columnar plant form; 'Hornibrookiana' - dwarf, glabrous form, slow growing

Pinus strobus
Eastern White Pine
USDA Hardiness Zones: 3b-7

DESCRIPTION

NATIVE HABITAT: Eastern United States and Southern Canada
PLANT TYPE: Evergreen, coniferous, needle-like leaves, large tree
MATURE SIZE: 50-80' tall by 25-35' wide
FORM/SHAPE: Symmetrical canopy outline when young; irregular, wide speading when mature
BARK: Smooth; greenish gray when young; forms fissures and ridges when mature; showy trunk with heavy resin production
FLOWER: Yellow male cone; male cone has heavy pollen production; inconspicuous; pinkish purple female cone; forms late Winter to Spring
FRUIT: Elongated, greenish purple cone turns brown when mature; covered in resin
FOLIAGE: Spiraled arrangement; simple, soft blue-green needles; three to five needle-like leaves per fascile; 3-4" long; older inner needles turn yellow to brown and shed in Fall and again in Spring as new growth begins

LANDSCAPE CHARACTERISTICS

GROWTH RATE: Fast   **DROUGHT TOLERANCE:** Moderate   **SALT TOLERANCE:** Low
SOIL REQUIREMENTS: Well-drained, acidic, loam or sandy soil; not suited for heavy clay soil
LIGHT REQUIREMENTS: Part shade to full sun; young trees tolerate part shade, mature trees prefer full sun
PEST PROBLEMS: White Pine weevil, mites, adelgids, bark beetle, black carpenter beetle, aphids, spider mites, Southern Pine beetle, Pine needle miner, bagworm, redheaded pin sawfly, sawfly, pales weevil, Deodar weevil, Nantucket tipmoth, Pine spittlebug, Pine scale, Pine webworm, Pine tortoise scale and other scale insects
DISEASE PROBLEMS: White Pine blister rust, canker, butt rot, *Fusarium*, *Ganoderma*, needle blight, needle rust, nutrient deficiencies, *Pestalotiopsis*, *Phytophthora*, pitch canker, sooty mold, gall, cone rust and Pine wood nematodes
ENVIRONMENTAL FACTORS: Roots close to surface; susceptible to injury from salt on roads; sensitive to air pollution
PRUNING: Allow tree to remain limbed to the ground; remove co-dominant leaders

ADDITIONAL NOTES

USES: Bonsai, hedge or screen, shade tree, specimen, Christmas tree and naturalizing
URBAN USES: No proven urban tolerance; sensitive to air pollution; not tolerant of compacted or water-logged soil
SUBSTITUTIONS: *Pinus glabra*, *Pinus armandii*, *Pinus monticola*
COMMENTS: *Pinus strobus* is one of the few Pines that make a nice hedge or screen. It is best if lower branches are kept full to ground. *Pinus strobus* is a good choice as a specimen, in group plantings or as a Christmas tree. Red Currants are hosts to White Pine blister rust and should not be planted within 300' of White Pines.
OTHER CULTIVARS: Dwarf, weeping and unusual plant forms and foliage are also known: 'Fastigiata', 'Blue Shag', 'Nana' and 'Prostrata'

Pinus taeda
Loblolly Pine
USDA Hardiness Zones: 6b-9

DESCRIPTION

NATIVE HABITAT: Eastern and Southern United States

PLANT TYPE: Evergreen, coniferous, long needle-like leaves, large tree

MATURE SIZE: 50-80' tall by 30-35' wide

FORM/SHAPE: Tall, narrow dome with irregular outline

BARK: Brown to gray-brown; furrowed, forming large, irregular plates

FLOWER: Greenish to purple male cone; green female cone matures to brown and remains on tree for three to four years; forms in late Winter to Spring

FRUIT: Brown, large, spiny; cones form in pairs; persistent and showy

FOLIAGE: Spiraled arrangement; three long, needle-like leaves per fascile; fragrant green foliage; older inner needles turn yellow-brown and shed in Fall and again in Spring at time of new growth

LANDSCAPE CHARACTERISTICS

GROWTH RATE: Fast   **DROUGHT TOLERANCE:** Moderate   **SALT TOLERANCE:** Moderate

SOIL REQUIREMENTS: Well-drained, acidic, clay, loam or sandy soil; will tolerate infrequently wet sites

LIGHT REQUIREMENTS: Full sun

PEST PROBLEMS: Black carpenter beetle, aphids, spider mites, Southern Pine beetle, Pine needle miner, bagworm, redheaded pin sawfly, sawfly, pales weevil, Deodar weevil, Nantucket tipmoth, Pine spittlebug, Pine scale, Pine webworm, Pine tortoise scale and other scale insects

DISEASE PROBLEMS: Canker, blister rust, butt rot, *Fusarium*, *Ganoderma*, needle blight, needle rust, nutrient deficiencies, *Pestalotiopsis*, *Phytophthora*, pitch canker, sooty mold, gall, cone rust and Pine wood nematodes

ENVIRONMENTAL FACTORS: Surface roots can lift sidewalks; reseeds into landscape, so it is not good for manicured landscapes

PRUNING: Prune to remove lower limbs as tree grows; self-limbing occurs but dead limbs may have to be removed

ADDITIONAL NOTES

USES: Reclamation plantings, screen planting, shade tree, specimen, parks and commercial landscapes

URBAN USES: No proven tolerance in urban areas

SUBSTITUTIONS: *Pinus rigida, Pinus serotina* or *Pinus elliottii*

COMMENTS: The Loblolly Pine loses its lower branches as the tree ages. It is the most common Pine tree species from upper Coastal to Piedmont regions of its indigenous range and it is often planted as a pulpwood and lumber tree.

OTHER CULTIVARS: No known commercial cultivars are presently grown

Pinus thunbergii
Japanese Black Pine
USDA Hardiness Zones: 6-8

DESCRIPTION

NATIVE HABITAT: Japan and Korea
PLANT TYPE: Evergreen, coniferous, long needle-like leaves, large tree
MATURE SIZE: 25-30' tall by 20-35' wide
FORM/SHAPE: Irregular to pyramidal
BARK: Rough; brown; fissures and ridges form plates with irregular patterns
FLOWER: Yellowish brown male cone; male cone has heavy pollen production; green female cone turns brown when mature
FRUIT: Oval, hard, dry, brown; medium-sized female cone; showy
FOLIAGE: Spiraled arrangement, simple, dark green, 4"-6" long needles; old inner needles turn yellowish-brown and shed in Fall and again in Spring as new growth begins

LANDSCAPE CHARACTERISTICS

GROWTH RATE: Moderate   **DROUGHT TOLERANCE:** High   **SALT TOLERANCE:** Moderate to High
SOIL REQUIREMENTS: Well-drained, acidic to alkaline, clay, loam or sandy soil; does well along the beachfront or in dry sandy soil
LIGHT REQUIREMENTS: Full sun
PEST PROBLEMS: Black carpenter beetle, aphids, spider mites, Southern Pine beetle, Pine needle miner, bagworm, redheaded pin sawfly, sawfly, pales weevil, Deodar weevil, Nantucket tipmoth, Pine spittlebug, Pine scale, Pine webworm, Pine tortoise scale and other scale insects
DISEASE PROBLEMS: Canker, blister rust, butt rot, *Fusarium*, *Ganoderma*, needle blight, needle rust, nutrient deficiencies, *Pestalotiopsis*, *Phytophthora*, pitch canker, sooty mold, gall, cone rust and Pine wood nematodes
ENVIRONMENTAL FACTORS: Broadleaf herbicides used on lawns will cause foliage damage or death to all pines if spray drift is absorbed
PRUNING: Minimal pruning for natural form; prune to create a central leader if tall tree-form or bonsai is preferred

ADDITIONAL NOTES

USES: Bonsai, container or planter planting, buffer strip plantings, specimen or as an accent tree and screening
URBAN USES: No proven urban tolerance; one cultivar has ozone tolerance
SUBSTITUTIONS: *Pinus ridiga, Pinus nigra, Pinus elliottii*
COMMENTS: Many dwarf, unusual foliage and unique plant forms are known for Japanese Black Pine. This is a good plant choice for sandy areas along the beachfront because it is tough and adaptable and grows into unusual, irregular plant forms.
OTHER CULTIVARS: 'Thunderhead' compact form, 'Oculus-draconis' variegated needles, Majestic Beauty® - good ozone tolerance

Pinus virginiana
Virginia Pine
USDA Hardiness Zones: 5-8

DESCRIPTION

NATIVE HABITAT: Eastern and Southern United States
PLANT TYPE: Evergreen, coniferous, short needle-like leaves, large tree
MATURE SIZE: 30-60' tall by 20-40' wide; can grow to 70' tall or larger
FORM/SHAPE: Pyramidal to rounded, open, irregular scrubby crown
BARK: Thin; orange-brown with thin exfoliating flakes; mature bark develops ridges and furrows with thicker flakes and plates
FLOWER: Yellowish orange-brown, male cones, light green, female cone; matures to reddish light brown; forms in late Winter to Spring; pollen may be a severe allergen problem for some people
FRUIT: Short, broad, cone, 1 1/2-3" long by 1 1/2-2" wide
FOLIAGE: Spiraled arrangemen;, two needles per fascicle; simple, twisted, needle-like foliage with stiff, sharp apex, 2-4" long, fragrant; needles held for three or more years

LANDSCAPE CHARACTERISTICS

GROWTH RATE: Slow to Moderate   **DROUGHT TOLERANCE:** Moderate to High   **SALT TOLERANCE:** Low
SOIL REQUIREMENTS: Well-drained, slightly alkaline to slightly acidic, clay, loam or sandy soil
LIGHT REQUIREMENTS: Full sun
PEST PROBLEMS: Black carpenter beetle, aphids, spider mites, Southern Pine beetle, Pine needle miner, bagworm, redheaded pin sawfly, sawfly, pales weevil, Deodar weevil, Nantucket tipmoth, Pine spittlebug, Pine scale, Pine webworm, Pine tortoise scale and other scale insects
DISEASE PROBLEMS: Canker, blister rust, butt rot, *Fusarium*, *Ganoderma*, needle blight, needle rust, nutrient deficiencies, *Pestalotiopsis*, *Phytophthora*, pitch canker, sooty mold, gall, cone rust and Pine wood nematodes
ENVIRONMENTAL FACTORS: Not tolerant of water-logged or flooded soil; reseeds in the landscape, so it is not good for manicured landscapes
PRUNING: Tolerates pruning and shearing; pruning creates a more dense, uniform plant; can develop new shoots on old growth when pruned, making it a good choice for Christmas trees

ADDITIONAL NOTES

USES: Buffer strips, parking lots, median strips, reclamation plantings, specimen, wind breaks and as a Christmas tree
URBAN USES: No proven urban tolerance; not tolerant of water-logged soil and air pollutants; short lived
SUBSTITUTIONS: *Pinus glabra, Pinus echinata, Pinus nigra, Pinus thunbergii* and cultivars or *Picea abies*
COMMENTS: The open, natural form makes the Virginia Pine a good choice for naturalizing and reclamation plantings. If the plant is sheared, it makes a good screen or buffer plant. Virginia Pine is a good choice as a Christmas tree due to shoot regeneration.
OTHER CULTIVARS: 'Wates Golden' - light green Summer foliage typical of species, develops golden foliage in Winter from cold temperatures and full sun, plant has open, broad form unless pruned for compactness

Prunus caroliniana 'Cherry Ruffle'
Cherry Ruffle Cherry Laurel
USDA Hardiness Zones: 7-10

NATIVE HABITAT: Southeastern United States; cultivar of nursery origin
PLANT TYPE: Evergreen, broadleaf, small tree
MATURE SIZE: 20-30' tall by 10-15' wide
FORM/SHAPE: Broad, pyramidal form when young; broad, rounded dome when mature
BARK: Smooth; dark gray with transverse lenticels when young; older trunks become more coarse and near gray-black
FLOWER: Small, white flowers on short racemes, 1/2-2" long; blooms in early Spring before leaves emerge; attracts insects
FRUIT: Green, ovate to subglabous shape, drupe fruit, 1/2-3/4"; dull black when ripe; attracts animals
FOLIAGE: Opposite, simple, ovate, entire margin, 2-4" long; glossy, dark green, thick and waxy leaves; new growth is medium green and turns a dark green color; in Fall, the older previous season's foliage turns yellow and sheds throughout the dormant season until the start of new growth in Spring

LANDSCAPE CHARACTERISTICS

GROWTH RATE: Moderate to Fast   **DROUGHT TOLERANCE:** Moderate   **SALT TOLERANCE:** Moderate
SOIL REQUIREMENTS: Well-drained, moist, fertile, humus rich, slightly acidic to slightly alkaline soil
LIGHT REQUIREMENTS: Full sun to light shade
PEST PROBLEMS: Peach tree borer, Dogwood borer, ambrosia beetles, white fringed beetle, Pear thrips, caterpillars, leafroller, Eastern tent caterpillar, treehopper, leaf miner, spider mites, eriophyid mites, sawfly, skeletonizer, Japanese beetle, Plum borer, shothole borer, Apple leafhopper, terrapin scale, white Peach scale and *Euonymus* scale
DISEASE PROBLEMS: *Alternaria*, leaf spot, black knot, blight, canker, collar rot, *Cylindrocladium*, *Ganoderma*, leaf blister, *Nectria, Phomopsis, Phytophthora,* powdery mildew, *Taphrina, Verticillium* wilt, Oak root rot, *Pseudomonas,* crown gall and virus disorder
ENVIRONMENTAL FACTORS: Not tolerant of water-logged soil; heavy fruit production poses a problem in pedestrian areas; flowers attract insects; produces many seedling plants
PRUNING: Tolerant of heavy pruning for hedges and screens; can be trained as a standard or multi-trunk tree

ADDITIONAL NOTES

USES: Hedges, screening, planters, specimen or accent tree, reclamation and naturalizing
URBAN USES: Very adaptable to soil types and pH levels; needs well-drained soil; not tolerant of water-logged soil
SUBSTITUTIONS: *Ilex cornuta* cultivars, *Ilex x* 'HL 10-90' PP 14,477 Christmas Jewel®, *Ligustrum* cultivars, *Myrica cerifera, Loropetalum* cultivars
COMMENTS: 'Cherry Ruffle' is more dense, upright and compact than the species. The unique 'ruffled' leaf gives the upright plant habit an unusually lacy look. In colder regions, the leaves take on a burgundy-red cast in Winter.
OTHER CULTIVARS: 'Bright-n-Tight'™ - glossy, dark green foliage, upright, narrow, pyramidal form, smaller and more compact than species

Quercus virginiana
Southern Live Oak
USDA Hardiness Zones: 7b-10b

NATIVE HABITAT: Coastal Plains of the Eastern and Southern United States to East Texas
PLANT TYPE: Evergreen to semi-evergreen, broadleaf, large tree
MATURE SIZE: 60-80' tall by 60-120' wide
FORM/SHAPE: Sprawling wide crown; one of the broadest spreading Oaks; usually possesses many curved trunks and branches
BARK: Smooth; tannish gray; matures to dark gray to blackish gray with thick, rough, deep fissures and ridges; becomes blocky with age
FLOWER: Olive-gray, male flower; gray, greenish brown female flower; inconspicuous; blooms in Spring
FRUIT: Variable size, oblong-ellipsoid to obovate, dark brown to black; can cause problems in public access areas
FOLIAGE: Alternate, simple, broadly oblong-elliptic, entire margin smooth to sparsely dentate; dark green leaf surface with olive-green leaf underside; inner foliage turns yellow to brown and sheds throughout Winter and at the time of new growth in Spring

LANDSCAPE CHARACTERISTICS

GROWTH RATE: Slow to Moderate   **DROUGHT TOLERANCE:** High   **SALT TOLERANCE:** Moderate to High
SOIL REQUIREMENTS: Well-drained, slightly acidic to alkaline, clay, loam or sandy soil; tolerates occasionally wet soil
LIGHT REQUIREMENTS: Part shade to full sun
PEST PROBLEMS: Mites (blister, Oak, eriophyid, *Platanus*), ambrosia beetles, Texas leafcutter ants, leaf miner, Cranberry rootworm, caterpillars, orange-striped Oakworm, Oak webworm, Oak skeletonizer, bud gall mite, flatheaded Apple tree borer, Red Oak and branch borer, Ash borer, broadnecked root borer, spittlebug, Oak lacebug, leafhopper, aphids, golden and red cottony cushion scale
DISEASE PROBLEMS: Anthracnose, Oak root rot, bleeding canker, canker rot, *Endothia*, *Ganoderma*, *Hypoxylon*, leaf blight, *Nectria*, Oak wilt, powdery mildew, root rot, *Phytophthora*, *Taphrina* and xylem limiting bacteria
ENVIRONMENTAL FACTORS: Roots can lift sidewalks, curbs and driveways
PRUNING: Prune when young to establish proper trunk and branch structure

ADDITIONAL NOTES

USES: Large parking lot islands, buffer strips around parking lots, reclamation plantings, shade tree and residential street tree
URBAN USES: Good choice for streets and medians; adaptable to many soil types, drought and high salt levels; moderately tolerant of air pollutants; needs large, well-drained growing area for root system and crown development
SUBSTITUTIONS: *Quercus* species, *Gingko* cultivars, *Lagerstroemia* cultivars, *Ulmus* cultivars, *Ilex* species and cultivars
COMMENTS: The Southern Live Oak is an excellent street tree to use in the Southern United States. The trunk can grow to be six feet in diameter. Live Oaks have varying leaf size, plant shape and cold hardiness.
OTHER CULTIVARS: 'SDLN' PP 12,015 Cathedral® - broad, pyramidal, fast growing, uniform habit and produced on its own roots; "QVTIA' PP 11,219 Highrise® - upright, broad, columnar, fast growing, uniform growth, produced on its own roots

Quercus virginiana 'QVTIA' PP 11,219
Highrise® Live Oak
USDA Hardiness Zones: 7b-10b

DESCRIPTION

NATIVE HABITAT: Coastal Plains of the Eastern and Southern United States to East Texas; cultivar of nursery origin
PLANT TYPE: Evergreen to semi-evergreen; broadleaf, large tree
MATURE SIZE: 30-40' tall by 12-18' wide
FORM/SHAPE: Upright, broad, columnar form
BARK: Smooth; tannish gray; matures to dark gray to blackish gray with thick, rough, deep fissures and ridges; becomes blocky with age
FLOWER: Olive-gray, male flower; gray, greenish brown, female flower; inconspicuous; blooms in Spring
FRUIT: Variable size, oblong-ellipsoid to obovate, dark brown to black; can cause problems in public access areas
FOLIAGE: Alternate, simple, broadly oblong-elliptic, entire margin smooth to sparsely dentate; dark green leaf surface with olive-green leaf underside; inner foliage turns yellow to brown and sheds throughout Winter and at the time of new growth in Spring

LANDSCAPE CHARACTERISTICS

GROWTH RATE: Moderate   **DROUGHT TOLERANCE:** Moderate to High   **SALT TOLERANCE:** Moderate to High
SOIL REQUIREMENTS: Well-drained, fertile, moist, humus rich, slightly acidic to slightly alkaline, clay, loam or sandy soil; tolerates infrequent flooding, but prefers well-drained soil
LIGHT REQUIREMENTS: Full sun, but will tolerate part shade
PEST PROBLEMS: Mites (blister, Oak, eriophyid, *Platanus*), ambrosia beetles, Texas leafcutter ants, leaf miner, Cranberry rootworm, caterpillars, orange-striped Oakworm, Oak webworm, Oak skeletonizer, bud gall mite, flatheaded Apple tree borer, Red Oak and branch borer, Ash borer, broadnecked root borer, spittlebug, Oak lacebug, leafhopper, aphids, golden and red cottony cushion scale
DISEASE PROBLEMS: Anthracnose, Oak root rot, bleeding canker, canker rot, *Endothia*, *Ganoderma*, *Hypoxylon*, leaf blight, *Nectria*, Oak wilt, powdery mildew, root rot, *Phytophthora*, *Taphrina* and xylem limiting bacteria
ENVIRONMENTAL FACTORS: Not tolerant of water-logged soil or compacted planting sites; shallow root system needs a large area for growth; limb breakage can occur in wind, ice and snow storms
PRUNING: Maintain central leader; remove limbs with acute branch to trunk angles and remove low hanging limbs

ADDITIONAL NOTES

USES: Parking lots, planters, specimen, street tree, medians, narrow areas around buildings and avenues
URBAN USES: Adaptable to many soil types, drought, and high salt levels; moderately tolerant of air pollutants; needs a large, well-drained growing area for its root system; narrow crown requires less space
SUBSTITUTIONS: *Ilex opaca*, *Ilex x attenuata*, *Ilex vomitoria*, *Quercus laurifolia*, *Quercus hemisphaerica*, *Quercus geminata*, *Quercus phillyreoides* 'Emerald Sentinel'
COMMENTS: Highrise® is very uniform and upright in form. It maintains high quality growth when produced on its own roots and is adaptable to container or field production. The tree also has good ball and burlap survival rate.
OTHER CULTIVARS: 'SDLN' PP 12,015 Cathedral® - broad, pyramidal, fast growing, uniform habit and produced on its own roots

Thuja occidentalis 'Degroot's Spire'
Degroot's Spire Arborvitae
USDA Hardiness Zones: 3-8

DESCRIPTION

NATIVE HABITAT: Eastern North America; cultivar of nursery origin
PLANT TYPE: Evergreen, coniferous, medium size tree
MATURE SIZE: 15' tall by 2' wide
FORM/SHAPE: Very narrow, columnar
BARK: Chestnut-brown, covered with thin flakes and fibers when young; matures to grayish brown plates and fissures
FLOWER: Yellow; inconspicuous; blooms late Winter to Spring
FRUIT: Small, oval, dry, brown, woody cone; 1/2" long; inconspicuous
FOLIAGE: Alternate, scale-like, vertical sprays; fragrant, dark green foliage; keeps dark green color through Winter

LANDSCAPE CHARACTERISTICS

GROWTH RATE: Moderate to Fast   **DROUGHT TOLERANCE:** Moderate   **SALT TOLERANCE:** Low to Moderate
SOIL REQUIREMENTS: Well-drained, moist, fertile, humus rich and slightly acidic to slightly alkaline soil; adaptable to many soils and fertility levels
LIGHT REQUIREMENTS: Full sun to part shade; best growth and color in full sun
PEST PROBLEMS: Cypress tip moth, leaf miner, Juniper midge, silver spotted tiger moth, spider mites, Cypress leaftier (mainly in Western North America)
DISEASE PROBLEMS: Canker, leaf blight, *Phomopsis*, root rot and wetwood
ENVIRONMENTAL FACTORS: Not tolerant of extremely dry or wet planting sites
PRUNING: Generally unnecessary, but can be pruned to control height and shape when needed; should be grown as a central leader tree

ADDITIONAL NOTES

USES: Narrow foundation specimen plant and planters
URBAN USES: Tolerant of sulfur dioxide air pollution and other air pollutants; tolerant of full sun or shaded environments; requires adequate water to become well established
SUBSTITUTES: *Ilex crenata* 'Sky Pencil', *Buxus sempervirens* 'Graham Blandy', *Osmanthus aurantiacus, Ilex x* 'HL 10-90' PP 14,477 Christmas Jewel®
COMMENTS: This is the best replacement for Italian Cypress in cold areas. 'Degroot's Spire' is very cold and heat tolerant and is easily grown with a single, main stem for a very narrow specimen in the landscape.
OTHER CULTIVARS: 'Emerald' - medium size,, narrow, pyramidal form, deep, bright green foliage; 'Europe Gold' - small, narrow, columnar form, golden yellow foliage, deep gold Winter foliage; 'Zmatlic' - small, very narrow, columnar form, dark green leaves, tight, congested fan-like foliage

Thuja occidentalis 'Emerald'
Emerald Arborvitae
USDA Hardiness Zones: 3-7

DESCRIPTION

NATIVE HABITAT: Eastern North America; cultivar of nursery origin
PLANT TYPE: Evergreen, coniferous, medium size tree
MATURE SIZE: 10-15' tall by 3-4' wide
FORM/SHAPE: Narrow, compact, pyramidal
BARK: Chestnut-brown, covered with thin flakes and fibers when young; matures to grayish brown plates and fissures
FLOWER: Yellow; inconspicuous; blooms late Winter to Spring
FRUIT: Small, oval, dry, brown woody cone; 1/2" long; inconspicuous
FOLIAGE: Alternate, scale-like, vertical sprays; fragrant, emerald green foliage; keeps dark green color through Winter

LANDSCAPE CHARACTERISTICS

GROWTH RATE: Moderate to Fast   **DROUGHT TOLERANCE:** Moderate   **SALT TOLERANCE:** Low to Moderate
SOIL REQUIREMENTS: Well-drained moist, fertile, humus rich and slightly acidic to slightly alkaline soil; tolerant of infrequent, short duration flooding
LIGHT REQUIREMENTS: Full sun to part shade
PEST PROBLEMS: Cypress tip moth, leaf miner, Juniper midge, silver spotted tiger moth, spider mites, Cypress leaftier (mainly in Western North America)
DISEASE PROBLEMS: Canker, leaf blight, *Phomopsis*, root rot and wetwood
ENVIRONMENTAL FACTORS: Not tolerant of extremely dry or wet planting sites
PRUNING: Generally unnecessary, but can be pruned to control height and shape when needed; should be grown as a central leader tree

ADDITIONAL NOTES

USES: Screen, specimen, narrow foundation specimen plant and planters
URBAN USES: Tolerant of sulfur dioxide air pollution and other air pollutants; tolerant of full sun or shaded environments; requires adequate water to become well established
SUBSTITUTES: *Ilex crenata* 'Sky Pencil', *Buxus sempervirens* 'Graham Blandy', *Osmanthus aurantiacus, Ilex x* 'HL 10-90' PP 14,477 Christmas Jewel®
COMMENTS: This is a good replacement tree for Italian Cypress in cold areas. Emerald Arborvitae is very cold and heat tolerant and it will hold green Winter color well. It is easily grown with a single main stem for a narrow specimen in the landscape.
OTHER CULTIVARS: 'Degroot's Spire' - very narrow, columnar, dark green foliage; 'Pyramidalis' - large, pyramidal, dark green foliage; 'Techny' syn. 'Mission' - medium size, pyramidal form, dark, bluish green foliage, does not bronze in Winter; 'Yellow Ribbon' - medium size, pyramidal, golden yellow foliage, deep golden color in Winter

Thuja x 'Green Giant'
Green Giant Arborvitae
USDA Hardiness Zones: 6-9

DESCRIPTION

NATIVE HABITAT: Cultivar of nursery origin
PLANT TYPE: Evergreen, coniferous, large tree
MATURE SIZE: 50' tall by 12' wide
FORM/SHAPE: Dense, pyramidal
BARK: Chestnut-brown, covered with thin flakes and fibers when young; matures to grayish brown plates and fissures
FLOWER: Male cones are yellow to brown; female cones are greenish yellow; matures to chestnut-brown, inconspicuous; blooms late Winter to Spring
FRUIT: Small, oval, dry, brown, woody cone; 1/2" long; inconspicuous
FOLIAGE: Alternate, scale-like, vertical sprays; fragrant, dark green foliage; keeps dark green color through Winter

LANDSCAPE CHARACTERISTICS

GROWTH RATE: Fast   **DROUGHT TOLERANCE:** Moderate once established   **SALT TOLERANCE:** Low
SOIL REQUIREMENTS: Well-drained, moist, fertile, humus rich and slightly acidic to slightly alkaline soil; adaptable to many soil and fertility levels
LIGHT REQUIREMENTS: Full sun; plant will adapt to light shade conditions
PEST PROBLEMS: Cypress tip moth, leaf miner, Juniper midge, silver spotted tiger moth, spider mites, Cypress leaftier (mainly in Western North America)
DISEASE PROBLEMS: Canker, leaf blight, *Phomopsis*, root rot and wetwood
ENVIRONMENTAL FACTORS: Not tolerant of extremely dry or wet planting sites
PRUNING: Can be pruned to control height and shape when necessary; should be grown as a central leader tree

ADDITIONAL NOTES

USES: Large specimen plant or mass planted as a large hedge or screen
URBAN USES: Tolerant of sulfur dioxide air pollution and other air pollutants; plant tolerates full sun or light shade environments; requires adequate water to become well established
SUBSTITUTES: *Thuja occidentalis* cultivars, *Thuja plicata* 'Excelsa', *Thuja plicata* 'Clemson Select', *Cryptomeria japonica* cultivars or *Cryptomeria japonica var. sinensis* 'Radicans'
COMMENTS: Green Giant Arborvitae is a very fast growing evergreen tree with as much as 3' of annual growth per year in optimal growing conditions. This tree is also adaptable to a wide range of climatic conditions. It makes a better choice for a screening tree than Leyland Cypress.
OTHER CULTIVARS: 'Excelsa' - very similar with slightly wider spread; 'Atrovirens' - fast growing, graceful form, very shade tolerant; 'Clemson Select' - more compact, adaptable to southern heat, very shade tolerant; 'Steeplechase' PP 16,094 - broader, finer textured and more dense

Tsuga canadensis
Canadian Hemlock
USDA Hardiness Zones: 3-7

DESCRIPTION

NATIVE HABITAT: Eastern to Northeastern United States to Southern Canada
PLANT TYPE: Evergreen, coniferous, large tree
MATURE SIZE: 40-70' tall by 25-35' wide
FORM/SHAPE: Broad, pyramidal
BARK: Smooth; grayish brown when young; scaly and flaky on maturing trees; older trees have deep furrows and ridges with angular plates
FLOWER: Male cones are tan with yellowish white pollen; female cones are brown to gray; blooms late Winter to Spring
FRUIT: Ovoid, stalked, slender cone, 1/2 to 1" long by 1/2" wide; brown when mature
FOLIAGE: Obtuse or acute, linear, almost regularly double ranked, needles 1/4-2/3" long by 1/8-1/12" wide; foliage yellow-green in early Spring; turns dark, glossy green in Summer; older inner leaves turn yellow to brown and shed during Winter and as new growth emerges in Spring

LANDSCAPE CHARACTERISTICS

GROWTH RATE: Moderate   **DROUGHT TOLERANCE:** Low   **SALT TOLERANCE:** Low
SOIL REQUIREMENTS: Well-drained, moist, fertile, humus rich, slightly acidic soil
LIGHT REQUIREMENTS: Light shade to full sun; when young, best growth and development in light shade; tolerant of full sun in its native range when mature
PEST PROBLEMS: Wooly adelgid, bud worms, leafroller, tussock moths, Japanese weevil, Hemlock borer, Hemlock looper, grape scale, Hemlock scale, spider mites, Spruce needle miner, black vine weevil, rust mite, Pine spittlebug, elongated Hemlock scale and Juniper scale
DISEASE PROBLEMS: Canker, rust, sapwood rot, *Phytophthora,* leaf blight, *Ganoderma* and wood rot
ENVIRONMENTAL FACTORS: Not tolerant of water-logged soil; wooly adelgid damage is causing major destruction in the Hemlock population of the Eastern United States; adelgids can be controlled with insecticides in the landscape, but it is only a temporary measure
PRUNING: Can be pruned if needed for size control; maintain a central leader when grown as a full size tree; best grown when limbed to the ground

ADDITIONAL NOTES

USES: Screens, specimen tree, topiaries, background plantings and naturalizing
URBAN USES: Very limited use due to wooly adelgid infestation; not tolerant of dry, windy sites or water-logged soil
SUBSTITUTIONS: *Thuja plicata* 'Clemson Select', *Thuja plicata* 'Atrovirens', *Thuja x* 'Green Giant', *Thuja occidentalis* cultivars, *Cryptomeria* cultivars, *Cedrus deodara* cultivars, *Chamaecyparis* cultivars, Juniper cultivars
COMMENTS: Canadian Hemlock is problematic. Disease and pests, especially wooly adelgid, are prevalent in some areas of its native range, and this limits the use for the tree. This is unfortunate because this is a graceful and beautiful tree for partly shaded conditions. Unique cultivars have been selected and are in commercial production.
OTHER CULTIVARS: 'Brandley' - dwarf, irregularly spreading mound; 'Pendula' - medium size, upright, weeping narrow mound; 'Sargents Weeping' - broad, medium size, spreading, weeping mound

x Cupressocyparis leylandii
Leyland Cypress
USDA Hardiness Zones: 6-9

DESCRIPTION

NATIVE HABITAT: Hybrid of garden origin
PLANT TYPE: Evergreen, coniferous, large tree
MATURE SIZE: 50-80' tall by 15-20' wide
FORM/SHAPE: Upright, conical, pyramidal
BARK: Young stems are green; quickly turns reddish brown; covered with thin flakes; matures to dark reddish brown with scales or plates
FLOWER: Inconspicuous; blooms late Winter to early Spring
FRUIT: Greenish brown cones; 3/8" long, eight scales
FOLIAGE: Scale-like, tightly appressed; dark green to bluish green leaves; foliage retained for several years

LANDSCAPE CHARACTERISTICS

GROWTH RATE: Moderate to Fast   **DROUGHT TOLERANCE:** Moderate to High   **SALT TOLERANCE:** Moderate
SOIL REQUIREMENTS: Prefers moist, well-drained soil, but is adaptable to drier conditions; not tolerant of extremely wet soil; important to lime soil and maintain a moderate pH level
LIGHT REQUIREMENTS: Full sun for best growth and to reduce twig and leaf diseases; not tolerant of shade
PEST PROBLEMS: Mites, bagworm, Cypress and Arborvitae leafminer, Cypress sawfly, cottony Cypress scale, Cypress bark scale, cottony cushion scale, Cypress mealybugs and Cypress bark beetle
DISEASE PROBLEMS: Canker, *Seiridium* twig dieback and canker, *Pestalotiopsis* twig dieback, root rot
ENVIRONMENTAL FACTORS: Heavy shade encourages disease and decline problems; not tolerant of wet soil; poorly developed root system and multi-leaders make trees prone to wind and ice damage
PRUNING: To maintain and control size or to develop density, trees should always have one central leader and extra leaders should be removed when trees are young

ADDITIONAL NOTES

USES: Nice specimen, large hedges and privacy screens due to rapid growth rate
URBAN USES: Good tolerance in urban conditions, but must have full sun and well-drained soil to avoid chronic disease problems
SUBSTITUTIONS: 'Green Giant' Arborvitae, *Cryptomeria* cultivars, *Ilex* species and cultivars, *Picea abies*, *Tsuga canadensis*, *Juniperus* species and cultivars
COMMENTS: Leyland Cypress is a general classification given to bi-generic hybrids of *Cupressus macrocarpa* (Monterey Cypress) *x Chamaecyparis nootkatensis* (Alaskan Cypress) which denotes as many as twenty cultivars with the following two most commonly known as Leyland Cypress: 'Haggerston Grey' is the most commonly known followed by 'Leighton Green' as the second most known.
OTHER CULTIVARS: 'Haggerston Grey' - more open growth, dark gray-green foliage with pale gray-green cast; 'Leighton Green' - green foliage in flattened sprays; 'Naylor's Blue' - gray-blue dark green foliage draping from limbs, very graceful form with open growth and pyramidal form; 'Gold Rider' - gold tinged yellow-green foliage, compact columnar form, does not suffer from foliage burn in Winter cold and Summer sun

Cold Hardy Palms

Butia capitata
Pindo Palm, Jelly Palm or Wine Palm
USDA Hardiness Zones: 8-10b

DESCRIPTION

NATIVE HABITAT: Argentina, Uruguay and Central to Southern Brazil

PLANT TYPE: Evergreen, monocot, small, single-stemmed, Palm tree; monoecious

MATURE SIZE: 15' tall

FORM/SHAPE: Vase-shaped, single trunk

TRUNK: Coarse; gray; thick covering of overlapping, stubby and woody leaf bases

FLOWER: Creamy yellow to reddish; separate male and female flowers on same inflorescence; 3-4' long; once branched inflorescence; blooms late Spring to early Summer

FRUIT: Yellow to orange, 1" globus-shaped; sweet; messy

FOLIAGE: Pinnately compound, reduplicate, stiffly arching; petiole 4-6' long with slender, fibrous, spines on petiole margin; blue-green color

LANDSCAPE CHARACTERISTICS

GROWTH RATE: Slow   **DROUGHT TOLERANCE:** High   **SALT TOLERANCE:** Moderate

SOIL REQUIREMENTS: Adaptable to a wide range of soil conditions from clay to sand; well-drained, slightly alkaline to slightly acidic soil

LIGHT REQUIREMENTS: Full sun for best growth and fruit development; tolerates light shade

PEST PROBLEMS: Scales, spider mites, Palm leaf skeletonizer and mealybugs

DISEASE PROBLEMS: *Ganoderma*, stigmina, leaf spot, graphiola false smut, *Phytophthora* bud rot and root rot

ENVIRONMENTAL FACTORS: Winter cold injury to growth terminal; not tolerant of water-logged soil

PRUNING: Remove old leaves down to leaf petiole base; leave petiole base on Palm trunk

ADDITIONAL NOTES

USES: Specimen plant, medians, planters, patio plant or as a large house plant in cool sunny area

URBAN USES: Medians and street avenues; tolerant of infrequent flooding; adaptable to many soil types, but soil should be well-drained

SUBSTITUTIONS: *Trachycarpus fortunei*

COMMENTS: *Butia capitata* is the most cold hardy of the feather-leafed Palms. Other Palms will not tolerate temperatures below thirty-two degrees fahrenheit. Several fan-type Palms are more cold hardy than Pindo. *Butia capitata* has tasty, edible fruit. The species is considerably variable in nature. Plants are seed produced and show variable trunk height, trunk thickness, leaf color, fruit color and taste. There is some variation in plant hardiness and adaptability. It grows better in zones colder than USDA Hardiness Zone 10b.

OTHER CULTIVARS: No known cultivars of *Butia capitata* in commercial production; all are seed produced; some variable foliage color leaf forms are known

Rhapidophyllum hystrix
Needle Palm

USDA Hardiness Zones: (6b-)7a-10b

DESCRIPTION

NATIVE HABITAT: Coastal Plain of the Southeastern United States

PLANT TYPE: Evergreen, monocot, clump-forming, shrub-like Palm; dioecious, but occasionally monoecious

MATURE SIZE: 8' tall by 5-8' wide

FORM/SHAPE: Clustering; essentially trunkless to short trunk form; stem prostrate or erect with numerous leaves per plant

TRUNK: Fiber-matted crown; covered with needle-like fibers formed at leaf attachments and leaf bases

FLOWER: Yellow, purple or reddish; separate male and female plants; occasionally both sexes on same plants; blooms from late Spring to early Summer

FRUIT: 1" long; purple-brown, wooly; ovoid to pyriform; acorn-like nut in clusters

FOLIAGE: Palmate, induplicate, divided deeply into fifteen to twenty blunt and jagged-tipped segments; 4' wide with segments 2' long and 3/4" wide; dark green above, silvery below; numerous leaves per plant; spiny leaf bases on trunk can be a human hazard

LANDSCAPE CHARACTERISTICS

GROWTH RATE: Slow   **DROUGHT TOLERANCE:** High   **SALT TOLERANCE:** Moderate

SOIL REQUIREMENTS: Adaptable to a wide range of soil conditions from clay to sand; requires well-drained, moist, fertile, humus rich, slightly acidic to slightly alkaline soil

LIGHT REQUIREMENTS: Full shade to full sun; best growth and development in part sun

PEST PROBLEMS: Spider mites, mealybugs and scales

DISEASE PROBLEMS: None reported

ENVIRONMENTAL FACTORS: Winter cold injury to growth terminal; must be planted in well-drained soil; tolerant of infrequent, short duration flooding

PRUNING: Not needed; remove old leaves as they turn yellow; avoid sharp needles

COMMENTS

USES: Specimen plant, container plant, foundation planting, shrub border, naturalized habitat

URBAN USES: Tough and adaptable; tolerates full shade to full sun, short duration flooding; very tolerant of many pests and diseases

SUBSTITUTIONS: *Sabal minor, Sabal palmetto* or *Trachycarpus fortunei*

COMMENTS: *Rhapiodophyllum hystrix* is very cold hardy. It is a tough, adaptable plant for varying soil and light conditions. It can be found growing in landscapes as far north as Washington D.C., Oregon and British Columbia. Because of the needles, care should be used in planting close to walks and public access areas. It should not be planted in or around playgrounds.

OTHER CULTIVARS: No other known cultivars, but two botanical forms are described; one with more finely divided leaves and more offset (suckers) found in dryer habitats; the other has wider divisions of the leaf blade, less offset (suckers) and a taller trunk

Sabal palmetto
Cabbage Palm, Sabal Palm or Common Palmetto
USDA Hardiness Zones: 8a-11

DESCRIPTION

NATIVE HABITAT: Coastal Plain of the Southeastern United States and along the Gulf Coast

PLANT TYPE: Evergreen, monocot, fan-leafed, Palm tree; monoecious

MATURE SIZE: 40-50' tall by 10-15' wide

FORM/SHAPE: Tall; straight or curved, topped with dense, round crown of smooth, fan-shaped Palm leaves with horizontal bands of leaf base scars

TRUNK: Gray

FLOWER: Whitish green; showy; 4-5' long stalks; blooms in Summer

FRUIT: Numerous green and black fruits are produced; can be messy in pedestrian and public access areas

FOLIAGE: Costapalmate, induplicate, strongly twisted downward at middle; 3'-6' wide leaf blade divided to about half in numerous segments, some stiff and some drooping; dark green color

LANDSCAPE CHARACTERISTICS

GROWTH RATE: Slow   **DROUGHT TOLERANCE:** High   **SALT TOLERANCE:** High

SOIL REQUIREMENTS: Well-drained, acidic to alkaline, clay, loam or sandy soil; will tolerate extended flooding

LIGHT REQUIREMENTS: Part shade to full sun

PEST PROBLEMS: Palm weevil on new transplants and Cabbage Palm caterpillar

DISEASE PROBLEMS: *Ganoderma*, butt rot (enters through injuries on lower trunk and roots) and graphiola false smut

ENVIRONMENTAL FACTORS: Winter cold injury to growth terminal; fruit on female plants can be messy in public access areas

PRUNING: Remove yellowing older leaves and shedding leaf bases ('boots'); rate of leaf base shedding varies on each plant

ADDITIONAL NOTES

USES: Specimen plant, groves, mixed with other trees or companion plant in coastal landscapes

URBAN USES: Good choice for urban areas, especially medians and street avenues

SUBSTITUTIONS: Chinese Windmill Palm, which is more cold hardy and has better growth where Summer temperatures are moderate

COMMENTS: *Sabal palmetto* transplants well but must be watered until established. At planting it is best to remove leaves or tie them up to reduce sun and wind dessication. *Sabal palmetto* can withstand the damage of hurricanes.

OTHER CULTIVARS: Some seed produced variety types are known; 'Lisa'- considered a naturally occurring form with a higher number of chromosomes; plant form and appearance more compact, shorter, thicker petiole and thicker, more ridged, less twisted leaves than species

Trachycarpus fortunei
Windmill Palm, Chusan, Chinese Windmill Palm or Hemp Palm
USDA Hardiness Zones: 7a-10b

DESCRIPTION

NATIVE HABITAT: China; species of genus found also in temperate and mountain forests of subtropical Asia

PLANT TYPE: Evergreen, monocot, single-stemmed, Palm tree; monoecious

MATURE SIZE: 15-25' tall by 6-10' wide

FORM/SHAPE: Rounded, single straight trunk

TRUNK: Slender; dark brown to gray fibers aging to gray; persistent protruding leaf base

FLOWER: Yellow; fragrant; separate male and female plants; blooms from late Spring to early Summer

FRUIT: Bluish black; 1/2" round

FOLIAGE: Palmate; induplicate; divided to base into forty to fifty stiff or drooping segments shortly split at tips; dark green above, silvery below; 2-3" wide segments 1 1/2-2' long, twenty to thirty leaves per tree; petioles are bluntly toothed and can be a human hazard

LANDSCAPE CHARACTERISTICS

GROWTH RATE: Slow   **DROUGHT TOLERANCE:** High   **SALT TOLERANCE:** Moderate

SOIL REQUIREMENTS: Adaptable to a wide range of soil conditions from clay to sand; requires well-drained, moist, fertile, humus rich, slightly acidic to slightly alkaline soil

LIGHT REQUIREMENTS: Full sun for best growth and development; tolerates part shade

PEST PROBLEMS: None reported

DISEASE PROBLEMS: *Phytophthora* bud rot; only moderately susceptible to lethal yellowing

ENVIRONMENTAL FACTORS: Winter cold injury to trunk terminal; fruit on female plants can be messy in public access areas

PRUNING: Not needed; remove old leaves that are yellowing; best to not remove base of petiole; the base and hairy fiber protect the trunk and are considered attractive

ADDITIONAL NOTES

USES: Tropical accent or specimen tree, planters, patio tree, foundation plantings in combination with other landscape plants or as a cold hardy replacement for *Sabal palmetto* and *Chamaerops humilis*

URBAN USES: Tough and adaptable; use in narrow planting spaces; lawn areas can be maintained under canopy crown

SUBSTITUTIONS: *Sabal palmetto*, *Chamaerops humilis* USDA Hardiness Zones 8-11

COMMENTS: *Trachycarpus fortunei* is one of the most cold hardy palms. It does not survive well in hot, tropical climates. The tree is more tolerant of yellowing disease. Old, large specimens are found growing in the upper Piedmont areas of the Carolinas in USDA Hardiness Zone 7a.

OTHER CULTIVARS: No known cultivars of Trachycarpus fortunei in commercial production; all are seed produced; some USDA Hardiness Zone 7a regional types may show better cold hardiness in their seedling offspring

Availability Reference

To assist your decision in selecting plant material to specify in designs or to grow at your nursery, we have provided this chart for reference. The categories of availability are Readily, Moderately and Limited. To find growers of this plant material, please contact the Plant & Supply LOCATOR at 1-800-475-2687.

DECIDUOUS TREES

Acer buergerianum	Trident Maple	Moderately
Acer buergerianum 'ABMTF'	Aeryn® Trident Maple	Limited
Acer palmatum	Japanese Maple	Moderately
Acer palmatum 'Bloodgood'	Bloodgood Japanese Maple	Moderately
Acer palmatum 'Sango kaku'	Coral Bark Japanese Maple	Moderately
Acer palmatum dissectum 'Seiryu'	Seiryu Japanese Maple	Moderately
Acer plantanoides 'Crimson King'	Crimson King Norway Maple	Moderately
Acer rubrum	Red Maple	Readily
Acer rubrum	Autumn Flame® Red Maple	Readily
Acer rubrum	October Glory® Red Maple	Readily
Acer rubrum 'Brandywine'	Brandywine Red Maple	Readily
Acer rubrum 'Franksred'	Red Sunset® Red Maple	Readily
Acer rubrum 'HOSR'	Summer Red® Red Maple	Readily
Acer saccharum	Sugar Maple or Northern Sugar Maple	Moderately
Acer saccharum	Green Mountain® Sugar Maple	Moderately
Acer saccharum 'Astis'	Steeple® Sugar Maple	Limited
Acer saccharum 'Legacy'	Legacy Sugar Maple	Moderately
Acer x freemanii 'Jeffers Red'	Autumn Blaze® Maple	Readily
Aesculus x carnea 'Fort McNair'	Fort McNair Red Horse Chestnut	Limited
Amelanchier x grandiflora 'Autumn Brilliance'	Autumn Brilliance® Serviceberry	Readily
Betula nigra	River Birch	Readily
Betula nigra 'BNMTF'	Dura-Heat® River Birch	Readily
Betula nigra 'Cully'	Heritage® River Birch	Readily
Carpinus betulus 'Fastigiata'	Pyramidal European Hornbeam	Moderately
Carpinus caroliniana	American Hornbeam or Blue Beech	Limited
Cercis canadensis	Eastern Redbud Tree	Readily
Cercis canadensis 'Covey'	Lavender Twist Weeping Redbud Tree	Limited
Cercis canadensis 'Forest Pansy'	Forest Pansy Redbud Tree	Readily
Cercis chinensis 'Avondale'	Avondale Redbud Tree	Moderately
Cercis reniformis 'Oklahoma'	Oklahoma Redbud Tree	Moderately
Chionanthus retusus	Chinese Fringetree	Moderately
Chionanthus virginicus	White Fringetree or Grancy Gray-beard	Moderately
Cladrastis kentukea (syn. lutea)	American Yellowwood	Moderately
Cornus florida	Dogwood	Readily
Cornus florida 'Cherokee Princess'	Cherokee Princess Dogwood	Moderately
Cornus florida rubra 'Comco #1'	Cherokee Brave Dogwood	Moderately
Cornus kousa	Chinese Dogwood	Readily
Crataegus phaenopyrum	Washington Hawthorn	Moderately
Crataegus viridis 'Winter King'	Winter King Hawthorn or Green Hawthorn	Moderately
Fagus grandifolia	American Beech	Limited
Fraxinus americana 'Junginger'	Autumn Purple® White Ash	Moderately
Fraxinus pennsylvanica 'Oconee'	Georgia Gem® Green Ash	Moderately
Fraxinus pennsylvanica 'Patmore'	Patmore Green Ash	Moderately
Fraxinus pennsylvanica 'Urbanite'	Urbanite® Green Ash	Moderately
Ginkgo biloba	Ginkgo Tree	Limited

Gleditsia triacanthos var. inermis 'Shademaster'	Shademaster® Honeylocust	Moderately
Gleditsia triacanthos var. inermis 'Skycole'	Skyline® Honeylocust	Moderately
Koelreuteria paniculata	Goldenrain Tree	Limited
Lagerstroemia fauriei 'Fantasy'	Fantasy Crape Myrtle	Readily
Lagerstroemia indica 'Carolina Beauty'	Carolina Beauty Crape Myrtle	Readily
Lagerstroemia indica 'Catawba'	Catawba Crape Myrtle	Readily
Lagerstroemia indica 'Potomac'	Potomac Crape Myrtle	Readily
Lagerstroemia indica 'Whit II'	Dynamite® Crape Myrtle	Readily
Lagerstroemia indica 'Whit III'	Pink Velour® Crape Myrtle	Readily
Lagerstroemia indica 'Whit IV'	Red Rocket® Crape Myrtle	Readily
Lagerstroemia (i. x fauriei) 'Biloxi'	Biloxi Crape Myrtle	Readily
Lagerstroemia (i. x fauriei) 'Choctaw'	Choctaw Crape Myrtle	Readily
Lagerstroemia (i. x fauriei) 'Miami'	Miami Crape Myrtle	Readily
Lagerstroemia (i. x fauriei) 'Muskogee'	Muskogee Crape Myrtle	Readily
Lagerstroemia (i. x fauriei) 'Natchez'	Natchez Crape Myrtle	Readily
Lagerstroemia (i. x fauriei) 'Sarah's Favorite'	Sarah's Favorite Crape Myrtle	Readily
Lagerstroemia (i. x fauriei) 'Sioux'	Sioux Crape Myrtle	Readily
Lagerstroemia (i. x fauriei) 'Tonto'	Tonto Crape Myrtle	Readily
Lagerstroemia (i. x fauriei) 'Tuscarora'	Tuscarora Crape Myrtle	Readily
Lagerstroemia (i. x fauriei) 'Tuskegee'	Tuskegee Crape Myrtle	Readily
Liquidambar styraciflua	Sweetgum	Moderately
Liquidambar styraciflua 'Rotundiloba'	Rotundiloba Sweetgum	Limited
Liquidambar styraciflua 'Slender Silhouette'	Columnar or Slender Silhouette Sweetgum	Limited
Liriodendron tulipifera	Tulip Poplar or Tulip Tree	Readily
Magnolia stellata	Star Magnolia	Moderately
Magnolia x soulangiana	Saucer Magnolia	Readily
Malus 'Prairifire'	Prairifire Crabapple	Moderately
Malus x 'Sutyzam'	Sugar Tyme® Crabapple	Limited
Malus x 'Zumi'	Zumi Crabapple	Limited
Metasequoia glyptostroboides	Dawn Redwood	Readily
Nyssa sylvatica	Black Gum	Moderately
Oxydendron arboreum	Sourwood	Limited
Pistacia chinensis	Chinese Pistache	Moderately
Platanus occidentalis	Sycamore	Readily
Platanus x acerifolia 'Bloodgood'	Bloodgood London Planetree	Readily
Platanus x acerifolia 'Yarwood'	Yarwood London Planetree	Limited
Prunus cerasifera 'Thundercloud'	Thundercloud Plum	Readily
Prunus serrulata 'Kwanzan'	Kwanzan Cherry	Readily
Prunus subhirtella 'Autumnalis Rosea'	Pink Autumn Flowering Cherry	Readily
Prunus x 'Okame'	Okame Cherry	Readily
Prunus x yedoensis	Yoshino Cherry	Readily
Pyrus calleryana 'Bradford'	Bradford Pear	Readily
Pyrus calleryana 'Glen's Form'	Chanticleer® Pear	Moderately
Quercus acutissima	Sawtooth Oak	Moderately
Quercus alba	White Oak	Limited
Quercus coccinea	Scarlet Oak	Moderately
Quercus laurifolia	Laurel, Swamp Laurel or Diamond-leaf Oak	Readily
Quercus lyrata	Overcup Oak	Readily
Quercus nuttallii	Nuttall Oak	Readily
Quercus palustris	Pin Oak	Readily
Quercus phellos	Willow Oak	Readily

Quercus phellos 'QPMTF'	Wynstar® Willow Oak	Limited
Quercus phellos 'QPSTA'	Hightower® Willow Oak	Moderately
Quercus rubra	Northern Red Oak	Readily
Quercus shumardii	Shumard Oak	Readily
Salix babylonica	Weeping Willow	Moderately
Styrax japonica	Japanese Snowbell	Moderately
Taxodium distichum	Bald Cypress	Readily
Taxodium distichum 'Mickelson'	Shawnee Brave® Bald Cypress	Moderately
Taxodium distichum 'Sofine'	Autumn Gold™ Bald Cypress	Moderately
Tilia cordata	Greenspire® Littleleaf Linden	Moderately
Ulmus americana 'Princeton'	Princeton Elm	Moderately
Ulmus parvifolia	Chinese Lacebark Elm	Moderately
Ulmus parvifolia 'BSNUPF'	Everclear® Elm	Limited
Ulmus parvifolia 'Drake'	Drake Chinese Elm	Readily
Ulmus parvifolia 'Emer I'	Athena® Elm	Limited
Ulmus parvifolia 'Emer II'	Allee® Elm	Readily
Ulmus parvifolia 'UPMTF'	Bosque® Elm	Readily
Vitex agnus-castus 'Shoal Creek'	Chastetree	Readily
Zelkova serrata	Green Vase® Zelkova	Readily
Zelkova serrata 'C Creek I'	Gold Falls® Zelkova	Limited
Zelkova serrata 'Musashino'	Musashino Zelkova	Moderately
Zelkova serrata 'Village Green'	Village Green Zelkova	Readily
Zelkova serrata 'ZSFKF'	Myrimar® Zelkova	Limited

EVERGREEN TREES

Cedrus deodara	Deodar Cedar	Moderately
Cedrus deodara 'BBC'	Bracken's Best Deodar Cedar	Moderately
Cedrus deodara 'Bill's Blue'	Bill's Blue Deodar Cedar	Moderately
Cedrus deodara 'Sander's Blue'	Blue Velvet™ Deodar Cedar	Moderately
Cryptomeria japonica 'Yoshino'	Japanese Cedar or Cryptomeria	Readily
Cryptomeria japonica var. sinensis 'Radicans'	Radicans Cryptomeria	Moderately
Cupressus arizonica var. glabra 'Carolina Sapphire'	Carolina Sapphire Arizona Cypress	Moderately
Cupressus sempervirens	Italian Cypress or Mediterranean Cypress	Readily
Eriobotrya japonica	Loquat	Readily
Ilex cornuta 'Burfordii'	Burford Holly	Readily
Ilex cornuta 'Needle Point'	Needle Point Holly	Readily
Ilex opaca 'Croonenburg'	Croonenburg American Holly	Limited
Ilex vomitoria	Yaupon Holly	Readily
Ilex vomitoria 'Pendula'	Weeping Yaupon Holly	Moderately
Ilex x 'Emily Bruner'	Emily Bruner Holly	Readily
Ilex x 'HL10-90'	Christmas Jewel® Holly	Limited
Ilex x 'Mary Nell'	Mary Nell Holly	Readily
Ilex x 'Nellie R. Stevens'	Nellie R. Stevens Holly	Readily
Ilex x attenuata 'East Palatka'	East Palatka Holly	Readily
Ilex x attenuata 'Foster No. 2'	Foster No. 2 Holly	Readily
Ilex x attentuata 'Greenleaf'	Greenleaf Holly	Moderately
Ilex x attenuata 'Savannah'	Savannah Holly	Readily
Juniperus chinensis 'Kaizuka'	Hollywood Juniper	Moderately
Juniperus silicicola 'Brodie'	Brodie Juniper	Limited
Juniperus virginiana	Eastern Red Cedar	Readily

Juniperus virginiana 'Burkii'	Burkii Red Cedar	Limited
Ligustrum japonicum 'Recurvifolium'	Wavy Leaf Ligustrum	Readily
Loropetalum chinense rubrum 'Zhuzhou Fuchsia'	Zhuzhou Red Leaf Loropetalum	Readily
Magnolia grandiflora 'Bracken's Brown Beauty'	Bracken's Brown Beauty Magnolia	Readily
Magnolia grandiflora 'Claudia Wannamaker'	Claudia Wannamaker Magnolia	Readily
Magnolia grandiflora 'D. D. Blanchard'	D. D. Blanchard Magnolia	Readily
Magnolia grandiflora 'Little Gem'	Little Gem Magnolia	Readily
Magnolia grandiflora 'Mgtig'	Greenback™ Magnolia or Migtig Magnolia	Readily
Magnolia grandiflora 'Southern Charm'	Teddy Bear® Magnolia	Moderately
Magnolia grandiflora 'TMGH'	Alta® Magnolia	Readily
Magnolia virginiana	Sweetbay Magnolia	Readily
Myrica cerifera	Wax Myrtle	Readily
Osmanthus fragrans	Fragrant Tea Olive	Readily
Osmanthus x fortunei	Fortune's Tea Olive	Readily
Picea abies	Norway Spruce	Moderately
Picea omorika	Serbian Spruce	Moderately
Picea pungens	Colorado or Blue Spruce	Moderately
Pinus elliottii	Slash Pine	Readily
Pinus nigra	Austrian Pine	Moderately
Pinus strobus	Eastern White Pine	Readily
Pinus taeda	Loblolly Pine	Readily
Pinus thunbergii	Japanese Black Pine	Moderately
Pinus virginiana	Virginia Pine	Readily
Prunus caroliniana 'Cherry Ruffle'	Cherry Ruffle	Limited
Quercus virginiana	Southern Live Oak	Readily
Quercus virginiana 'QVTIA'	Highrise® Live Oak	Moderately
Thuja occidentalis 'Degroot's Spire'	Degroot's Spire Arborvitae	Limited
Thuja occidentalis 'Emerald'	Emerald Arborvitae	Moderately
Thuja x 'Green Giant'	Green Giant Arborvitae	Readily
Tsuga canadensis	Canadian Hemlock	Limited
x Cupressocyparis leylandii	Leyland Cypress	Readily

PALM TREES

Butia capitata	Pindo Palm, Jelly Palm or Wine Palm	Readily
Rhapidophyllum hystrix	Needle Palm	Readily
Sabal palmetto	Cabbage Palm, Sabal Palm or Common Palm	Readily
Trachycarpus fortunei	Windmill, Chinese Windmill, Chusan or Hemp Palm	Readily

How to Properly Plant Trees

1.   Dig the desired hole 2-3 times (the wider the hole the better) the width of the container or rootball. If the soil becomes smooth or compressed on the sides of the hole (mostly in clay soils) loosening of those areas is recommended to allow easier root expansion. Some suggest that loosening dirt in the bottom of the hole is beneficial, but it can cause the heavy rootball to settle below the desired depth.

2.   Before placing the tree in the hole, remove the container and other plastic or synthetic non-biodegradable wrapping from roots. Leave only biodegradable burlap wrapping on rootball if the tree is a B&B tree. Always handle tree by its rootball and not by the trunk. Plant the tree with the top surface of the rootball a few inches above the existing grade.

3.   Once the tree is in the ground, remove any rope or twine at the surface of the rootball as well as the burlap at the surface of the rootball.

4.   Backfill with the original surrounding soil, if possible, to allow for better root transition. Water the entire disturbed area after backfilling (as per diagram) to remove air pockets surrounding the rootball. The addition of composted organic matter and nutrient amendments to backfill soil prior to filling greatly benefits the tree. Have a soil test to determine the amount of nutrients needed.

5.   Apply a 2-4" layer of mulch over the entire planting area, but keep mulch a few inches away from the tree trunk to eliminate excess moisture and increase oxygen flow around tree trunk.

6.   Watering and fertilization applications may vary in your planting location.

7.   Stake the tree if needed for additional support.

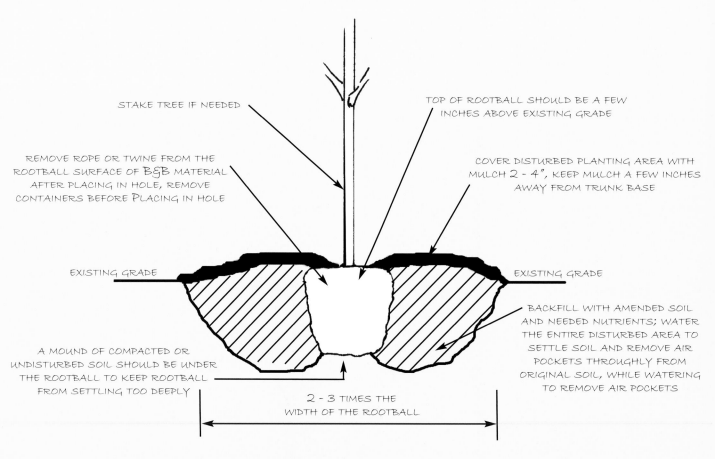

STAKE TREE IF NEEDED

TOP OF ROOTBALL SHOULD BE A FEW INCHES ABOVE EXISTING GRADE

REMOVE ROPE OR TWINE FROM THE ROOTBALL SURFACE OF B&B MATERIAL AFTER PLACING IN HOLE, REMOVE CONTAINERS BEFORE PLACING IN HOLE

COVER DISTURBED PLANTING AREA WITH MULCH 2 - 4", KEEP MULCH A FEW INCHES AWAY FROM TRUNK BASE

EXISTING GRADE

EXISTING GRADE

A MOUND OF COMPACTED OR UNDISTURBED SOIL SHOULD BE UNDER THE ROOTBALL TO KEEP ROOTBALL FROM SETTLING TOO DEEPLY

BACKFILL WITH AMENDED SOIL AND NEEDED NUTRIENTS; WATER THE ENTIRE DISTURBED AREA TO SETTLE SOIL AND REMOVE AIR POCKETS THROUGHLY FROM ORIGINAL SOIL, WHILE WATERING TO REMOVE AIR POCKETS

2 - 3 TIMES THE WIDTH OF THE ROOTBALL

Rootball Size Chart

Rootball sizes and weights will vary depending on equipment, plant selection, soil and moisture content. (These are general approximations only)

Deciduous Trees

Caliper	Recommended Rootball Size	Approximate Rootball Weight (lbs)
2"	24"	300
2.5"	28"	600
3"	32"	750
3.5"	38"	1100
4"	42"	1500
4.5"	48"	2500
5"	54"	3200
6"	60"	5000
7"	70"	6000

Evergreen Trees

Height	Recommended Rootball Size	Approximate Rootball Weight (lbs)
6-7'	22"	250
7-8'	24"	300
8-9'	28"	600
9-10'	30"	700
10-12'	34"	900
12-14'	38"	1100
14-16'	42"	1500
16-18'	46"	2000
18-20'	50"	2800

USDA Hardiness Zone Map

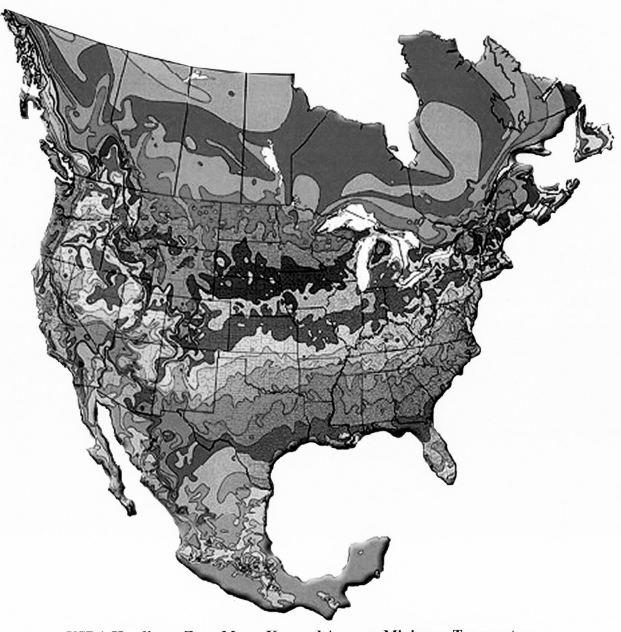

USDA Hardiness Zone Map - Key and Average Minimum Temperature

Zone 1		Below -50 F	**Zone 6b**		-5 to 0 F
Zone 2a		-50 to -45 F	**Zone 7a**		0 to 5 F
Zone 2b		-45 to -40 F	**Zone 7b**		5 to 10 F
Zone 3a		-40 to -35 F	**Zone 8a**		10 to 15 F
Zone 3b		-35 to -30 F	**Zone 8b**		15 to 20 F
Zone 4a		-30 to -25 F	**Zone 9a**		20 to 25 F
Zone 4b		-25 to -20 F	**Zone 9b**		25 to 30 F
Zone 5a		-20 to -15 F	**Zone 10a**		30 to 35 F
Zone 5b		-15 to -10 F	**Zone 10b**		35 to 40 F
Zone 6a		-10 to -5 F	**Zone 11**		Above 40 F

Tree Hardiness Zone Chart

USDA Hardiness Zones	3	4	5	6	7	8	9	10
Botanical Name								
Acer buergerianum - Trident Maple			X	X	X	X	X	
Acer buergerianum 'ABMTF'			X	X	X	X	X	
Acer palmatum - Japanese Maple			X	X	X	X		
Acer palmatum 'Bloodgood'			X	X	X	X		
Acer palmatum 'Sango kaku'			X	X	X	X	X	
Acer palmatum dissectum 'Seiryu'				X	X	X		
Acer plantanoides 'Crimson King'	X	X	X	X	X			
Acer rubrum - Red Maple		X	X	X	X	X	X	
Acer rubrum - Autumn Flame®	X	X	X	X	X	X		
Acer rubrum - October Glory®			X	X	X	X		
Acer rubrum 'Brandywine'		X	X	X	X	X		
Acer rubrum 'Franksred'		X	X	X	X	X		
Acer rubrum 'HOSR'			X	X	X	X	X	
Acer saccharum - Sugar Maple	X	X	X	X	X	X		
Acer saccharum - Green Mountain®	X	X	X	X	X	X		
Acer saccharum 'Astis'		X	X	X	X	X		
Acer saccharum 'Legacy'			X	X	X	X	X	
Acer x freemanii 'Jeffers Red'	X	X	X	X	X	X		
Aesculus x carnea 'Fort McNair'			X	X	X			
Amelanchier x grandiflora 'Autumn Brilliance'		X	X	X	X			
Betula nigra - River Birch				X	X	X	X	
Betula nigra 'BNMTF'		X	X	X	X	X	X	
Betula nigra 'Cully'		X	X	X	X	X	X	
Butia capitata - Pindo Palm						X	X	X
Carpinus betulus 'Fastigiata'			X	X	X	X		
Carpinus caroliniana - American Hornbeam	X	X	X	X	X	X	X	
Cedrus deodara - Deodar Cedar					X	X	X	
Cedrus deodara 'BBC'					X	X	X	
Cedrus deodara 'Bill's Blue'					X	X	X	
Cedrus deodara 'Sander's Blue'					X	X	X	
Cercis canadensis - Eastern Redbud Tree		X	X	X	X	X	X	
Cercis canadensis 'Covey'			X	X	X			
Cercis canadensis 'Forest Pansy'				X	X	X	X	
Cercis chinensis 'Avondale'				X	X	X	X	
Cercis reniformis 'Oklahoma'				X	X	X	X	
Chionanthus retusus - Chinese Fringetree				X	X	X	X	
Chionanthus virginicus - White Fringetree			X	X	X	X	X	
Cladrastis kentukea (syn. lutea) - Yellowwood	X	X	X	X	X	X		
Cornus florida - Dogwood			X	X	X	X	X	
Cornus florida 'Cherokee Princess'			X	X	X	X	X	
Cornus florida rubra 'Comco #1'			X	X	X	X	X	

USDA Hardiness Zones	3	4	5	6	7	8	9	10
Cornus kousa - Chinese Dogwood			X	X	X	X		
Crataegus phaenopyrum - Washington Hawthorn		X	X	X	X	X	X	
Crataegus viridis 'Winter King'		X	X	X	X	X	X	
Cryptomeria japonica 'Yoshino'				X	X	X		
Cryptomeria japonica var. sinensis 'Radicans'				X	X	X	X	
Cupressus arizonica var. glabra 'Carolina Sapphire'					X	X	X	
Cupressus sempervirens - Italian Cypress					X	X	X	
Eriobotrya japonica - Loquat						X	X	X
Fagus grandifolia - American Beech	X	X	X	X	X	X		
Fraxinus americana 'Junginger'		X	X	X	X	X	X	
Fraxinus pennsylvanica 'Oconee'				X	X	X	X	
Fraxinus pennsylvanica 'Patmore'	X	X	X	X	X			
Fraxinus pennsylvanica 'Urbanite'			X	X	X	X		
Ginkgo biloba - Gingko Tree		X	X	X	X	X		
Gleditsia triacanthos var. inermis 'Shademaster'		X	X	X	X	X		
Gleditsia triacanthos var. inermis 'Skycole'		X	X	X	X	X		
Ilex cornuta 'Burfordii'				X	X	X	X	
Ilex cornuta 'Needle Point'				X	X	X	X	
Ilex opaca 'Croonenburg'			X	X	X	X	X	
Ilex vomitoria - Yaupon Holly					X	X	X	
Ilex vomitoria 'Pendula'					X	X	X	
Ilex x 'Emily Bruner'					X	X	X	
Ilex x 'HL10-90'				X	X	X	X	
Ilex x 'Mary Nell'					X	X	X	
Ilex x 'Nellie R. Stevens'				X	X	X	X	
Ilex x attenuata 'East Palatka'					X	X	X	
Ilex x attenuata 'Foster No. 2'				X	X	X	X	
Ilex x attenuata 'Greenleaf'				X	X	X	X	
Ilex x attenuata 'Savannah'				X	X	X	X	
Juniperus chinensis 'Kaizuka'			X	X	X	X	X	
Juniperus silicicola 'Brodie'				X	X	X	X	
Juniperus virginiana - Eastern Red Cedar	X	X	X	X	X	X	X	
Juniperus virginiana 'Burkii'	X	X	X	X	X	X	X	
Koelreuteria paniculata - Goldenrain Tree			X	X	X	X	X	
Lagerstroemia fauriei 'Fantasy'					X	X	X	
Lagerstroemia indica 'Carolina Beauty'				X	X	X	X	
Lagerstroemia indica 'Catawba'				X	X	X	X	
Lagerstroemia indica 'Potomac'				X	X	X	X	
Lagerstroemia indica 'Whit II'				X	X	X	X	
Lagerstroemia indica 'Whit III'				X	X	X	X	
Lagerstroemia indica 'Whit IV'				X	X	X	X	
Lagerstroemia (i. x fauriei) 'Biloxi'					X	X	X	
Lagerstroemia (i. x fauriei) 'Choctaw'					X	X	X	
Lagerstroemia (i. x fauriei) 'Miami'					X	X	X	
Lagerstroemia (i. x fauriei) 'Muskogee'				X	X	X	X	X
Lagerstroemia (i. x fauriei) 'Natchez'					X	X	X	

USDA Hardiness Zones	3	4	5	6	7	8	9	10
Lagerstroemia (i. x fauriei) 'Sarah's Favorite'					x	x	x	
Lagerstroemia (i. x fauriei) 'Sioux'					x	x	x	
Lagerstroemia (i. x fauriei) 'Tonto'					x	x	x	
Lagerstroemia (i. x fauriei) 'Tuscarora'					x	x	x	
Lagerstroemia (i. x fauriei) 'Tuskegee'					x	x	x	
Ligustrum japonicum 'Recurvifolium'				x	x	x	x	x
Liquidambar styraciflua - Sweetgum			x	x	x	x	x	x
Liquidambar styraciflua 'Rotundiloba'				x	x	x	x	x
Liquidambar styraciflua 'Slender Silhouette'				x	x	x	x	
Liriodendron tulipifera - Tulip Poplar			x	x	x	x	x	
Loropetalum chinense rubrum 'Zhuzhou Fuchsia'				x	x	x	x	
Magnolia grandiflora 'Bracken's Brown Beauty'			x	x	x	x	x	
Magnolia grandiflora 'Claudia Wannamaker'					x	x	x	x
Magnolia grandiflora 'D. D. Blanchard'				x	x	x	x	x
Magnolia grandiflora 'Little Gem'					x	x	x	
Magnolia grandiflora 'Mgtig'					x	x	x	x
Magnolia grandiflora 'Southern Charm'					x	x	x	
Magnolia grandiflora 'TMGH'					x	x	x	
Magnolia stellata - Star Magnolia		x	x	x	x	x		
Magnolia virginiana - Sweetbay				x	x	x	x	x
Magnolia x soulangiana - Saucer				x	x	x	x	
Malus 'Prairifire'		x	x	x	x	x		
Malus x 'Sutyzam'		x	x	x	x	x		
Malus x 'Zumi'		x	x	x	x			
Metasequoia glyptostroboides - Dawn Redwood				x	x	x		
Myrica cerifera - Wax Myrtle					x	x	x	x
Nyssa sylvatica - Black Gum		x	x	x	x	x		
Osmanthus fragrans - Fragrant Tea Olive					x	x	x	
Osmanthus x fortunei - Fortune's Tea Olive					x	x	x	
Oxydendron arboreum - Sourwood			x	x	x	x		
Picea abies - Norway Spruce	x	x	x	x	x			
Picea omorika - Serbian Spruce		x	x	x	x			
Picea pungens - Colorado Spruce		x	x	x	x			
Pinus elliottii - Slash Pine					x	x	x	x
Pinus nigra - Austrian Pine			x	x	x	x		
Pinus strobus - Eastern White Pine	x	x	x	x	x			
Pinus taeda - Loblolly Pine					x	x	x	
Pinus thunbergii - Japanese Black Pine					x	x	x	
Pinus virginiana - Viginia Pine			x	x	x	x		
Pistacia chinensis - Chinese Pistache				x	x	x	x	
Platanus occidentalis - Sycamore		x	x	x	x	x		
Platanus x acerifolia 'Bloodgood'			x	x	x	x		
Platanus x acerifolia 'Yarwood'				x	x	x	x	
Prunus caroliniana 'Cherry Ruffle'					x	x	x	x
Prunus cerasifera 'Thundercloud'			x	x	x	x		
Prunus serrulata 'Kwanzan'			x	x	x	x	x	

USDA Hardiness Zones	3	4	5	6	7	8	9	10
Prunus subhirtella 'Autumnalis Rosea'			X	X	X	X		
Prunus x 'Okame'			X	X	X	X	X	
Prunus x yedoensis			X	X	X	X		
Pyrus calleryana 'Bradford'			X	X	X	X	X	
Pyrus calleryana 'Glen's Form'			X	X	X	X	X	
Quercus acutissima - Sawtooth Oak			X	X	X	X	X	
Quercus alba - White Oak	X	X	X	X	X	X		
Quercus coccinea - Scarlett Oak		X	X	X	X	X		
Quercus laurifolia - Laurel Oak				X	X	X	X	X
Quercus lyrata - Overcup Oak				X	X	X	X	
Quercus nuttallii - Nuttall Oak				X	X	X		
Quercus palustris - Pin Oak		X	X	X	X	X		
Quercus phellos - Willow Oak				X	X	X	X	
Quercus phellos 'QPMTF'				X	X	X	X	
Quercus phellos 'QPSTA'				X	X	X	X	
Quercus rubra - Northern Red Oak			X	X	X	X		
Quercus shumardii - Shumard Oak			X	X	X	X	X	
Quercus virginiana - Live Oak					X	X	X	X
Quercus virginiana 'QVTIA'					X	X	X	X
Rhapidophyllum hystrix - Needle Palm				X	X	X	X	X
Sabal palmetto - Sabal Palm						X	X	X
Salix babylonica - Weeping Willow		X	X	X	X	X		
Styrax japonica - Japanese Snowbell			X	X	X	X		
Taxodium distichum - Bald Cypress			X	X	X	X	X	X
Taxodium distichum 'Mickelson'			X	X	X	X		
Taxodium distichum 'Sofine'			X	X	X	X	X	X
Thuja occidentalis 'Degroot's Spire'	X	X	X	X	X	X		
Thuja occidentalis 'Emerald'	X	X	X	X	X			
Thuja x 'Green Giant'				X	X	X	X	
Tilia cordata - Greenspire® Littleleaf Linden	X	X	X	X	X			
Trachycarpus fortunei - Windmill Palm					X	X	X	X
Tsuga canadensis - Canadian Hemlock	X	X	X	X	X			
Ulmus americana 'Princeton'	X	X	X	X	X	X		
Ulmus parvifolia - Chinese Elm			X	X	X	X	X	X
Ulmus parvifolia 'BSNUPF'			X	X	X	X		
Ulmus parvifolia 'Drake'					X	X	X	X
Ulmus parvifolia 'Emer I'			X	X	X	X	X	X
Ulmus parvifolia 'Emer II'			X	X	X	X		
Ulmus parvifolia 'UPMTF'			X	X	X	X		
Vitex agnus-castus 'Shoal Creek'					X	X	X	X
x Cupressocyparis leylandii - Leyland Cypress				X	X	X	X	
Zelkova serrata - Green Vase® Zelkova			X	X	X	X		
Zelkova serrata 'C Creek I'			X	X	X	X		
Zelkova serrata 'Musashino'			X	X	X	X	X	
Zelkova serrata 'Village Green'			X	X	X	X		
Zelkova serrata 'ZSFKF'			X	X	X	X		

Flowering Trees by Season

Fall Flowering

Osmanthus fragrans
Osmanthus x fortunei
Prunus subhirtella 'Autumnalis Rosea'

Winter Flowering

Amelanchier x grandiflora 'Autumn Brilliance'
Eriobotrya japonica
Osmanthus fragrans
Prunus cerasifera 'Thundercloud'
Prunus x 'Okame'

Spring Flowering

Aesculus x carnea 'Fort McNair'
Cercis canadensis
Cercis canadensis 'Covey'
Cercis canadensis 'Forest Pansy'
Cercis canadensis 'Avondale'
Cercis reniformis 'Oklahoma'
Chionanthus retusus
Chionanthus virginicus
Cladrastis kentukea (syn. lutea)
Cornus florida
Cornus florida 'Cherokee Princess'
Cornus florida rubra 'Comco #1'
Cornus kousa
Crataegus phaenopyrum
Crataegus viridis 'Winter King'
Ligustrum japonicum 'Recurvifolium'
Loropetalum chinese rubrum 'Zhuzhou Fuchsia'
Magnolia stellata
Magnolia x soulangiana
Malus 'Prairifire'
Malus x 'Sutyzam'
Malus x 'Zumi'
Osmanthus fragrans
Pyrus calleryana 'Bradford'
Pyrus calleryana 'Glen's Form'
Prunus caroliniana 'Cherry Ruffle'
Prunus serrulata 'Kwanzan'
Prunus subhirtella 'Autumnalis Rosea'
Prunus x yedoensis

Summer Flowering

Koelreuteria paniculata
Lagerstroemia fauriei 'Fantasy'
Lagerstroemia indica 'Carolina Beauty'
Lagerstroemia indica 'Catawba'
Lagerstroemia indica 'Potomac'
Lagerstroemia indica 'Whit II'
Lagerstroemia indica 'Whit III'
Lagerstroemia indica 'Whit IV'
Lagerstroemia (i. x fauriei) 'Biloxi'
Lagerstroemia (i. x fauriei) 'Choctaw'
Lagerstroemia (i. x fauriei) 'Miami'
Lagerstroemia (i. x fauriei) 'Muskogee'
Lagerstroemia (i. x fauriei) 'Natchez'
Lagerstroemia (i. x fauriei) 'Sarah's Favorite'
Lagerstroemia (i. x fauriei) 'Sioux'
Lagerstroemia (i. x fauriei) 'Tonto'
Lagerstroemia (i. x fauriei) 'Tuscarora'
Lagerstroemia (i. x fauriei) 'Tuskegee'
Magnolia grandiflora 'Bracken's Brown Beauty'
Magnolia grandiflora 'Claudia Wannamaker'
Magnolia grandiflora 'D. D. Blanchard'
Magnolia grandiflora 'Little Gem'
Magnolia grandiflora 'Mgtig'
Magnolia grandiflora 'Southern Charm'
Magnolia grandiflora 'TMGH'
Magnolia virginiana
Oxydendrum arboreum
Sabal palmetto
Styrax japonica

Unique Tolerance Levels

Light Shade to Shade Tolerant

Acer buergerianum
Acer buergerianum 'ABMTF'
Acer palmatum
Acer palmatum 'Bloodgood'
Acer palmatum 'Sango kaku'
Acer palmatum 'Seiryu'
Aesculus x carnea 'Fort McNair'
Amelanchier x grandiflora 'Autumn Brilliance'
Butia capitata
Cercis canadensis 'Covey'
Chionanthus retusus
Chionanthus virginicus
Cornus florida
Cornus florida 'Cherokee Princess'
Cornus florida rubra 'Comco #1'
Cornus kousa
Eriobotrya japonica
Fagus grandifolia
Ginkgo biloba
Ligustrum japonicum 'Recurvifolium'
Loropetalum chinense rubrum 'Zhuzhou Fuchsia'
Magnolia virginiana
Myrica cerifera
Osmanthus fragrans
Osmanthus x fortunei
Prunus caroliniana 'Cherry Ruffle'
Rhapidophyllum hystrix
Thuja x 'Green Giant'
Tsuga canadensis

High Salt Tolerance

Gleditsia triacanthos var. inermis 'Skycole'
Ilex vomitoria
Ilex vomitoria 'Pendula'
Juniperus silicicola 'Brodie'
Quercus rubra
Sabal palmetto

Short Duration Flood Tolerant

Butia capitata
Fraxinus pennsylvanica 'Patmore'
Fraxinus pennsylvanica 'Urbanite'
Ilex opaca 'Croonenburg'
Liquidambar styraciflua

Liquidambar styraciflua 'Rotundiloba'
Liquidambar styraciflua 'Slender Silhouette'
Magnolia virginiana
Platanus x acerifolia 'Bloodgood'
Platanus x acerifolia 'Yarwood'
Platanus occidentalis
Quercus laurifolia
Quercus nuttallii
Quercus palustris
Quercus phellos
Quercus phellos 'QPMTF'
Quercus phellos 'QPSTA'
Quercus shumardii
Rhapidophyllum hystrix
Sabal palmetto
Salix babylonica
Taxodium distichum
Taxodium distichum 'Mickelson'
Taxodium distichum 'Sofine'
Thuja occidentalis 'Emerald'
Ulmus americana 'Princeton'

High Drought Tolerance

Acer buergerianum
Butia capitata
Cercis canadensis
Cercis reniformis 'Oklahoma'
Cupressus arizonica var. glabra 'Carolina Sapphire'
Cupressus sempervirens
Gleditsia triacanthos var. inermis 'Skycole'
Ilex vomitoria
Nyssa sylvatica
Pinus elliottii
Pinus nigra
Pinus thunbergii
Pistacia chinensis
Platanus x acerifolia 'Bloodgood'
Platanus occidentalis
Quercus shumardii
Rhapidophyllum hystrix
Sabal palmetto
Taxodium distichum
Taxodium distichum 'Mickelson'
Taxodium distichum 'Sofine'
Ulmus americana 'Princeton'
Ulmus parvifolia 'BSNUPF'
Ulmus parvifolia 'Drake'
Ulmus parvifolia 'Emer I'
Ulmus parvifolia 'Emer II'
Ulmus parvifolia 'UPMTF'

Street Trees

Acer buergerianum
Acer buergerianum 'ABMTF'
Acer rubrum
Acer rubrum - Autumn Flame®
Acer rubrum - October Glory®
Acer rubrum 'Brandywine'
Acer rubrum 'Franksred'
Acer rubrum 'HOSR'
Acer saccharum
Acer saccharum - Green Mountain®
Acer saccharum 'Astis'
Acer saccharum 'Legacy'
Acer x freemanii 'Jeffers Red'
Aesculus x carnea 'Fort McNair'
Butia capitata
Carpinus betulus 'Fastigiata'
Carpinus caroliniana
Fraxinus americana 'Junginger'
Fraxinus pennsylvanica 'Oconee'
Fraxinus pennsylvanica 'Patmore'
Fraxinus pennsylvanica 'Urbanite'
Ginkgo biloba
Gleditsia triacanthos var. inermis 'Shademaster'
Gleditsia triacanthos var. inermis 'Skycole'
Ilex vomitoria
Liquidambar styraciflua 'Slender Silhouette'
Pistacia chinensis
Platanus occidentalis
Platanus x acerifolia 'Bloodgood'
Platanus x acerifolia 'Yarwood'
Pyrus calleryana 'Bradford'
Pyrus calleryana 'Glen's Form'
Quercus acutissima
Quercus alba
Quercus coccinea
Quercus lyrata
Quercus nuttallii
Quercus palustris
Quercus phellos
Quercus phellos 'QPMTF'
Quercus phellos 'QPSTA'
Quercus rubra
Quercus shumardii
Ulmus americana 'Princeton'
Ulmus parvifolia
Ulmus parvifolia 'BSNUPF'
Ulmus parvifolia 'Emer I'
Ulmus parvifolia 'Emer II'
Ulmus parvifolia 'UPMTF'
Zelkova serrata
Zelkova serrata 'C Creek I'
Zelkova serrata 'Musashino'
Zelkova serrata 'Village Green'
Zelkova serrata 'ZSFKF'

Screening Trees

Aesculus x carnea 'Fort McNair'
Cedrus deodara
Cedrus deodara 'BBC'
Cedrus deodara 'Bill's Blue'
Cedrus deodara 'Sander's Blue'
Crataegus phaenopyrum
Crataegus viridis 'Winter King'
Cryptomeria japonica var. sinensis 'Radicans'
Cryptomeria japonica 'Yoshino'
Cupressus arizonica var. glabra 'Carolina Sapphire'
Cupressus sempervirens
Ilex cornuta 'Burfordii'
Ilex cornuta 'Needle Point'
Ilex opaca 'Croonenburg'
Ilex vomitoria
Ilex x 'Emily Bruner'
Ilex x 'HL10-90'
Ilex x 'Mary Nell'
Ilex x 'Nellie R. Stevens'
Ilex x attenuata 'East Palatka'
Ilex x attenuata 'Foster No. 2'
Ilex x attenuata 'Greenleaf'
Ilex x attenuata 'Savannah'
Juniperus silicicola 'Brodie'
Juniperus virginiana
Juniperus virginiana 'Burkii'
Ligustrum japonicum 'Recurvifolium'
Magnolia grandiflora 'Bracken's Brown Beauty'
Magnolia grandiflora 'Claudia Wannamaker'
Magnolia grandiflora 'D. D. Blanchard'
Magnolia grandiflora 'Little Gem'
Magnolia grandiflora 'Mgtig'
Magnolia grandiflora 'Southern Charm'
Magnolia grandiflora 'TMGH'
Myrica cerifera
Osmanthus fragrans
Osmanthus x fortunei
Picea abies
Picea omorika
Picea pungens
Pinus elliottii
Pinus nigra
Pinus strobus
Pinus taeda
Pinus thunbergii
Pinus virginiana
Prunus caroliniana 'Cherry Ruffle'
Pyrus calleryana 'Bradford'
Pyrus calleryana 'Glen's Form'
Quercus virginiana
Quercus virginiana 'QVTIA'
Quercus laurifolia
Salix babylonica
Taxodium distichum
Taxodium distichum 'Mickelson'
Taxodium distichum 'Sofine'
Thuja occidentalis 'Emerald'
Thuja x 'Green Giant'
Tsuga canadensis
x Cupressocyparis leylandii

Optimal Fruit Appearance/Season

Amelanchier x grandiflora 'Autumn Brilliance' - (Summer to Fall)
Cornus florida - (Fall through Winter)
Cornus kousa - (Fall through Winter)
Crataegus phaenopyrum - (Fall through Winter)
Crataegus viridis 'Winter King' - (Fall through Winter)
Ilex cornuta 'Burfordii' - (Fall through Winter)
Ilex cornuta 'Needle Point' - (Fall throughWinter)
Ilex vomitoria 'Pendula' - (Fall through Winter)
Ilex vomitoria - (Fall through Winter)
Ilex x attenuata 'East Palatka' - (Fall through Winter)
Ilex x attenuata 'Foster No. 2' - (Fall through Winter)
Ilex x attenuata 'Greenleaf' - (Fall through Winter)
Ilex x attenuata 'Savannah' - (Fall through Winter)
Ilex x 'Emily Bruner' - (Fall through Winter)
Ilex x 'HL10-90' - (Fall through Winter)
Ilex x 'Mary Nell' - (Fall through Winter)
Ilex x 'Nellie R. Stevens' - (Fall through Winter)
Juniperus chinensis 'Kaizuka' - (Fall through Winter)
Juniperus virginiana 'Burkii' - (Fall through Winter)
Juniperus virginiana - (Fall through Winter)
Koelreuteria paniculata - (Summer through Fall)
Malus 'Prairifire' - (Fall through Winter)
Malus x 'Sutyzam' - (Fall through Winter)
Malus x 'Zumi' - (Fall through Winter)
Styrax japonica - (Fall through Winter)

Unique Bark/Trunk

Acer buergerianum
Acer buergerianum 'ABMTF'
Acer palmatum 'Sango kaku'
Betula nigra
Betula nigra 'BNMTF'
Betula nigra 'Cully'
Fagus grandifolia
Ginkgo biloba
Lagerstroemia fauriei 'Fantasy'
Lagerstroemia indica 'Carolina Beauty'
Lagerstroemia indica 'Catawba'
Lagerstroemia indica 'Potomac'
Lagerstroemia indica 'Whit II'
Lagerstroemia indica 'Whit III'
Lagerstroemia indica 'Whit IV'
Lagerstroemia (i. x fauriei) 'Biloxi'
Lagerstroemia (i. x fauriei) 'Choctaw'
Lagerstroemia (i. x fauriei) 'Miami'
Lagerstroemia (i. x fauriei) 'Muskogee'
Lagerstroemia (i. x fauriei) 'Natchez'
Lagerstroemia (i. x fauriei) 'Sarah's Favorite'
Lagerstroemia (i. x fauriei) 'Sioux'
Lagerstroemia (i. x fauriei) 'Tonto'
Lagerstroemia (i. x fauriei) 'Tuscarora'
Lagerstroemia (i. x fauriei) 'Tuskegee'
Magnolia x soulangiana
Metasequoia glyptostroboides
Oxydendron arboreum
Taxodium distichum
Taxodium distichum 'Mickelson'
Taxodium distichum 'Sofine'
Platanus x acerifolia 'Bloodgood'
Platanus x acerifolia 'Yarwood'
Ulmus americana 'Princeton'
Ulmus parvifolia

Ulmus parvifolia 'BSNUPF'
Ulmus parvifolia 'Drake'
Ulmus parvifolia 'Emer I'
Ulmus parvifolia 'Emer II'
Ulmus parvifolia 'UPMTF'
Zelkova serrata - Green Vase®
Zelkova serrata 'C Creek I'
Zelkova serrata 'Musashino'
Zelkova serrata 'Village Green'
Zelkova serrata 'ZSFKF'

Excellent Fall Color

Acer buergerianum 'ABMTF'
Acer palmatum
Acer palmatum 'Bloodgood'
Acer palmatum dissectum 'Seiryu'
Acer rubrum - October Glory®
Acer rubrum 'Brandywine'
Acer rubrum 'Franksred'
Acer saccharum - Green Mountain®
Acer saccharum 'Astis'
Acer saccharum 'Legacy'
Acer x freemani 'Jeffers Red'
Amelanchier x grandiflora 'Autumn Brilliance'
Cornus florida
Cornus florida 'Cherokee Princess'
Cornus florida rubra 'Comco #1'
Cornus kousa
Ginkgo biloba
Lagerstroemia fauriei 'Fantasy'
Lagerstroemia indica 'Carolina Beauty'
Lagerstroemia indica 'Catawba'
Lagerstroemia indica 'Potomac'
Lagerstroemia indica 'Whit II'
Lagerstroemia indica 'Whit III'
Lagerstroemia indica 'Whit IV'
Lagerstroemia (i. x fauriei) 'Biloxi'
Lagerstroemia (i. x fauriei) 'Choctaw'
Lagerstroemia (i. x fauriei) 'Miami'
Lagerstroemia (i. x fauriei) 'Muskogee'
Lagerstroemia (i. x fauriei) 'Natchez'
Lagerstroemia (i. x fauriei) 'Sarah's Favorite'
Lagerstroemia (i. x fauriei) 'Sioux'
Lagerstroemia (i. x fauriei) 'Tonto'
Lagerstroemia (i. x fauriei) 'Tuscarora'
Lagerstroemia (i. x fauriei) 'Tuskegee'
Liquidambar styraciflua
Liquidambar styraciflua 'Slender Silhouette'
Liriodendron tulipifera
Metasequoia glyptostroboides
Nyssa sylvatica
Oxydendron arboreum
Pistacia chinensis
Pyrus calleryana 'Bradford'
Pyrus calleryana 'Glen's Form'
Quercus alba
Quercus coccinea
Quercus lyrata
Quercus nuttallii
Quercus palustris
Quercus rubra
Quercus shumardii
Taxodium distichum
Taxodium distichum 'Mickelson'
Taxodium distichum 'Sofine'
Zelkova serrata 'C Creek I'

Botanical Name Index

Botanical Name Index Continued

Common Name Index

Glossary

Acidic: soil or conditions with a pH level less than 7.0

Acorn: fruit of the *Quercus* genus

Acute: two sides of an angle forming a narrow point

Alkaline: soil or conditions with a pH level more than 7.0

Alternate: refers to the arrangement of the leaves on the stem; leaves are attached across from each other in a staggered pattern on the stem; only one leaf at each node

Anther: pollen containing portion of the stamen (male reproductive flower organ)

Apex: end or terminal point of any plant part

Ascending: having an upward turned limb habit

Asexual Reproduction: formation of a new plant (clone or daughter plant) from the vegetative plant parts (stems, leaves, roots, tubers, stolons or rhizomes) of a plant (mother plant) that is genetically identical

Awl-like: leaves that are narrow, stiff and sharp

Axillary Cluster: grouping of leaves or flowers that rise from the leaf axil

Axis: central stem or support of a plant

Ball and Burlap: trees or shrubs dug and the rootball is wrapped in burlap, the burlap is tied or pinned and usually placed in a wire basket

Bark: outer surface of the stem or root of a plant

Berry: fleshy fruit containing seeds that are protected by pulpy flesh

Bipinnate: twice pinnate

Botanical Name: also known as Scientific Name; recognized Latin name of a plant; three parts; first part of the name is the genus and is always capitalized and in italics; second part is the species name and is always lower case and in italics followed by the cultivar name that is capitalized with single quotes and no italics

Bract: leaf-like structure at the base of the flower or inflorescence

Broadleaf: term that distinguishes plants with a leaf that has a broad, flattened blade

Bud: beginning stage of a flower or shoot; meristematic tissue at the apex of a shoot

Capsule: dry, hard fruit that splits open to release a seed or seeds

Chlorosis: leaf discoloration (yellow or whitening) caused by mineral deficiency or disease; loss of chlorophyll

Circling Root: roots that grow in a circle instead of spreading out; can lead to root girdling and will cause problems if not corrected at a young age; common in root-bound container grown plants

Clay: soil made of very small particles usually formed from the weathering of low silica rock

Clefted: divided or separated near the midpoint or apex

Co-dominant leader: having two or more main trunks instead of one; can cause breakage problems in plants with multiple, main trunks

Common Name: non-scientific name commonly used when referring to a plant; many plants may have several common names

Compacted Soil: soil that is dense or compressed

Cone: dry fruit made of scales that are arranged around a main axis

Coniferous: cone-bearing

Corymb: flat topped inflorescence or a modified raceme where the stalks of the lower flowers are elongated to be even with the upper flowers; lower flowers open first

Crenate: rounded teeth along the leaf margin

Crossing Limbs: limbs or branches that intersect or cross over each other; can cause crowding of the crown

Crotch: refers to the limb or branch crotch; where the limb or branch is attached to the trunk

Crown: part of the tree located on the upper portion of the trunk system where branches, twigs, leaves, flower and fruit are held

Cyme: flat topped inflorescence where the upper flowers open first

Cultivar: non-Latin name for a cultivated variety; placed after botanical name, always put in single quotations

Deciduous: loses its leaves for part of the year; usually loses leaves in Fall through dormant season of Winter

Defoliate: loss or shedding of leaves

Dehiscent: opening or splitting of a structure containing the seeds of a plant

Dentate: row of spines or teeth along the leaf margin that are perpendicular instead of pointing forward

Dense: full, thick

Descending: downward drooping limb habit

Dioecious: male and female organs (flowers) borne on separate plants

Distal: located near the apex, not at the base (refers to the foliage)

Dormant: a state of rest or reduced metabolic activity where a plant's tissue remains alive but does not grow

Drupe: a seed and surrounding structure encased in fleshy pulp

Elliptic: in the shape of an ellipse; usually pointed or narrow at the ends

Entire: smooth or unindented leaf margins; leaves are without teeth or lobes

Espalier: plant that is trained along a trellis or wall in a horizontal or spreading manner

Evergreen: leaves remain green and on the plant throughout one or more years; old foliage may shed during the dormant season

Exfoliating Bark: bark that flakes or peels off in layers, plates or strips

Fascile: tight cluster of leaves or stems

Fastigiate: having vertical to upright, closely arranged twigs, limbs and trunks

Female Flower: flower that has only female reproductive organs; contains no functional male organs

Fertility Level: level of mineral nutrients found in the soil

Fissure: groove or deep furrow

Flower: reproductive organ of a plant; contains pistils, stamens or both; as well as other organs associated with the pistil or stamen

Foliage: leaves or needles

Frost Injury: injury caused by frost or freezing temperatures; normally occurs in late Spring or early Fall; leaves, young shoots and flowers usually affected

Fruit: mature ovary, usually containing seeds; sometimes includes reproductive structures of the plant (berry, drupe, samara, nut, cone)

Genus: group of different species with similar common flower traits but have different physical characteristics

Girdling Root: roots that grow around and across the trunk; restricting the flow of carbohydrates and sap through the phloem (inner bark); caused by limited planting spaces, planting too deeply or root-bound container grown plants

Glabrous: lacking hairs or scales

Glandular: containing glands

Globose: round-shaped

Glossy: shiny

Grafted Tree: asexual plant propagation technique where the tissue of one plant is fused to another plant; trees are often grafted on another tree's root system with similar traits in the same genus or species

Humus: soil that contains high organic content (decayed trees, plant litter and animal tissue or waste); improves soil moisture and nutrient content

Hybrid: cross between two or more plants within a genus or rarely, between two different genera

Included Bark: bark embedded between two limbs or a trunk and a limb that creates a weak union

Inconspicuous: not showy; unnoticeable

Inflorescence: flower producing, modified branches or stalks

Internode: space between two nodes

Knees: the pointed or conical woody growths projecting from the roots of some swamp-growing trees (Bald Cypress); are often rising out of water saturated soil

Lanceolate: long and narrow; tapering to a point (as in Weeping Willow leaf)

Leader: Main trunk or terminal of a stem

Leaf: photosynthetic structure of a plant

Leaf Scar: mark left on stem or trunk where a leaf was attached

Lenticel: small corky bark outgrowth on the trunk that allow gas exchange between the plant and atmosphere

Lime: mineral additive to soil; used to neutralize acidic soils; mainly calcium and magnesium

Loam: soils with a balanced mix of clay, sand and silt

Lobe: projecting section of the leaf

Male Flower: flower that has only male reproductive organs; contains no functional female organs

Margin: edge of the leaf

Mature: old; nearing full growth and development

Meristematic Tissue: plant cells that are not differentiated and can develop into distinctive tissue in the shoot tip or root tip; (example: shoot tip meristematic tissue may form leaf, shoot, xylem, phloem or flower tissue)

Monocot: has only one primary seed leaf (Palms)

Monoecious: male and female organs (flowers) borne on same plant

Mottled Pattern: puzzle-shaped outline

Mycorrihizal: fungus that enters the root tissue and forms a relationship with the plant; the fungus digests organic matter creating additional nutrients for the plant and better moisture uptake from soil

Multi-stem/Multi-trunk: having more than one main branch or trunk; smaller trees or shrubs can be trained in this manner

Naturalized: natural or woody area; process by which the cultivated area is blended with the natural habitat

Needle: leaves that are extremely narrow and usually square or rounded

Node: a point along a stem, normally swollen or constricted, containing a bud of meristematic tissue from which a shoot may arise

Nutlet: small nut-like seed attached to a modified leaf bract in axillary clusters (*Carpinus* fruit)

Oblanceolate: leaf shape that is narrow at the ends and widest at the midpoint

Obovate: broadest point above middle of leaf

Oblong: leaves are longer than wide; almost parallel margins; almost rectangular-shaped

Obtuse: rounded; almost a circular shape

Opposite: refers to the arrangement of the leaves on the stem; leaves are attached across from each other at the node; leaves are paired

Ovoid: egg-shaped

Palmate: fan or palm-like

Palmately Compound: leaf that is divided into leaflets attached at a central point

Panicle: repeatedly branched inflorescence (refers to the flower); usually a branched raceme

Pendulous: weeping or hanging limb habit

Petiole: the stalk of a leaf

pH Level: scale or range from 0 to 14 by which the soil's acidity and alkalinity are measured (0-very acidic; 14-very alkaline)

Pinnate: feather-like

Pinnately Compound Leaf: leaf that is divided into leaflets; leaflets are arranged on either side of the axis

Pistil: female organ or organs in a flower

Pith: soft, white or light colored soft or spongy tissue in the center of the stem or twig

Plate: thin, flat sheet; usually refers to bark especially peeling or shedding

Pollen/Pollination: yellowish to white (and occasionally other colors) very small grain-like structure produced by the anthers; the male element which fertilizes the ovule

Pome: fleshy fruit with several seed (Crabapple or Pear)

PPAF: plant patent applied for

PP: plant patent number

Pubescent: short, fuzzy hair along the leaf surface

Pyramidal: pyramid-shaped; broadest at base

Raceme: an elongated inflorescence with short floral stalks

Racemose: flowers arranged in a raceme

Root: woody underground portion of a plant responsible for anchoring it and extracting water and nutrients from the soil

Root Flare: uppermost point on trunk where roots emerge

Root Pruning: trimming or cutting the roots prior to digging or transplanting a plant; method helps roots develop and can prevent circling or girdling roots

Samara: dry, winged fruit that contains a seed

Sandy: soil made up of fine, granular matter; gritty texture

Scale: modified leaf or bract

Seed: mature fertilized embryo

Serrate: toothed or saw-like points along the leaf margin

Sessile: having no stalk

Simple: leaf that is undivided and entire, containing only one blade

Slough: to shed or cast-off the outer layer

Smooth: not rough or ridged

Species: an individual organism within a genus that has similar traits and the ability to cross and reproduce a similar or like individual; does not exclude the ability to self-pollinate

Spine: needle-like point or points along a leaf margin or apex and woody, sharp pointed projection on a stem or petiole

Spiral Leaf Arrangement: leaves arranged in a spiral around a main axis

Stamen: male organ or organs in a flower

Standard: small tree or shrub that has been trained or grafted to have a clear, single-stem and a tight head

Stem: organ or structure of the plant that supports the leaves and flowers

Subrhombic: somewhat diamond-shaped; a parallelogram with equal sides having two acute angles and two oblique angles

Sucker: vigorous shoot which grows from a root system below or at ground level

Sunscald: burning or scorching of a plant's leaf or bark from harsh sun exposure and hot temperatures

Terminal: tip or apex

Tomentose: layer of wooly hairs on the leaf

Topiary: pruning or clipping a plant into an ornamental shape or sculpture

Unisexual Flower: flower containing only female or male reproductive organs but not both

Variegated: patterned, mottled, marginated or striped white or gold coloring on a green leaf

Variety: see Cultivar

Water-logged Soil: soil saturated with water

Weeping: drooping or pendulous limb habit

Well-drained Soil: soil with adequate aeration

Whorled: refers to the arrangement of the leaves on the stem; having three or more leaves arising from the same node and symmetrically placed around the stem

Winterscald: damage to a plant's leaf or bark from exposure to harsh wind, direct sun and freezing temperatures

Xylem: the woody part of the plant stem or trunk that transports nutrients and water from the root system up to the plant leaves

Bibliography

Bailey, L.H. (1942). *The Standard Cyclopedia of Horticulture.* New York, NY: MacMillan Company (Original work published 1900).

Bloom, A., & Bloom, R. (2002). *Gardening With Conifers.* Buffalo, NY: Firefly Books.

Brickell, C. (Ed.). (1976). *The Royal Horticultural Society A-Z Encyclopedia of Garden Plants.* London: Dorling Kindersley Limited.

Broschat, T.K., & Meerow, A.W. (1991). *Betrock's Reference Guide to Florida Landscape Plants.* Hollywood, FL: Betrock Information Systems, Inc.

Clemson University Cooperative Extension. http://www.clemson.edu/extension

Coombes, A.J. (1992). *Dorling Kindersley Handbooks: Trees.* New York, NY: Dorling Kindersley Limited.

Dirr, M.A. (1975). *Manual of Woody Landscape Plants: Their Identification, Ornamentals Characteristics, Culture, Propagation and Uses.* Champaign, Illinois: Stipes Publishing Co.

Galle, F. (1997). *Hollies, The Genus Ilex.* Portland, OR: Timber Press, Inc.

Godfrey, R.K. (1988). *Trees, Shrubs and Woody Vines of Northern Florida and Adjacent Georgia and Alabama.* Athens, GA: University of Georgia Press.

Harris, C.W., & Dines, N.T. (1998). *Time-Saver Standards for Landscape Architecture: Design and Construction Data* (2nd ed.). New York, NY: McGraw-Hill, Publishing Company Inc.

Hillier Nurseries. (1995). *The Hillier Manual of Trees and Shrubs* (6th ed.). Great Britain: Redwood Books.

Johnson, W.T., & Lyon, H.H. (1976). *Insects That Feed On Trees and Shrubs* (2nd ed.). Ithaca, NY & London: Comstock Publishing Associates, a division of Cornell University Press.

Meerow, A.W. (2005). *Betrock's Cold Hardy Palms.* Hollywood, FL: Betrock Information Systems, Inc.

Prendergast, D., & Prendergast, E. (2003). *The Tree Doctor: A Guide to Tree Care and Maintenance.* Buffalo, NY: Firefly Books Inc.

Radford, A.E., & Attles, H.E., & Bell, C.R. (1987). *Manual of the Vascular Flora of the Carolinas.* Chapel Hill, NC: The University of North Carolina Press.

Sinclair, W.A., Lyons, H.T., & Johnson, W.T. (1987). *Diseases of Trees and Shrubs.* Ithaca, NY & London: Comstock Publishing Associates, a division of Cornell University Press.

South China Institute of Botany and The Chinese Academy of Sciences. (2004). *Magnolias of China.* Hong Kong: Hong Kong Science and Technology Press.

Toogood, A. (1990). *The Garden Trees Handbook: A Complete Guide To Choosing, Planting And Caring For Garden Trees.* New York, NY: Swallow Publishing Ltd.

van Gelderen, C.J., & van Gelderen, D.M. (2000). *Maples for Gardens A Color Encyclopedia.* Portland, OR: Timber Press, Inc.

van Gelderen, D.M., & van Hoey Smith, J.R.P. (1995). *Conifers* (2nd ed.). (G.J.E. Ten Kate, Trans.) Portland, OR: Timber Press, Inc.

Wasson, E. (Cons.). (2001). *Trees & Shrubs: Illustrated A-Z of Over 8,500 Plants.* Willoughby, NSW Australia: Global Book Publishing Pty Ltd.

Whittle, T. (1997). *The Plant Hunters: Tales of the Botanist-Explorers Who Enriched Our Gardens.* New York, NY: Lyons and Burford Publishers.

Photo Acknowledgments

We would like to extend our sincere gratitude to the individuals and wholesale nurseries that contributed to the many photographs used in this book. Their contributions have made it possible to illustrate and showcase the beauty of these featured trees. If you would like to inquire about any of these quality wholesale nurseries, please contact the Plant & Supply LOCATOR at 1-800-475-2687 to obtain their contact information.

A. McGill & Sons, *Oregon*

Alan W. Meerow, *Florida*

Athena Trees, Inc., *Georgia*

Betrock Information Systems, *Florida*

Bold Spring Nursery, *Georgia*

Charlie's Creek Nursery, *South Carolina*

Cherry Creek Nursery, *Tennessee*

Cleveland Tree Company, *Georgia*

Cole Jenest & Stone, P.A., *North Carolina*

Gary's Nursery, *North Carolina*

Gateway Farms, *Florida*

GreenSource Direct, *South Carolina*

Head Ornamentals, *South Carolina*

Hillside Nursery, *North Carolina*

Horticultural Portraits, *Oregon*

Images by BA, *South Carolina*

J. Frank Schmidt & Son Company, *Oregon*

Jennifer Orr, *South Carolina*

King's Sunset Nursery, *South Carolina*

Kokopelli Nursery, *Kansas*

Lake Tree Growers, *Georgia*

Mack Bros. Landscape Nursery, *Florida*

Merritt Brothers Tree Farm, *South Carolina*

Moon's Tree Farm, *Georgia*

Pritchard Nursery, *Georgia*

Ray Bracken Nursery, *South Carolina*

Scott Coile, *Georgia*

Shady Grove Plantation & Nursery, *South Carolina*

Southeastern Growers, *Georgia*

Stockhaven Nursery, *South Carolina*

Sugar Hill Nurseries, *Georgia*

The LandArt Design Group, *South Carolina*

Three Oaks Contractors, Inc., *South Carolina*

Tree Introductions, *Georgia*

Tri Scapes, *Georgia*